D1134502

RUGBY
On This Day

RUGBY
On This Day

History, Facts & Figures from Every Day of the Year

ADRIAN HILL

RUGBY
On This Day
History, Facts & Figures from Every Day of the Year

All statistics, facts and figures are correct as of 1st July 2009

© Adrian Hill

Adrian Hill asserted his rights in accordance with the Copyright, Designs and Patents Act 1988 to be identified as the author of this work.

Published By:
Pitch Publishing (Brighton) Ltd
A2 Yeoman Gate
Yeoman Way
Durrington
BN13 3QZ

Email: info@pitchpublishing.co.uk
Web: www.pitchpublishing.co.uk

First published 2009
Reprinted 2012

A catalogue record for this book is available from the British Library.

10-digit ISBN: 1-9054116-4-2
13-digit ISBN: 978-1-9054116-4-1

Typesetting and origination by Pitch Publishing. Printed in Great Britain.
Manufacturing managed by Jellyfish Print Solutions Ltd.

For Clare, Sean and Gemma

INTRODUCTION

Welcome to *Rugby On This Day*. When I told non-followers of the sport that I was writing a book selecting two rugby union stories from every day of the year I got some quizzical looks... "What are you going to write about in the summer?" or "What about when the Six Nations isn't on?"

Fifty years ago that sentiment would have carried some weight but rugby is now a 12-months of the year activity, so the ancient and the more modern have been combined as I've tried to offer a flavour of one of the most colourful sports there is.

It's a pursuit which millions of people around the globe not just play or follow, it becomes a part of their life. Friends are made and experiences shared through the passion for rugby.

I've trawled the internet, visited libraries, scoured my own collection of books, conducted interviews and relied on recollections from nearly 20 years writing about the sport for broadcasters and the written media to, I hope, produce not just an historic record of great matches and feats, but also the more whimsical, unusual and plain daft happenings in the curious oval ball game.

It's a very different sport at the pinnacle to what it was even 15 years ago, let alone a century past. I've tried to add some historical context, shine a light on a variety of issues which have changed the way rugby is played or administered through the years and have strived, where possible, to link stories on given days together by a common thread.

Inevitably there will be matches and tales that I have not selected for the book (some days were very competitive!). The idea was to make it as entertaining as possible, and not to focus too much on any one country or sector of the rugby scene. Some tough decisions were made and if I have omitted one of your favourites I apologise... There's only so much space to fill!

I hope you enjoy reading this snapshot of rugby history as much as I've enjoyed writing it. Perhaps you'll reminisce, learn something new and even chuckle the odd time.

Adrian Hill, July 2009

ACKNOWLEDGEMENTS

Thanks to all at Pitch Publishing for giving me the opportunity to write this, my first book, my wife Clare for all her love and support which has helped me through the long days and nights it took to research and tap away on the keyboard, and to Sean and Gemma for showing great patience while Dad toiled away in the spare room!

This project would not have been possible if it was not for the legion of rugby journalists, record keepers and historians over the past 200 years. There are too many to name, but those of you still with us know who you are. Your passion for the sport comes shining through in the welter of information I have waded through to complete the book. Hope you enjoy it.

RUGBY
On This Day

JANUARY

JANUARY 1

France, a powerhouse of world rugby... Well, it was not always the case. A fledgling team faced Wales in Swansea on New Year's Day 1910, as their country made its official debut in the International Championship. The Five Nations was born! The celebratory mood among the French was soon quashed, though, as Wales taught them a lesson 49-14. William Bancroft kicked eight conversions in the match (still a Championship record for Wales) and the margin of victory was a Welsh record in the event for 98 years.

"I vow to thee my country" actually used to be plural for some in rugby union. On January 1 2000 the International Rugby Board amended its rules to preclude a player from switching allegiance after appearing for a team at Full, "A" or Sevens level. Brian Smith, appointed by Martin Johnson to his England coaching staff, was an example. He played six times for his Aussie homeland (appearing in the 1987 World Cup), before his studies at Oxford and ancestry raised the interest of the Irish selectors, who picked him nine times at fly-half. Smith – a Shamrock Wallaby seen wearing the English rose!!

JANUARY 2

Many aspire to change how we see the world, few actually achieve it. In 1967, during the depths of apartheid, a white child was born in Vereeniging, who would be involved in an epoch-making event in 1995. Francois Pienaar was the man who led South Africa to victory in the World Cup on home soil in their first appearance in the event. And the man who handed him the trophy – wearing the Springbok shirt Pienaar had presented to him prior to the final – was President Nelson Mandela. As a symbol of the transformation of South African society it was just perfect.

On the subject of immense personalities, how about earning a nickname of "Pine Tree"? Colin Meads played 55 Tests for New Zealand between 1955 and 1971, mostly in the second row, and his towering presence (literally and figuratively) earned the respect of players and public alike. On January 2 2001 he became a Distinguished Companion of the New Zealand Order of Merit (the equivalent of a Knighthood), following on from being hailed as "All Black of the 20th century". He once said rugby was the greatest thing ever to happen to him... Many in the Land of the Long White Cloud would still suggest that it should be the other way round.

JANUARY 3

Lawrence Dallaglio picked this day at the start of 2008 to announce his immediate retirement from Test rugby and plans to quit playing altogether that May. Big Lol ("Lawrence Bruno Nero" to the birth registrars) is a true icon of the professional era. He inspired England to some famous victories with his rampaging presence (memorably dragging half the Welsh team over the line with him during a Six Nations game) and drove Wasps, almost by force of will at times, to a procession of Premiership and Heineken Cup titles. We will not see his like too often in the future.

Talking of Dallaglio and his beloved Wasps... In 1999, the early days of a new era for English club rugby, the Premiership was a league populated by what can be seen now as a rare old mixture of clubs. And so it was that on this day Dallaglio, Josh Lewsey, Kenny Logan and other Wasps celebrities trotted out in front of 2,000 freezing diehards at West Hartlepool's Victoria Park. Surely a foregone conclusion but no, Toby Handley's try was the vital score that beat the southern aristocrats 21-17. So what of West? They finished bottom that season and now reside in the regional leagues, while Wasps went on to claim trophy after trophy. Such is the way of professional sport...

JANUARY 4

Here's a tale of political unrest, Russian royalty, a fabulous try and the All Blacks... Prince Alexander Obolensky, who had fled the Russian Revolution in 1917, made his England debut against New Zealand in 1936. His searing pace helped him score the first try and he then eluded several despairing Kiwis to dot down in the corner and lift those not already standing at Twickenham to their feet. England won 13-0 (still their best win against the All Blacks); Obolensky played in three more internationals but was killed when his fighter plane crashed in Norfolk early in the Second World War. The RFU named a restaurant at HQ in his honour.

Obolensky's thoughts on events at Twickenham exactly 46 years later would have been interesting to hear... England were playing Australia and amid the half time team talks and sucking of oranges (on the pitch in those days) there was a sudden commotion from the crowd. On to the pitch swept a topless (and amply proportioned) Erica Roe – Twickenham's first streaker. Upon which, England scrum-half Steve Smith allegedly remarked to his skipper, Bill Beaumont: "Bill, there's a guy just run on the park with your backside on his chest!"

JANUARY 5

Yorkshire had become used to welcoming superstar rugby league players and cricketers to the county. Then, in 2005, at last, union fans in the broad acres could crow about an overseas legend coming into their midst when it was confirmed that Leeds had signed Justin Marshall – the New Zealand scrum-half. Big ambitions, broken dreams... It never really worked out and Marshall left after just one desultory season ended in relegation. Sedgley Park, away, in League One was not in the plan for the great All Black, so he decamped to the Swansea-based Ospreys for two campaigns and has since plied his trade for Montpellier and Saracens.

Wales – the passion, the singing, the scintillating back play... and the contradictions. A country that prides itself on its Celtic heritage, yet where speaking the lyrical national language is a minority pursuit. Michael Owen, the 2005 Wales Grand Slam-winning captain, revealed two years later that he was learning to communicate in Welsh, so he can speak to those in the team who use the ancient tongue. Owen will always live in the shadow of his footballer namesake but was reportedly amused when, just a few days after the Grand Slam was clinched, a Welsh shopkeeper asked him if he had "seen the rugby at the weekend"!

JANUARY 6

Fly-half is the pivotal position in a rugby team. The No.10 can run the show and exert his personality on a match. No-one exemplified this more than the man they called "The King"... Barry John was born on this day in 1945. His genius was fleeting – a mere 30 Tests (25 for Wales and 5 for the Lions) – but his mesmeric running and ball skills place him among the greatest, and most graceful, ever to play the game. The Lions' triumph in New Zealand in 1971 saw John at his elusive best. He was referred to as a "ghost" by Scottish journalist Norman Mair: "What a relief it was to see Barry John leaving by the door, rather than simply drifting through the wall!"

Here's a question for you... What rugby organisation was actually a football body? You'll find the answer in Canada... The Ontario Rugby Football Union was formed on January 6 1883 but for 111 years existed as a governing body for Canadian Football – the cousin of the American version (Gridiron). Non-Canadian readers will be relieved to learn that the Ontario Rugby Union actually does "what it says on the tin" and administers a 15-a-side code involving scrums and line-outs...

JANUARY 7

The South African rugby team is renowned for its ferocious will to win, sometimes seemingly at all costs (witness the 1974 Lions tour and 2002 at Twickenham) but the 1960/61 tourists, although not in that overtly violent tone, perhaps coined the expression "the result is more important than the performance". A drab 5-0 victory over England followed 3-0 and 8-3 "triumphs" over Wales and Ireland, before they ran amok by making double figures (12-5) in Scotland, to complete the most sheepish of Grand Slam tours. They fielded Dave Stewart at fly-half at Twickenham, but sweet dreams were not made of this...

A dream that did come true in 1996 was the first Heineken Cup final, held in Cardiff. Toulouse beat the Welsh capital's club 21-18 after a period of extra time. To coincide with the announcement of professionalism, a hastily arranged tournament had been launched in the summer of 1995 involving 12 teams from Ireland, France, Wales, Italy and Romania to decide the champions of European club rugby. England and Scotland gave it a miss, but joined the party for the next season. The Heineken Cup has now developed into the foremost club tournament in the world, a rollercoaster ridden and enjoyed by fans around the globe.

JANUARY 8

The Scots and the Welsh have always had one common enemy – the English. After having had their own rugby dust-ups with the dreaded Anglos, the Celtic duo decided it was about time blue should meet red so, in 1883, they organised the first Scotland-Wales international at Raeburn Place in Edinburgh. The scoring system in those days was an anachronism by modern standards – tries didn't count, with matches decided on the most goals scored. Scotland's Bill MacLagan was successful with three kicks, to opposition kicker Charles Lewis' one, and the Scots ruled the roost. It would take a further five matches before Wales achieved their first win in the fixture.

Matches decided by the boot? That sounds right up Jonny Wilkinson's street when, of course, he's fit to take the field. A Heineken Cup match for Newcastle in Perpignan in 2005 was the occasion when a knee ligament injury left England's golden boy stricken on the Catalonian turf. He was ruled out for two months – his third major injury sustained since the 2003 World Cup. This, however, was merely a prelude to a horrendous run of setbacks for the world's most prolific points scorer...

JANUARY 9

A good old Celtic row was stirred when Arthur Gould, the most celebrated Welsh player of the 19th century, won his last cap against England on January 9 1897. Gould had led Wales to their first Triple Crown four years earlier and was acknowledged as the "inventor" of centre play. To celebrate the end of a record-breaking career, the Welsh Rugby Union bought Gould a house – an amazing gift in those Corinthian days. However, this really irked the self-styled guardians of the game in Edinburgh and Dublin, who ruled that this was an act of professionalism and promptly cancelled Scotland and Ireland's fixtures with the Dragons.

If Gould had been alive in the latter part of the 20th century he could have safely bet his property on Michael Lynagh kicking goals. The Aussie was a thorn in many international sides with his world record 911 points for the Wallabies and, after packing away his green and gold caps, he decided, in 1996, to sign for ambitious English club Saracens. Two seasons in North London produced a cup win in 1998 and appeared to usher in a period of success for the "men in black". However, Lynagh retired and it all went to pot with, at the time of writing, not a single trophy more in Sarries' trophy cabinet since.

JANUARY 10

Props, the workhorses of the game putting their heads in where it most definitely hurts and leaving the glory to others... Hang on, not so fast with that stereotype... In recent times we have regularly seen All Black Tony Woodcock cross the whitewash and, in the mists of time, we find another scrum machine hitting the high notes... An injury crisis forced Wales to field Jehoida Hodges as an emergency wing against England in 1903. The front rower enjoyed the wide open spaces to such an extent that he scored a hat-trick of tries in a 21-5 victory. How about Shane Williams helping to take a few "against the head"? Can't see it, can you?

Adaptability was one of the watch-words of one of the masters of the art of coaching – Carwyn James. The Welshman, who coached the 1971 Lions to victory in New Zealand, died in 1983 at the age of 53. He had some great players, but there have been many coaches who have had great material but were unable to weave the pattern. James had a rugby brain as astute as the game has seen.

JANUARY 11

A significant date in the history of French rugby. The South West – the traditional stronghold of the Gallic game – was granted its first Test match when South Africa beat France at Bordeaux's Stade Municipal in 1913. It was also the first time Les Bleus had taken on the Springboks. How curious that only once more (Toulouse in 1925) did the French Federation stage international rugby outside Paris until 1953. In 1948, France achieved their first victory over one of the southern powers when Australia were vanquished 13-6 in well, of course, Paris.

From those early days of being makeweights of the international game, France became a world force, certainly too powerful on home soil most of the time for British and Irish sides. Scotland suffered eight defeats and celebrated just three victories in Paris between 1930 and 1965, but then managed to win at Stade Colombes on consecutive visits in 1967 and 1969. This last match was also the first time a replacement had been used in the Five Nations – Ian McCrae coming on for the injured Gordon Connell in the first half.

JANUARY 12

England, the dominant European rugby nation between the world wars, fell into a slump as competitive sport sprang back to life after Hitler had been seen off. There had been just one outright championship win since the end of hostilities, and no Grand Slam since 1928, as the 1957 season dawned. They needed inspiration, and found it in the shape of 36-year-old Eric Evans, who died on this day in 1991. The Sale hooker led his country to the Slam and was only denied back-to-back clean sweeps by draws with Scotland and Wales in 1958 – not a bad "Indian summer". Evans died with just two Slams added to England's tally since his day and then, like London buses, two came along together in 1991 and 92.

If England are among the biggest fish in the international pool, Leicester certainly hold a similar status in the club game. Under Dean Richards in the early 21st century, they were the first side to take the emerging Heineken Cup by the scruff of the neck and virtually claim possession. Consecutive triumphs in 2001 and 2002 was a unique achievement and included 11 straight match wins, a spell only broken by Llanelli at Stradey Park on this day in 2002.

JANUARY 13

If the French rugby team, shortly after the ravages of World War II, could be described as an untreated lump of metal then Lucien Mias was the welder who managed to transform it into an efficient machine. Second row Mias made his international debut on this day in 1951 against Scotland in Paris. He scored a try in a 14-12 victory, a prelude to a career that would see him lead the French to a Test series win in South Africa in 1958 and a first outright Five Nations title the following year. Mias helped made French packs believe in themselves and work as a unit – the world was made to sit up and take notice.

Stade Colombes was Mias' Parisien stamping ground for many years but, with its facilities falling behind other stadia, the French Rugby Federation needed a new venue to showcase the talents of its exciting team. Parc des Princes, the original home of Les Bleus, was renovated and became a cauldron of Gallic emotion on Five Nations Saturdays for 24 colourful years. The first such occasion was against Scotland in 1973. The Scots lost 16-13 and suffered 12 further defeats there with just a solitary victory. France often played like Princes, and the Dax band played on, in the suffocating concrete bowl.

JANUARY 14

There is an old saying that "records are made to be broken", often repeated through gritted teeth by the person who has just lost a cherished accolade. A handful, though, just seem to be unobtainable. In 1905, Wales beat England 25-0 in Cardiff – a massive score at the time, when getting to double figures was a struggle, and still the biggest Welsh win against the English. All hail to turn-of-the-century legends such as Willie Llewellyn, captain and a try scorer that day, and Dickie Owen for a performance that has stood the test of time.

The idea of a defence coach, let alone an Englishman who used to play rugby league, working with the Wales team would have been anathema to the boys of 1905. Professional rugby dictates, though, that if you want to be the best, get the best. Shaun Edwards had proved himself to be right at the top of the tree with Wasps and so when his old mentor, Warren Gatland, was appointed Wales boss there was only one man he wanted by his side – albeit on a "part-time" basis.

SHAUN EDWARDS – PART-TIME WALES COACH, BUT TOTALLY COMMITTED

JANUARY 15

People have played for two different countries and some have achieved international caps in separate sports under the same flag, but how about two nations in two sports? Clive van Ryneveld made his debut for the England rugby team against Wales on January 15 1949, while studying at Oxford University, and went on to appear in all four games in that season's Five Nations. Not content with that, van Ryneveld gave up on rugby and concentrated on cricket, throwing his lot in with his homeland and winning the first of 19 Springbok caps in the summer game AGAINST England at Trent Bridge in 1951.

An unwritten law of rugby was tested on the opening weekend of the 1977 Five Nations in Cardiff – "A player has a right to settle a score on the pitch before returning to the business of playing the game." When Wales lock Geoff Wheel punched Ireland's Stuart McKinney, after he deemed that the flanker had illegally disrupted a line-out, Willie Duggan retaliated by clobbering Allan Martin. Both would have just expected a ticking off. They were wrong... Scottish ref Norman Sanson made history by making not just the first sending off in the Championship's history but also the first double sending off in any international.

JANUARY 16

France wing Eric Bonneval can look back on his brief career with a self-satisfied glow. It was 1988, England were in Paris (with a certain Will Carling making his debut) and for Bonneval this was to be his eighth, and last, Five Nations match having been on the winning side in the previous seven. Laurent Rodriguez's try made the difference in a 10-9 win for the French. Eccentric selection policies meant that was that for Bonneval, but he retired having equalled Charles Wade's unblemished eight-match Championship sequence set a century before.

On this day in 2008 Steve Borthwick announced he was leaving Bath to join Saracens, having been "sold the club" by incoming director of rugby Eddie Jones. Less than a month later he led England for the first time and the season ended with European Challenge Cup success with Bath. However, a troublesome England tour of New Zealand (on and off the pitch), record international defeats in the autumn, criticism of his captaincy after a string of Six Nations sin-bins, a South African takeover of Sarries and Jones leaving the club towards the end of another mediocre campaign made 2008/9 a nightmare.

JANUARY 17

Some people are just, well, driven... Take Wavell Wakefield, who made his England debut on January 17 1920. What did he achieve? How about a Red Rose record 31 caps that stood for 42 years, being acknowledged as the originator of modern forward play, leading England to back-to-back Grand Slams, serving in World War I, RAF 440-yards champion, Member of Parliament, RFU President, knighted, made a Lord, first Englishman inducted to rugby's International Hall of Fame and lived to the age of 84. If only he had pulled his finger out and done something with his life...

Another English stalwart ended his distinguished career exactly 61 years after Wakefield's debut with the same number of caps – Fran Cotton. That Cotton managed to extend his time at the top to 31 appearances was testament to the fortitude that enabled him to be one of the legendary 1974 Lions in South Africa. On his third Lions tour as a player, in 1980, he was stricken by chest pains and had to return home. Surely his career was over... No, Cotton played on, before earning the respect of a new generation with his handling of the successful 1997 Lions trip as manager.

JANUARY 18

You've got to be good to be known as "The Invincibles" and for decades rugby aficionados have bowed their heads in reverence to the 1924/25 New Zealand squad. They beat France in the last match of their European tour – played 30, won 30. The outstanding individual, who incredibly played in every game, was a 19-year-old Maori called George Nepia. The world was at his feet, but the South African government would not allow him to set those feet inside their country for the 1928 series with the ironically-named All Blacks, due to the colour of his skin.

Invincible is a word almost appropriate to describe Munster at Thomond Park, Limerick. Gloucester ventured there in 2003 knowing they had "only" to avoid defeat by 27 points, and prevent Munster from scoring four tries, to qualify for the Heineken Cup quarter-finals. With a minute left they had achieved it, but then John Kelly's try (Munster's fourth) and Ronan O'Gara's conversion produced a 33-6 score – no wonder they call it the "Miracle Match". It compounded a sorry weekend for the Cherry and Whites... A Limerick taxi driver claimed a member of the Gloucester entourage left notes on their game-plan in the back of his cab, which were passed on to Munster.

JANUARY 19

The combination of passion for rugby and widely voiced antipathy for the English has always made the Welsh appear to try just that little bit harder against their neighbours over the years. Particularly on home soil, where the "Hwyl" sweeps both fans and players along on a tide of emotion to repel the old enemy from the East. England won in Cardiff in 1963, but then endured decades of hurt in the fabled Arms Park, as Wales coupled historical enmity with some of the greatest teams in Five Nations history to frequently outclass the men in white. Finally, Will Carling's 1991 Grand Slam team managed to end the curse 28 years to the day after Richard Sharp's side had triumphed.

It's bad enough being English for Ireland, Scotland and Wales but when, in 1999, it was perceived that the Anglos were doing better financially out of their relationship with them it really made the Celtic blood boil. The RFU had a deal with satellite broadcasters BSkyB, granting exclusive live coverage of England's Championship home games from 1998-2002. When some of this money was not paid to the Celts, the Five Nations committee expelled England from the event. The expulsion lasted just 20 hours before agreement was hammered out in Glasgow on January 19 1999.

JANUARY 20

In 2007, Leicester Tigers did what 31 previous teams had failed to do – beat Munster in a Heineken Cup match in the west of Ireland. Thomond Park in Limerick had become a fortress for the reigning European champions. Even miracles (see January 18) could happen in front of a baying crowd, where an omnipresent slogan "Irish by birth, Munster by grace of God" sums up the esprit de corps. Tries from a Leinsterman (Geordan Murphy) and Ollie Smith showed future visitors how the west could be won.

Today was the day in 2009 when Matt Stevens went public and admitted that he had a drug addiction. The Bath and England prop, speaking to Sky Sports News in emotional terms, confirmed that he had failed a test following a Heineken Cup match a month earlier. His statement paved the way for a two-year suspension from all rugby. "It is pretty distressing talking about this when I think how much time and effort so many people have put into my career. I have thrown it away through irresponsible behaviour," confessed a shame-faced Stevens.

JANUARY 21

Rugby has traditionally been a sport pursued by those in high places, but it may be a surprise to read that a former resident of the White House is among that number. As Bill Clinton was inaugurated as the 42nd President of the United States, I wonder if he recalled the days when he was dabbling with the oval ball during his time at Oxford University in the late 1960s? Gordon Brown is another high profile politician with a penchant for rucks and mauls, although Brown's experiences left him blind in his left eye, after suffering a detached retina during a game at Edinburgh University.

The 2008 banking crisis had Mr Brown preaching financial discipline... Ah, yes, the "D" word synonymous with rugby. Yellow cards can be costly – just ask Martin Johnson. French referee Patrick Thomas was the first official to brandish such a card in an international, when England's Ben Clarke was the offending player against Ireland in Dublin in 1995. In those days it was simply a "warning" but five years to the day later the law-makers decided to introduce sin-bins. Ten minutes on the touchline to make players think again and punish teams for foul play or persistent infringement.

JANUARY 22

This is a date resonant with history for France and Scotland. The "Auld Alliance" countries first played each other on the rugby field in 1910, at Inverleith in Edinburgh. The Scots won 27-0, scoring five tries – two from wing Ian Robertson (no, not the BBC Radio commentator, although some in the press box might claim it was that long ago that "Robbo" played for Scotland). There was no indication then that France would come back 11 years later and mount an impenetrable defence for a 3-0 victory.

Fast forward to 1927 and France visited the spanking new Murrayfield for the first time. Their expulsion from the Five Nations, amid allegations of professionalism, and World War II contributed to a 25-year gap before Les Bleus won at the ground. Another factor was the tournament structure dictating that France always had to play in Edinburgh in freezing January. In those amateur days, France were renowned for being far more effective with the sun on their backs and the Scots were doughty competitors under a leaden sky with a nip in the air. Edinburgh is known as the "Athens of the North", but it's nothing to do with the weather.

JANUARY 23

Ireland arrived at the 1982 Five Nations as apparent no-hopers. White-washed the previous year, on a run of seven straight defeats and with an ageing pack, it appeared to be a desperate measure to pluck Army captain Ciaran Fitzgerald to lead the side. The hooker had been frozen out of the team for two years. However, tries by wings Moss Finn (2) and Trevor Ringland, plus assured goal-kicking from Ollie Campbell, gave the Irish victory over Wales – the initial step to a first Championship since 1974 and the Triple Crown after a 33-year break.

Today's stars live on a diet of rugby in front of large crowds, playing week-in, week-out against fellow professionals. It was different in 1988 when, seven days after taking on France in front of 50,000 in Paris, Wasps' England men made the trek to Cumbria and sneaked a 13-6 win against Aspatria in the third round of the English Cup before 3,500. Five leagues separated them, and the gap remains. Now, Wasps solely swan around with the likes of Leicester and Toulouse, while Aspatria settle for Pontefract and Driffield, with no prospect of any red letter day against the top pros. The magic of the cup has been lost from the game.

JANUARY 24

"He took the ball in his arms and ran with it"... Fact or fiction? Was rugby invented by a schoolboy named William Webb Ellis? The debate has raged for decades, and will linger for as long as the game is played. The central character of the tale passed away on this day in 1872. 115 years after his death, he was officially recognised by the sport at the highest possible level with the naming of the World Cup in his honour and, in 2006, was inducted into the game's Hall of Fame. Not bad for apparently cheating in a game of football!!

If Webb Ellis is deemed to be the innovator of running rugby, Ian Smith was one of the first great practitioners of the art. The "Flying Scotsman", who was born in Australia, scored a world record 24 Test tries between 1924 and 1933 – a mark that stood for 54 years. Having scored three tries on debut against France the previous year, he notched four against the French in 1925, before completing another quad against Wales two weeks later. Eight tries in a Championship season, let alone across two matches, has yet to be bettered by anyone.

JANUARY 25

As Ireland beat Wales to end a 61-year Grand Slam drought in 2009, the legend that is Jack Kyle took it all in at the Millennium Stadium. Kyle is the most celebrated Irish fly-half in history and was the inspiration behind the clean sweep in 1948. The year before that momentous season he had made his Test bow, alongside 13 other debutants, in a defeat by France – Ireland's first international match since the war. Skipper and full-back Cornelius Murphy was the only member of the team who had donned the Ireland shirt before!

Brazil – land of magical footballers and... female rugby players. The Brazilian women's rugby team picked up the South American Sevens title in January 2009, making it five years unbeaten on their home continent in any match in the abbreviated form. It was as easy as a day on Copacabana beach for the Samba girls, as they conceded just two tries on their way to the crown. That earned them a place at the inaugural World Sevens in Dubai... Canada (38-0) and Spain (19-0) were both too good for them there, but they were runners-up in a tight consolation Bowl final to another emerging rugby nation... China.

JANUARY 26

Now here's one for all you "blazers" out there... This was the day, in 1871, when the Rugby Football Union held its first meeting, at the Pall Mall Restaurant near Trafalgar Square. A total of 21 clubs and schools were represented, as the RFU agreed the first firm set of rules, including Harlequins, Richmond and the now defunct Flamingoes. Wasps were absentees, apparently their delegation turned up at the wrong venue at the wrong time on the wrong day... At least they have been getting things right on the field in recent years. The Pall Mall is no more, but a plaque resides where it used to stand recognising its place in rugby history.

Certain dates and locations are special to certain people. Christian Darrouy, the French try-scoring machine of the 1950s and 60s, made his debut in 1957 against Ireland in Dublin and then, six years later to the day, and at the same ground, became just the second Frenchman to score a hat-trick of tries in a Championship match. Darrouy and the Boniface brothers really made the Gallic back-line sing and laid a marker for generations to come. It took Serge Blanco to erase Darrouy's tally of 23 tries in 40 Tests from the French record books.

JANUARY 27

We take the replacement of players for granted nowadays. When someone can no longer play a full part due to injury, a substitute comes on. However, up until the late 1960s this was simply not part of the game. There was no-one warming the bench, sides went one man (or more) down or walking wounded shouldered on. It took Ireland lock Mick Molloy, playing with a broken arm against France in 1968, to make the authorities realise the risks involved and the law was changed to allow subs. As for Molloy, he became the International Rugby Board's Medical Officer nearly 30 years after his act led to rugby becoming a safer game.

For rugby fans of a certain age, there will always be one try that sums up the beauty of the sport, and it happened today in 1973... Barbarians fly-half Phil Bennett mesmerised the All Blacks in front of his posts with three magical side-steps. JPR Williams showed strength in a tackle. John Pullin linked, and then there was a dummy so subtle from John Dawes you have to watch it again and again to appreciate it. Tom David to Derek Quinnell and then, as Cliff Morgan's classic commentary entreats... "This is Gareth Edwards, a dramatic start (as Edwards launches himself like a salmon to touch down in the corner)... WHAT A SCORE!!"

JANUARY 28

Having been thumped by England in their first ever match the year before, Wales got off the mark with victory over Ireland in the first red v green Test at Lansdowne Road in 1882. Wales notched four tries, but they didn't count in those Corinthian days, so skipper Charles Lewis' two goals was the difference between the sides. Imagine Gareth Edwards' try in 1973 not counting!! Or telling David Campese that his 64 touchdowns were irrelevant – "We only care about Michael Lynagh's goals, mate"...

Kicking at goal, or kicking full stop, was never Sevens wizard Waisale Serevi's idea of fun. The Fijian thrilled crowds the world over with his artistry and uncanny ability to wriggle out of the tightest of spots. How sad when the man who helped put his country truly on the rugby map was dismissed as Sevens player/coach by the Fijian Rugby Union in 2009 for "insubordination". Apparently, Serevi had deigned to criticise the selection policy and had been "repeatedly warned" about his conduct. Administrators shouldn't mess with genius...

JANUARY 29

New Zealand have always had strength in depth but sometimes it's just a little bit scary... The All Blacks won the World Cup Sevens for the first time in Mar del Plata, Argentina, in 2001 – despite losing Eric Rush, one of the greatest exponents of the shortened game, to a broken leg in one of the pool matches. For any other country it would have been a grievous blow to their chances but who should the ABs whistle up as a replacement? None other than Jonah Lomu!! Old enemy Australia were seen off 31-12 in the final... Crisis, what crisis?

Talking of crisis... Money matters off the field have grown steadily in importance since the game went professional. When the banking industry imploded in 2008, the ripples reached the English Premiership, so tournament organisers came up with a solution; more matches equals more money through the gate. The RFU, casting itself as the guardian of the paying public, threw out the plan to shoe-horn six extra league matches into the season from 2009-10. "You are going back to fans to foot the bill in very tough times," said Rob Andrew, while quietly the RFU announced an extra England game at Twickenham for autumn 2009...

JANUARY 30

There have been many great full-backs, but only one great Scott. Bob of that ilk followed in the footsteps of George Nepia as New Zealand's next great last line of defence. In the 1950s Scott was imperious, never more so than in 1954 when England found it impossible to penetrate the All Black line. *The Spectator* said of Scott: "It seemed that danger vanished at the sight of him." Nepia and Scott's successors in the black No.15 shirt include Don Clarke, Joe Karam, Allan Hewson, John Gallagher, Glen Osborne, Christian Cullen and Mils Muliaina... some list!

In Ireland it can seem like all roads lead to Dublin. In January 1999 it appeared to be literally true, as half of Ulster descended on Lansdowne Road for Ulster's Heineken Cup final against Colomiers. The fact that a predominately Protestant-supported team was playing on "home" turf in the capital of the Republic, on such an auspicious occasion, had great significance just nine months after the signing of the Good Friday agreement. David Humphreys inspired his side to become the first Irish winners of the trophy, amid tumultuous scenes. Rugby had again united a divided land.

JANUARY 31

A mighty tradition began at the conclusion of January 1948... The Barbarians had for years been a celebrated touring side without a ground but they were cast as a home team when they took on Australia at Cardiff Arms Park. The idea was a match from which the proceeds would pay for the Wallabies' trip home. The 45,000 attendance more than covered this and it became a template for a rugby carnival at the end of every major tour. The demands placed on professional players makes fulfilling the fixture more of a struggle these days.

The Heineken Cup final was moved away from Cardiff for the first time in 1998, and what an occasion it was in Bordeaux. Title holders Brive had 40,000 voices shouting for them against a small, but passionate, group of Bath fans willing their heroes on. It wasn't the greatest game, but the spectacle was amazing and ensured that the competition was recognised as the pinnacle of European club rugby. Jon Callard scored all Bath's 19 points to Brive's 18 – Bath, the kings of English rugby for so long, were champions of Europe. However, it marked the end of an era... The trophy cabinet at The Rec was bare for 10 years afterwards.

RUGBY
On This Day

FEBRUARY

FEBRUARY 1

It really doesn't matter when a match-winning score comes, but there's always something special about a last minute intervention. So it was in 1958 as, with the score at 6-6 and England down to 14 men due to injury, Peter Jackson received the ball 30 yards from Australia's line. He eluded opposing wing Roderick Phelps and glided outside full-back Terence Curley before diving headlong for a sensational score. Jackson was a celebrated player of his day, compared to both football legend Sir Stanley Matthews and ballet star Nijinsky.

Exactly 28 years before Jackson's heroics, Scotland were thankful to fly-half Herbert Waddell for a last-gasp winning drop goal against Wales. It was to be a glorious way to end an 18-cap career wearing the thistle. Waddell's kick was his 5th drop goal for his country, a Scottish record he held for over 50 years until one of his successors as playmaker, John Rutherford, came along. Waddell, a member of the first Scottish Grand Slam squad in 1925, died in 1988 having seen Rutherford play a key role in securing a second tartan clean sweep in 1984.

FEBRUARY 2

The act of kicking can be a thing of beauty... Barry John used to seemingly caress the leather as he guided a perfectly weighted grubber through the opposition defence and Phil Bennett slotted goals with calm precision and a limited back-lift. However, Jean-Patrick Lescarboura, the French fly-half of the mid 1980s, was a brute when it came to propelling the oval. If rugby balls had feelings they would have been quivering whenever the mighty man from Dax prepared to launch them into the stratosphere. In 1985, three enormous Lescarboura drop goals against England equalled the world record for an international match and earned a 9-all draw, in front of a gasping Twickenham crowd.

Scotland full-back Andy Irvine was famed more for his thrilling counter-attacking than kicking but it should be recognised that the Murrayfield icon of the 1970s was a prolific and reliable points accumulator. Irvine amassed a world record 301 before the World Cup era produced more opportunities for points machines such as Lynagh, Fox, Hastings and Wilkinson to soar past him. One of his stellar moments was a last minute penalty to win the 1974 Calcutta Cup match, in front of his adoring Edinburgh public.

FEBRUARY 3

There must definitely be something about the crisp February air that allows kickers of all shapes and sizes to achieve amazing feats. Take Scotland No.8 Peter Kininmonth against Wales in 1951... The Welsh were reigning Grand Slam champions and tipped to run riot at Murrayfield, with 11 members of the 1950 Lions in their ranks. However, with the home side 3-0 up, Kininmonth, from near the touchline in between the Wales 25 and halfway, struck an epic drop goal. Scotland won 19-0, the heaviest Welsh defeat for 26 years, a match ranking alongside the 1984 and 1990 Grand Slam clinchers in the pantheon of Scottish rugby.

We can't leave the subject of kicking without a mention of Scotland's regular nemesis... Jonny Wilkinson. In 2007, after over three years of injury heartache, England's pride and joy kicked a ball on the international stage for the first time since the most famous drop goal in history against the Scots at Twickenham. And what a return... Wilkinson took out all those long months of frustration on the Scots with a bravura show of 27 points – a Calcutta Cup best to add to his litany of records.

FEBRUARY 4

Say what you like about the Rugby Football Union (and many do) but the august organisation now based at Twickenham always seems to create news... The 1888 International Championship began on this day, but England did not take part. Scotland, Wales and Ireland agreed not to play against them after the RFU refused to join the International Rugby Football Board (set up by the other Home Nations), arguing that it required greater representation through having the most clubs and did not want the IRFB to be a law-making entity. The same stand-off occurred in 1889 before the RFU finally agreed to sign up to the world governing body in 1890.

The RFU in the amateur era was not held in a great deal of esteem by the general public, so perhaps it's appropriate to next reflect on a difference of opinion between English rugby HQ and an equally derided body – Wimbledon FC. In 1991, the "Crazy Gang" were struggling to compete with the big boys on meagre crowds at Crystal Palace and came up with the idea to play their home games at Twickenham. It must have taken a while for the gin and tonics to settle, but eventually the RFU threw the suggestion out of court. Vinny Jones playing on the hallowed turf? That would never do...

FEBRUARY 5

Many have brought a touch of class to proceedings on a rugby field, but how about a touch of glass... The 19th century Ireland full-back Dolway Walkington made his debut against England in 1887 – wearing a monocle. Strange but true... According to reports, Walkington would remove the eyepiece to make a tackle and on one occasion against Wales collected a clearance kick, calmly took out the circular corrective lens and slotted a magnificent drop goal!! Don't try this at home, kids...

In the year 2000, Italy played Scotland in Rome to inaugurate the Six Nations Championship. The Italians, who had been knocking on the door of the dining room where European rugby's aristocracy had feasted for decades, took their place at the table and made their presence felt immediately with a 34-20 win at Stadio Flaminio. Diego Dominguez scored 29 points – a record for the ancient Championship whether in its Four, Five or Six Nation guise. Oh well, the Scottish fans had the consolation of an exotic new city in which to drown their sorrows.

FEBRUARY 6

It was 1971 and a golden generation of Welsh players were embarking on a magical decade for the Dragons. Up against them on this day was a fired-up Scotland side and a huge crowd filling the Murrayfield terraces. It was a match to remember, a real battle. Scotland appeared to have an epic victory in their grasp until, with five minutes remaining, JPR Williams sent Gerald Davies on his elusive way to the corner. Now it was up to flanker John Taylor to add the extras... "JT" swung his left boot and the ball sailed through the posts – it was coined as "the greatest conversion since St Paul".

Never turn up late for a game. Scotland faced Wales 28 years to the day since that special occasion in 1971, and one of their flock of "kilted Kiwis" – John Leslie – made the record books with a try barely nine seconds after kick-off. The fastest try in the history of Test rugby. Scotland won 33-20, fielding three New Zealand-born players – Leslie, his brother Martin and Glenn Metcalfe. Perhaps they had a few cold "Steinys" and a "Fusch 'n' Chup" supper on Princes Street to celebrate...

FEBRUARY 7

Scotland likes to keep it in the family. With their relatively small playing numbers, the Scots have frequently selected brothers for international rugby matches. The most celebrated have been the Hastingses – Gavin and Scott appeared in 50 Tests together. It's a practice that has been going on for a long time, but rarely in multiples... In 1891, the Neilson brothers (George and William) began a Scottish rugby dynasty by making their debuts against Wales, which was carried on by Walter (won his solitary cap against England in 1894 in place of big brother George) and youngest sibling Robert (1898-1900).

The Neilsons shared the thrill of being picked to represent their country. The letter, telegram or phone call to confirm that first treasured cap – you've made it! Well, not quite in the case of Ken McLeod... He was selected at the age 15 to play against Wales in 1903, which would have made him the youngest ever Scotland international. Only thing was his headmaster at Fettes College in Edinburgh – the redoubtable Dr Heard – refused him permission to play!! "Your studies are more important, McLeod". The disappointed wing's time eventually came at the grand old age of 17 and he went on to appear 10 times for the Scots.

FEBRUARY 8

Two of the game's great entertainers made their Test debuts in England v Ireland fixtures on this day – Mike Gibson and David Duckham. The pair were comrades in arms on the famous 1971 tour of New Zealand. Gibson started as he was to go on in 1964, a match-winning performance as the Irish won at Twickenham for the first time since the Grand Slam team in 1948. It was to be the first of a then world record 81 caps for Ireland and the Lions over a 15-year career. If the World Cup had been around in his day, Gibson would surely have been the first to reach a ton.

Exactly five years after Gibson's entrance, he was directly opposed at inside centre by new boy Duckham at Lansdowne Road. The Coventry man scored a try but could not prevent a 17-15 defeat. The side-step at pace is his legacy... "You could see it coming but he still left you stranded," according to former Wales captain Mervyn Davies. It was a shame for England fans, and a relief to everyone else, that Duckham only received an estimated three passes per match from the desultory England teams of 1969-76. What an appalling waste of talent.

FEBRUARY 9

Rugby union is designed to be a sport for all shapes and sizes. Powerful props, lanky locks, and diminutive scrum-halves all add to the spectacle but there's something special about an elusive, fast winger. Shane Williams is the heir to a tradition handed down by the likes of Tony O'Reilly, David Duckham, JJ Williams and David Campese – men who could tease and sprint away from the opposition in the style of a matador. Williams went out on his own as Wales' leading Six Nations try scorer with his 10th and 11th against Scotland in 2008 and was to add four more, as Wales secured the Grand Slam, to equal Maurice Richards' Welsh record for a season set in the 1969 Five Nations.

Williams was a major reason why Wales climbed to their highest ever IRB World Ranking of fourth on February 9 2009. Some decry the rankings but rugby needs such a ladder to stimulate publicity for the game. World Cup seedings are now based on the list, and simply adds to the importance every Test match has. The Lithuanias, Israels and Moroccos have something to aim for, as Wales looked down on them from their lofty perch.

FEBRUARY 10

One of the more startling developments in the professional era has been, quite literally, Super Rugby in the southern hemisphere. The New Zealand and South African provinces were combined to create nine new franchises, while Australia forged ACT Brumbies to join New South Wales and Queensland, and Super 12 was born in 1996. The next stage was to add The Force from Western Australia and The Cheetahs from South Africa to create Super 14. In 2006 the Wellington-based Hurricanes beat the Blues, hailing from Auckland, in the first S14 match. In 2011 the tournament expands to 15.

Not all things in the southern garden are rosy... On the eve of the 2008 Super 14 season, Force scrum-half Matt Henjak took exception to team-mate Haig Sare in a Fremantle bar and walloped him – causing the wing to suffer a broken jaw. Nine days later The Force gave Henjak the sack. It wasn't the first time Henjak had been involved in controversy. Two separate alleged incidents in South African nightclubs, one while with The Brumbies in 2004 and the other on the Australia tour a year later, had called his temperament into question. Henjak eventually found "sanctuary" in the French Top 14 with Toulon... Mind how you go...

FEBRUARY 11

It would appear to be a prerequisite of rugby to get your hands dirty. Some, though, prefer to keep their extremities clean. The modern era has seen the introduction of fingerless mittens to help the ball `stick`, but the concept had been adopted many years before by the eccentric Basil MacLear. The Ireland fly-half made his debut in 1905 against England, the country of his birth, wearing white (yes, white) gloves fully covering his digits. Snooker referees may approve but today's harassed kit men would shake their heads.

While MacLear created his little mark in Irish rugby history, a real barrier was broken in 2007 when Dublin's Croke Park, the citadel of Gaelic games, staged an international in a "foreign" sport for the first time. Ireland welcomed France to one of the finest arenas in Europe while Lansdowne Road was being rebuilt – an occasion unthinkable for decades. Some wondered what all the fuss had been about, and why millions of Euros were being spent updating a ground when a better stadium could be used down the road. Those cynics fail to understand the unique power and position held by the GAA in Ireland.

FEBRUARY 12

While the all-time greats scattered around the Wales teams of the 1970s cast their shadows over the decade, two of the outstanding performers of that era among the other Home Nations were Ireland flanker Fergus Slattery and Scotland centre Jim Renwick, both born on this day. The Irishman was among those to redefine an openside's role into that of an all-action hero. Renwick, whose balding pate made him look older then he was, delighted Murrayfield with some inspired passages of play in concert with the likes of Andy Irvine and John Rutherford.

From sublime Scottish memories to one of the most unfortunate in tartan rugby history... Scott Murray was doing what he does best against Wales at Cardiff in 2006 – being a nuisance to the opposition; impressive at the line-out, good in the loose and with more than 70 caps worth of know-how. Irritated by a late tackle from opposing second row Ian Gough, Murray lashed out with his foot and struck Gough in the head. Kiwi referee Steve Walsh took a dim view and Murray was shown the red card – the first Scotland player to be sent off in a Championship match and just the second in 135 years of international rugby.

FEBRUARY 13

It's easy to make facile comparisons between today's professionals and the "gentlemen amateurs" of yore, but occasionally there's a reminder that those early players had more on their plates than just a mere game. The Reverend Matthew Mullineux, who led the 1899 British team to Australia, died on February 13 1945 with the Military Cross against his name. In May 1918, the army chaplain took charge of a regimental aid post in France, dressed the wounded and supervised evacuation. In the words of the news reports of the time: "But for his prompt assistance there would have been serious congestion of the wounded."

When 21-year-old Tom Kiernan trotted out at Twickenham in 1960 to make his debut, few could have imagined the impact he would have. Kiernan was selected for two Lions tours, was the first Irishman to win 50 caps, coached his country and became President of the Union. Kiernan was inducted into the International Hall of Fame and if Ireland ever created one he would have to have a wall to himself. Oh, and nephew Michael Kiernan won 43 caps, set Irish points scoring records and achieved Triple Crown success in 1982 and 1985.

FEBRUARY 14

Mixing business with pleasure can be a dangerous game, particularly when playing rugby at the highest level. Wing Tony O'Reilly was recalled by Ireland against England in 1970 after a seven-year absence, during which time he had progressed to become the "Baked Bean King" (MD of Heinz). The morning papers said that he had been spotted being driven to training on the eve of the match in a Rolls Royce. So when O'Reilly was caught at the bottom of a ruck and was "brought down to earth", so to speak, by the England forwards, a voice in the crowd bellowed: "And while you're at it, kick his bloody chauffeur as well!!"

Valentines Day 1962 produced an event that would lead to drooling two decades later from all lovers of scintillating back play – the birth of Philippe Sella. The quicksilver centre was a fixture in the French midfield for 13 years, accumulating a World Cup runners-up medal, a Grand Slam, six Five Nations titles (including three shared), 30 tries and a then world record 111 caps. Sella was the first man to hit the magical 100-cap barrier, a figure beyond imagination for any player when he began his career.

FEBRUARY 15

The parting of the ways between rugby union and league happened in 1895. A century of serial antagonism from both sides of the fence made it feel like a lot longer. Relations have improved greatly. Harlequins now play both codes, a raft of players and coaches have moved from league to union and Challenge Cup finals have been staged at Twickenham, Murrayfield and the Millennium Stadium. However, certain names remain entrenched in either code so it may be a surprise to learn that Dewsbury, in the heart of Yorkshire RL country, staged an International Championship match on this day in 1890. An historic occasion, it was the first Welsh win against the English.

Imagine Michael Ballack scoring for Germany against England at Wembley, receiving a standing ovation and being chaired off to the acclaim of the home fans. Difficult, isn't it? Back in 1964, All Black captain Wilson Whineray scored the concluding try of a 36-3 win over the Barbarians. The conversion went over, the referee blew his whistle and Whineray was carried off shoulder-high with the crowd singing "For he's a jolly good fellow", to mark the end of a 34-match tour, that saw just one defeat.

FEBRUARY 16

Throughout the 1960s and 70s, England always seemed to need a little bit of help to overcome Wales. The Welsh nation was buoyed by a clear superiority over their neighbours in the glory years, when the Red Rose wilted against the fire of the Dragon. In 1980, England recorded just their second win in the fixture in 17 years, and it was done against 14 men for over half the match at Twickenham. Flanker Paul Ringer was sent off for striking fly-half John Horton in the face or, according to Welsh cheerleader Max Boyce: "Taking mascara out of Horton's eye." Dusty Hare kicked three penalties to seal a 9-8 win and Bill Beaumont's side were on the way to a first Grand Slam for 23 years.

Among Beaumont's heroes was the late Maurice Colclough, who at the time was sampling a change of lifestyle with Angouleme. While Colclough was very much the exception to the rule in his day, there has recently been a procession of players following in his footsteps to France. James Haskell, Riki Flutey and Tom Palmer announced their intentions to swap Roast Beef for Moules Marinieres, to the consternation of the RFU. It seems the English can do little about French owners with deep pockets...

FEBRUARY 17

Dean Richards, that great bear of a man, is someone players want to follow. Whether initiating a driving maul for England or scheming on the training paddock as a director of rugby. On this day in 1998, Leicester Tigers decided to hand "Deano" the reins after the acrimonious departure of Bob Dwyer. What a move it was... Four straight Premiership titles, plus back-to-back Heineken Cups... but two trophy-less seasons saw opinion turn against him and he was sacked in 2004 – hero to zero. You can't keep a good man down, though, and Harlequins are stirring under his command.

February 17 2001 is a red letter date for rugby statisticians. The archetypal "record-breaking day" saw Wales goal-kicking machine Neil Jenkins become the first man to notch 1000 points in Test rugby during the 28-all draw against Scotland, which was just the third stalemate between the old Celtic rivals in 105 matches. While down at Twickenham, England amassed a Championship record score and win against Italy (80-23) with Jonny Wilkinson getting his fill with a record 35 points. Lies, lies and damned statistics... Outclassed Italy's score was their best tally against England.

FEBRUARY 18

This day has seen a queue of people occupying international rugby's "naughty step"... In 1995, Wales prop John Davies became the first player to be shown a red card when he was sent off against England for kicking the man who earlier that year became the first to clap eyes on a yellow card – Ben Clarke. A couple of years later, Andre Markgraaf was sacked in disgrace as South Africa coach after the broadcasting of racist remarks about black rugby officials and politicians. A South Africa coming out of long years of apartheid was a particularly unforgiving environment for such views.

In between Davies and Markgraaf, "robust" Ireland prop Peter Clohessy was banned for 26 weeks – that will be half a year – after being cited for stamping on France lock Oliver Roumat. Clohessy pleaded that his action "happened in the momentum of a gathering ruck situation and was without malicious intent." Rugby's administrators cocked a snoot at that and puffed their chests out in pride that new citing procedures using video evidence had been used, after public condemnation of the sight of Clohessy using Roumat like a doormat. Their task may have been helped by Ireland's national broadcaster showing the incident a reported 50 times on the day of the game!!

FEBRUARY 19

A good nickname adds to the fun of sport. Rugby has had its fair share – "Pinetree", "Mighty Mouse", "No-one" and "Chariots" have been monikers handed out to Messrs Meads, McLauchlan, Eales and Offiah, but another one sticks out for its sheer eccentricity. Esteemed journalist Frank Keating referred to speedy Ireland wing Simon Geoghegan as "looking like Bambi on Benzedrine", reflecting on Geoghegan's match-winning try against England on February 19 1994. With his bustling running style and spindly legs it was an act of literary genius!

Jonny Wilkinson has written his name over countless pages of the England record book with his points scoring feats. History should also relate that he has been far more than just a goal-kicker. At his peak, his defence was ferocious, stronger in the tackle than any fly-half in history. At the Stade de France in 2000, France wing Emile Ntamack, all bristling pace and power, was descending on the England line... wham!! He was stopped in his tracks by a shuddering waist high assault by Wilkinson. The Frenchman, and home crowd, were stunned by the ferocity of the relatively diminutive England No.10.

FEBRUARY 20

In 1982, Ireland at last won another Triple Crown. Ollie Campbell stroked six penalties and a drop goal against Scotland to send the Irish rugby nation into raptures, 33 years after the last time the thistle and rose had been cut down alongside a slain Dragon in one season. The Grand Slam remained elusive, France too good for the men in green in Paris, but Ciaran Fitzgerald's men had proved the prophets of doom who predicted the wooden spoon wrong.

While Dublin was heaving with revelling Irishmen, Paris was the scene of some very bizarre celebrations on February 20 1982 – even by the often extreme standards of rugby... England had just achieved consecutive wins in the French capital for the first time since 1923-25. Off the players went to toast their success in the traditional manner... Maurice Colclough teased his team-mates by using sleight of hand to swap the contents of bottles of water and after shave and then appeared to "down in one" the potent scent. Not to be outdone, prop Colin Smart produced an undoctored flask of après rasage, shoved it down his throat and had to be rushed to the nearest hospital to have the burning fluid pumped out of his stomach...

FEBRUARY 21

Modern day All Blacks are walking in the footsteps of legends. One such figure is Kel Tremain, born on this day in 1932. Tremain was an immense rugby figure in the 1960s, a flanker who showed that the position can be a constructive, as well as destructive, force on the pitch. He scored nine tries in 38 Tests, a staggering ratio for a forward in his day, and a magnificent 136 tries in 268 first-class matches. When he was dropped by the All Blacks in 1969 it was described in Napier, where he lived, as the biggest shock since the tragic 1932 earthquake devastated the city.

Tremain performed his heroics in television's black and white era, colour broadcasts brought the sport alive in the 1970s and 20 years on another significant milestone was reached when satellite stations began to take rugby around the globe. In 1998, England's 60-26 thrashing of Wales at Twickenham was the first International Championship match to be shown on subscription television, when Sky Sports began their controversial five-season deal with the RFU. In 2003 the BBC regained the right to show Six Nations games live from Twickenham.

FEBRUARY 22

In February 2004, almost a decade after the beginning of professionalism, Ireland were accepted as a nation that had met the challenge the right way. Welsh rugby, which initially allowed clubs free rein, was in its first season of regional rugby. The WRU had decided to change tack and follow the Irish example of concentrating the pro game on a handful of organisations under the control of the Union. Events on the pitch had showed the Welsh what could be done, and the Irish rubbed it in further by winning a record 5th straight match against the Dragons, scoring six tries to two in a convincing 36-15 win in Dublin.

Japanese society is based on the principle of honour and the "right way" to behave. Much as in life, so in rugby, with a decision surely unthinkable anywhere else in the world... The 2009 National Championship semi-finals took place without Toshiba, who had qualified. The club voluntarily stood down "in the spirit of rugby values" after one of its players failed a drugs test. Christian Loamanu was suspended indefinitely from playing in any official games in Japan after testing positive for Cannabinoid. Toshiba further cleansed its soul by chucking Loamanu out of the club.

FEBRUARY 23

The often bitingly cold conditions seen in February in the UK have seen various techniques used to allow important rugby matches to beat the cold. Under-soil heating, for instance, has saved many a fixture from being bracketed with that dreaded word... Postponed. The innovation had not reached Twickenham in 1963 (Murrayfield was the first stadium in the country to install in 1960) and, with a harsh frost threatening the Five Nations match against France, blowers were successfully employed on the pitch to keep the chill at bay. So there you have it – hot air emitted at Twickenham.

Scotland may have wished that a freak blizzard could have struck Stade de France in 2003 after they were put to the sword by France. The score of 38-3 was their worst defeat in Paris and was, sadly for the Scots, an accurate rehearsal for the World Cup match between the sides later that year (51-9). The French ran in four tries to nil, under the direction of scrum-half Fabien Galthie, with a Chris Paterson penalty the only reply.

FEBRUARY 24

Certain events feel the weight of history upon them... In 2007, there was a massive build-up to the Ireland v England match, which was to be the first time a British team had played at Dublin's Croke Park. Of even greater significance was the planned rendition of "God Save The Queen" at a stadium that saw the killing of 14 civilians by the British Army during a Gaelic football match in 1920, as southern Ireland struggled to free itself from the crown. Politicians beat their chests, predicting disturbances, but the Irish crowd respected the pre-match rituals impeccably and were rewarded by a rousing 43-13 victory for their heroes.

Also in 1997, at Murrayfield, a staggering start to a Six Nations match as Italy crossed the Scotland line three times in the first six minutes to set up an emphatic 37-17 victory – their first success in the tournament away from Rome. There had been no sign before (or since) of such a performance by the Azzurri, who have perpetually struggled to mix it on the scoreboard with the big boys since their elevation. Their meaty packs have packed a punch and been very competitive, but oh for an inventive back-line...

FEBRUARY 25

The England team either side of World War I was one of the most successful in the history of the International Championship. Five Grand Slams in seven seasons between 1913 and 1924 is an eye-catching performance and a key figure in their success was fly-half WJA "Dave" Davies. The 11-all draw with France in 1922 was the only one of Davies' 21 Five Nations matches that he failed to win and his half-back partnership with fellow sailor Cyril Kershaw has gone down in legend. That acknowledged rugby innovator Wavell Wakefield said that Davies was the "artist and philosopher of my rugby learning."

Scotland and Ireland have been pretty evenly matched over the years. The Grand Slam Irish team won in 2009 but the Scots led the series 62-55 after 123 meetings, with five draws and one abandoned in that time. However, playing at Murrayfield appears hardly to have been an advantage for the thistle against the shamrock. Ireland's 5-3 victory in 1967, thanks to a captain's try from Noel Murphy, was the 13th time in 18 visits that the Irish had cause for celebration in Edinburgh and Ireland achieved 22 wins and a draw from their first 42 visits.

FEBRUARY 26

George Lindsay, capped just four times by Scotland in the 19th century, died at the tragically young age of 42 in 1905. His rugby legacy lives on, though, as he continues to hold the oldest record in the book... On February 26 1887, at Raeburn Place in Edinburgh, Lindsay notched five tries against Wales. The feat remains the most tries scored by a player in an International Championship match and the dozen touchdowns in total by the Scotland team that day has also yet to be beaten. The irony is that the record is so old that it pre-dates points scoring, so the result is listed as a mere four goals to nil!!

France were not even playing international rugby when Lindsay was racking up his tries. The French joined the Championship in 1910 and made their mark at the evocative Stade Colombes in Paris. Progress demanded more modern facilities and, in 1972, Les Bleus played their 97th and last international at the venue for the 1924 Olympics and 1938 football World Cup final. They enjoyed themselves, scoring six tries in beating England 37-12 – a fitting way to say au revoir to a great ground.

FEBRUARY 27

A dreadful day for Welsh rugby as news of the death of all-time great scrum-half Dicky Owen came through from Swansea in 1932. Owen, who was actually registered at birth as Owens but was known throughout his career by the singular form, tragically took his own life in the pub he ran in the city. He was a member of the so-called "first Golden era" team, winning three Grand Slams, four Triple Crowns, six Championships and 35 caps between 1901 and 1912 – a tally unsurpassed by a Welshman until Gareth Edwards came along.

Suicides such as Owen's remind us that there are far more important concerns in life than the almighty lathers rugby followers sometimes get themselves into. The 2009 Six Nations tried the experiment of a first-ever Friday night match – France v Wales at Stade de France. The idea came from French television, with their impressive viewing figures for domestic matches at the end of the working week. However, there were howls of protests from fans concerned about having to take time off work and traditionalists who believed weekend afternoons should be the sole precinct for 6N games... Perhaps we should play the matches in black and white as well then...

FEBRUARY 28

The Calcutta Cup, the oldest international rugby trophy, was first awarded on this day in 1880, when England beat Scotland at Whalley Range in Manchester. For those not in the know, the reason why two British teams compete for a bauble named after an Indian city is because the trophy was donated to the RFU by former members of the defunct Calcutta Football Club in 1878. The English and Scottish ex-pats gave best to a climate more suited to cricket than rugby, disbanded the club, and had the silver rupees in its bank account melted down and made into an ornate cup.

Talking of skilled craftsmen, in 1953 England centre Jeff Butterfield and French forward totem Michel Celaya made their debuts in opposition at Twickenham. Butterfield, who scored a try in an 11-0 win, was a graceful presence in the English midfield for six years and played in all four Tests on the 1955 Lions tour of South Africa, scoring three tries in the drawn series. Celaya won 50 caps at lock and No.8, joining forces with Michel Crauste and Francois Moncla in the great back row of the 1961 Championship-winning team.

FEBRUARY 29

One of the better ideas to come from the RFU was a clubs' cup competition. For over 30 years, teams from across the English rugby spectrum took part, but "giant killings" were very rare. It's tough to defend a 50-metre line for 80 minutes against more powerful and skilful players. However, Birmingham's curiously named Pertemps Bees saw off mighty Wasps in the 2004 quarter-finals – just three months before their victims were crowned European champions. It was the Bees' (beaten in the semis) and the minnows' last hurrah... In 2005/6, the cup became the sole preserve of the Premiership clubs and Welsh regions.

The big professional clubs may have consigned matches against smaller fry to history but even they struggle when the weather does its worst... In 2008, Newcastle Falcons' home game against Wasps was called off just 90 minutes before kick-off after 60mph winds ripped off part of the roof of a stand and snapped one of the goalposts. Referee Tony Spreadbury was forced to make it a wasted journey north for himself and the Londoners but, as then Newcastle director of rugby John Fletcher put it: "I don't think (Falcons full-back) Mat Tait would have enjoyed it had a post come down and whacked him on the head."

RUGBY
On This Day

MARCH

MARCH 1

Disasters, such as Ibrox, Hillsborough and Valley Parade, led to the implementation of all-seater stadia. More seats mean fewer spectators and gone forever are mass gatherings such as the 104,000 who were recorded as seeing Scotland beat Wales 12-10 at Murrayfield in 1975 – a world record for a rugby union match. The old ground's huge terraces were teeming with a jovial mix of red and blue, plus the odd leek, to see the likes of Irvine, Renwick, McLauchlan and Brown see off JPR, Edwards, the Pontypool front row et al.

Palmerston North is a name to conjure with... A university city north of Wellington on New Zealand's North Island, it has its own little piece of rugby history... In 1996, the Hurricanes were beaten 36-28 by the Blues in the first-ever Super Rugby match (Super 12 in those days), and also the first fully professional rugby union match ever held in the southern hemisphere. The city hosts two matches in the 2011 World Cup, having been the venue for Tonga v Wales in the 1987 tournament, and is also home to the New Zealand Rugby Union's museum.

MARCH 2

The day after St David's Day, two of Welsh rugby's most famous full-backs were born. In 1871, Billy Bancroft entered the world. A renowned goal-kicker, Bancroft played 33 consecutive internationals from 1890 to 1901, leading Wales on 11 occasions. He died the day after his 88th birthday, when the boy who was to break his record for most caps as last line of Welsh defence was just 10... John Peter Rhys Williams was to become a living legend, known to all as "JPR". Never has there been a more dependable No.15. The old saying: "Who would you want to catch a rugby ball if your life depended on it?" was made for him.

On the other side of the coin, March 2 1981 was the day Scottish rugby mourned the passing of Phil MacPherson, who led them to their first Grand Slam in 1925. He was part of the celebrated "Jocks-ford" three-quarter line, alongside centre partner George Aitken and wings Ian Smith and Johnnie Wallace. All four were Oxford University students and formed a thrilling combination, with Smith's eight tries that season still a record for the Championship. MacPherson was also a fine athlete, claiming the Scottish long jump title in 1929, and was a brigadier in World War II.

MARCH 3

As the sport slid inexorably towards the line in the sand of August 1895 when rugby league was born, allegations of "professionalism" were rife. Arguably the most unfortunate befell Halifax's JP Clowes in 1888. Clowes, asked to join the first British team (forerunner of the Lions) to tour Australia and New Zealand, was disqualified and declared professional by the RFU on the eve of departure. Clowes was charged with playing in a Yorkshire Cup tie against Dewsbury, after receiving £15 from the tour organisers to purchase clothes for the trip. Clowes still toured, but didn't touch a ball in anger for fear of the opposition refusing to play against him and the whole squad being "professionalised" by his presence.

Who do English rugby fans like thrashing the most... the Scots, the French, the Aussies? It doesn't happen that often against the latter two but the old enemy from the North have taken some fearful batterings at Twickenham. The worst humbling (43-3) occurred in 2001, when the Red Rose Grand Slam team was in full bloom. They racked up six tries to eclipse the 91-year-old record of 21 for a Championship season. A year earlier Scotland had denied their bitter rivals the Grand Slam... This was savage revenge, of sorts.

MARCH 4

Playing two sports at international level simultaneously has gone with crowded fixture lists and player "burn-out". The likes of Andrew (AE) Stoddart are from a bygone age. Uniquely, Stoddart found the time to captain England at both cricket and rugby. He won the last of his 10 oval ball caps against Scotland on March 4 1893, a year after scoring 134 runs against Australia in Adelaide and four months before a home Ashes series. Remarkable, but sadly his mercurial lifestyle beat him in the end... He committed suicide at the age of 52.

Blackheath was at the forefront of rugby in Stoddart's day. Founder members of the RFU, "The Club" (as it likes to be known) celebrated its centenary in 1959 with a match against the Barbarians. The Baa-baas won 21-8 but had the small advantage of 13 internationals to the opposition's one. While Richmond, their age-old rivals, withered on the vine of professionalism, Blackheath chose to pay only within their means and have stabilised in the lower reaches of national rugby. No cups, no big crowds, but no bankruptcy for this most traditional of rugby clubs.

MARCH 5

Dan Carter is one of the new professionals who can subtly manipulate the sport to try to meet their own ends. Carter, born on this day in 1982, shocked New Zealand by announcing that he was going to play in France for Perpignan and bypass the 2009 Super 14 season, before returning for the Tri-Nations. The NZRU, who say only NZ-based players can pull on the black shirt, bent their rules to accommodate him. They recognised that money talks and feared the fly-half might walk away from the All Blacks if they didn't agree. Fate can be cruel, though; Carter ruptured his Achilles tendon in January 2009...

I wonder if Carter would oust Rob Andrew from Bill McLaren's all-time "World XV" named in 2001, if he had another go now? Andrew's selection caused uproar, particularly in Wales where it was unimaginable that Cliff Morgan, Barry John and Phil Bennett could be superseded by an Englishman. Another one for debate was McLaren's preference for Andy Irvine at full-back over Serge Blanco, Christian Cullen and JPR Williams.

MARCH 6

Of all the marvellous performances by Wales in the 1970s, the victory over France in 1976 that clinched a record-equalling 7th Grand Slam stands out. Two unbeaten sides clashed on the penultimate Saturday of the Championship. Wales built a 16-9 lead, Jean-Luc Averous scored a controversial try – the TV replay showed that JPR Williams got to the loose ball first, but the video ref hadn't been invented yet – and then the defining moment. Jean-Francois Gourdon sped down the wing and prepared to dive in at the corner when he was stopped in his tracks by a shuddering JPR tackle – what a player, what a match.

While those Welsh legends gained notoriety solely through their deeds on the pitch, some of the modern stars are wrapped up in "celebrity culture"... Gavin Henson and Danny Cipriani are seen almost as regularly at the front of the papers as the back. In 2008, Cipriani was snapped leaving a Mayfair nightclub in the early hours, just two days before a Calcutta Cup match that would have been his first England start. Brian Ashton dropped him for "inappropriate behaviour", despite Cipriani protesting that he only spent 10 minutes at the venue delivering match tickets to mates, and didn't have a drink... Beware the paparazzi.

MARCH 7

Will Carling was widely derided outside England but his team of the early 1990s achieved something even the Welsh legends of the 1970s failed to do – win back-to-back Grand Slams. Having ended an 11-year title drought in 1991, Carling's England sealed the first consecutive clean sweeps since 1923/24 with a 24-0 thumping of Wales at Twickenham. England's 118 points in the season eclipsed the Five Nations record set by Wales in 1976, while full-back and surgeon Jonathan Webb took his tally to a tournament best 67 over the campaign.

The Sevens World Cup had been dominated by New Zealand and Fiji. Apart from England's surprise victory in 1993, the All Blacks and their Pacific neighbours had carved it up between them... That's until a group of unheralded Welshmen pulled off one of the most stunning upsets in the history of the sport in 2009. The Dubai desert provided the backdrop and, appropriately enough, Wales skipper Lee Beach lifted the Melrose Cup after his side beat Argentina in the final, having disposed of the All Blacks in the last eight. "It was the first time we have made any Sevens final, and it was the World Cup final," gasped Beach.

MARCH 8

The first major British rugby team to tour overseas left for Australia and New Zealand on this day in 1888. The trip was the brainchild of England cricketers Alfred Shaw, Arthur Shrewsbury and Andrew Stoddart, who had revelled in the concept of travelling to the far-off colonies in the early Ashes tours. The RFU refused to support the venture and, as such, many of the leading players of the day didn't feel inclined to go. An extraordinary itinerary saw 53 matches in just five months, 18 of which were under "Victorian Rules" – Australian Rules Football, as we know it now – and Swinton's Harry Eagles played in every one of them!

In 1924, Ireland handed debuts to the raw talents of the teenage Hewitt brothers at Cardiff Arms Park. Fly-half Frank, at 17 years and 157 days, became the youngest ever Five Nations player, a mark that has not been surpassed since. While wing Tom was a relative old stager on the brink of his 19th birthday. In a dream start for the Hewitt boys, both scored tries as Ireland won 13-10 – the first Irish victory in Wales for 25 years... They had literally never seen anything like it!

MARCH 9

Two of England's greatest captains were born on this day... Under Bill Beaumont's astute leadership England broke through the shackles of more than two decades of under-achievement to claim the Grand Slam in 1980. For years, bizarre selection decisions had contributed to a dire sequence of results. Beaumont brought stability and a core of players from the North of England side he led to victory against the All Blacks in 1979. The big Lancastrian was rewarded with the 1980 Lions captaincy.

In 1970, as Beaumont was celebrating becoming 18, Martin Johnson entered the world he was to shake up with his brooding presence on the rugby field. Highlights of a life less ordinary have been leading England to the 2003 World Cup and Grand Slam, guiding the Lions to a series victory in South Africa in 1997, lifting two Heineken Cups and four Premiership titles with Leicester and 90 Test caps, 84 for England (a record for a lock) and six for the Lions. And now he bids to be the first man to captain and coach a World Cup-winning team... It's a tough ask but "Johnno" has been pushing back the boundaries for years...

MARCH 10

These days, we have 22-man international teams and supplementary players of 18 or more who don't even have to get changed for combat. In 1894, Ireland used just 18 players across the three games they required to win their first Championship and Triple Crown. On March 10, they beat Wales 3-0 in Belfast, having vanquished England 7-5 at Blackheath and Scotland 5-0 in Dublin. The parochial nature of Irish rugby of the time meant 13 of the players hailed from Dublin clubs, with not a single man from the west – unthinkable now...

Ireland and Wales have served up many landmark occasions. The 1951 fixture ended in a rare draw, allowing the Irish to clinch the Championship, with Wales fielding for the first time a man who would become one of their legends... Later to become a renowned commentator and TV executive, Cliff Morgan was a will 'o' the wisp fly-half, who bewitched defences with his footballing skills and speed off the mark. He would win 29 Wales caps, plus four Lions Test appearances, before calling it a day in 1958. Most of those were alongside the devastating centre partnership formed by his Cardiff club-mates, Bleddyn Williams and Jack Matthews.

MARCH 11

Lansdowne Road, one of the most evocative venues in rugby. The crowd, so close to the pitch, created an "extra man" for Ireland with a ferocity equal to the frequently inclement conditions created by a winter's day in Dublin. Post-match, all visitors were assured of a warm welcome in the hostelries nearby, providing pleasant memories of a trip to one of the game's historic sites. The first international played at the ground was held on this day in 1878, when England won by two goals to nil. Let's hope the new, £300m redeveloped stadium serves up just as many magic moments as the old, rickety but atmospheric "bear-pit"... It's a hope, but somehow it just won't be the same...

Great Lansdowne memories but sadly this day also recalls a tragedy that unfolded after a Welsh visit to the ground in 1950. Wales had clinched a first Triple Crown for 39 years with a 6-3 victory and the travelling hordes were in joyous mood... All that was transformed the next day by the realisation that 78 of their number had perished in what was then the world's worst civil aviation disaster; their plane had crashed in a field approaching Llandow airfield. Only five survived, the dead mostly coming from the Llanharan and Abercarn clubs.

MARCH 12

The need to find talent from whatever quarter has never been so profound since the sport went professional. However, Wales and Scotland were found out in 2000, when first evidence of the so-called "Grannygate" scandal appeared in the *Sunday Herald* newspaper. New Zealand-born duo Brett Sinkinson and Shane Howarth were both revealed to not hold any qualifications to play for Wales. Both had claimed to have grandparents from the Principality, but this was not the case, and the malaise spread to engulf Scotland prop Dave Hilton, when his "Edinburgh-born grandfather" was found to have actually come from... Bristol.

Accidents happen but nothing prepares for a truly tragic injury... In 2005, England U-21 prop Matt Hampson was taking part in a scrummaging session when he suffered a devastating injury that caused him to become paralysed from the neck down. After 18 months of intensive treatment, Hampson was able to return home and begin a courageous battle to improve his quality of life via the Matt Hampson Trust. Hampson has earned the admiration of the rugby community and is seen as an example of the "spirit of rugby".

MARCH 13

When Brian O'Driscoll lifted the Six Nations trophy in 2009 it set the seal on Ireland's second Grand Slam. The first was settled on this day in 1948, with a tense 6-3 triumph over Wales at Ravenhill. Prop John Daly scored the decisive try at the citadel of Ulster rugby, as fans from both sides of the politically divided island were united in elation. Some got a little carried away, though, literally tearing the shirt off Daly's back – which gives a lie to the view that modern shirts are not as tough as those in days of yore.

In 2005, Wales beat Scotland by a record 46-22 at Murrayfield, signalling that their own long wait for a Grand Slam could really be nearing its end. The ghosts of 1978 had lingered over the valleys but for Gareth Edwards, Mervyn Davies and Gerald Davies read Dwayne Peel, Michael Owen and Shane Williams, as a six-try demolition concluded leg four of the five-match journey to the Holy Grail. As if to make the point, the victory meant Wales had beaten the Scots three times in succession for the first time since that glory era.

MARCH 14

In the dying embers of the 19th century, after two decades of international rugby and with crowds steadily increasing, the search was on for bigger and better match venues. With the concept of Murrayfield still some way off, Scotland used football's Hampden Park in 1896 for the Calcutta Cup match. The 20,000 (modest by football standards) who turned up were rewarded with an 11-0 victory. The Scottish Rugby Union has only taken the national team across to Glasgow three times since.

Rugby is a confrontational sport and the aggression required often spills over into scuffles. Sadly, in 1993, Middlesex League player Seamus Lavelle was a victim of a dust-up with tragic consequences. Hendon No.8 Lavelle was struck by a punch from Centaurs' William Hardy that led to a fatal head injury. Hardy was charged with manslaughter, but was acquitted after his plea of self-defence was accepted. The court heard how Hardy had been hit by Lavelle and had reacted with an uppercut which felled the forward, who hit the back of his skull on the ground. The resultant swelling around the brain led to Lavelle's death, a brutal reminder that there is no such thing as a harmless punch.

MARCH 15

Two England Grand Slams, 67 years apart, were clinched on this day... In 1913, Aussie born prop Bruno Brown scored the only try to seal victory over Scotland at Twickenham and an initial English clean sweep. In 1980, there was a relative try bonanza at Murrayfield as John Carleton scored a hat-trick, a feat not achieved by an Englishman for 56 years, to put the "tin hat" on Bill Beaumont's achievement of leading his country to a first Grand Slam since 1957.

Another English victory, and another Triple Crown, but in 1997 the significance was lost amid a welter of Welsh emotion at the last-ever match at the National Stadium in Cardiff – better known to most as the Arms Park. The Millennium Stadium was built on the same site, but the pitch lies in a different plane and the old ambience of the horseshoe went with the demolition and subsequent erection of a larger, all-seated, fully enclosed venue with a character of its own. The Arms Park was the first true cathedral of rugby, where the singing of Land of My Fathers was an event on its own. Its successor has carried on the tradition.

MARCH 16

Will Carling and Rory Underwood, iconic English rugby figures of the late 20th century, achieved landmarks for different reason in 1996. The 28-15 win against Ireland was to be Underwood's last cap, hanging up his Test boots with 49 tries – an English record that will stand for a good while yet. For Carling, it was his 59th and final match as Red Rose captain. He was victorious on 44 of those occasions although, perhaps, it will be the defeats by Scotland (1990), Australia (1991 World Cup Final) and New Zealand (1995 World Cup semi-final) for which he will be remembered by many.

Remember Eric Cantona's "kung fu" moment at Selhurst Park? Well, Trevor Brennan provided rugby's answer in 2007 when the Irishman, exiled in Toulouse, literally crossed the line and attacked Ulster fan Patrick Bamford in the stands during a Heineken Cup match. On March 16 of that year, two months after the incident, Brennan was banned for life from all rugby activity. However, the flanker appealed and the sanction was eventually reduced to five years. Brennan's loss of self-control hit him hard in the wallet... A €25,000 fine, and €5,000 compensation to Bamford, putting a hole in any windfall from his time in France.

MARCH 17

It might be St Patrick's Day but this date is indelibly linked with the Scotland rugby team. Two of their three Grand Slams were clinched on March 17. The Thistle's clean sweep in 1984 was just its second in history, and 59 years after the first. Jim Calder scored the only try as he led his country to triumph against France at Murrayfield, with two unbeaten sides fighting for the Five Nations title. With the score at 12-all late in the second half, Calder clutched a Colin Deans line-out throw and plunged over the line. Peter Dods added 17 points, and the Scots won 21-12.

Six years on and it was another Grand Slam decider at Murrayfield... But this one was extra special because the Scots faced up to auld enemy England in the most famous Calcutta Cup match ever played. The occasion was given added poignancy by David Sole marching his team slowly on to the field and Flower of Scotland being played for the first time as Scotland's anthem at Murrayfield. The magic moment for the Scots was wing Tony Stanger beating Rory Underwood to Gavin Hastings hopeful punt, to cancel out Jeremy Guscott's first half try. The Scots won 13-7 and Edinburgh went delirious.

MARCH 18

Twickenham was built for massive occasions such as Calcutta Cup matches, first held there in 1911. In the late 19th and early 20th century the Scots felt very comfortable at places such as Richmond and Blackheath, recording three wins at each venue. England went into the 1911 match not having won the cup at home since Manchester in 1897 and, remarkably, could not claim a victory over the Scots in London for 27 years. Anthony Henniker-Gotley became the first England captain to hoist the Calcutta Cup at Twickenham.

In 1978, the golden era of Welsh rugby ended with a 16-7 victory over France in Cardiff, a second Grand Slam in three seasons and the end of two superb careers. Gareth Edwards and Phil Bennett formed one of the great half-back partnerships. For five years they weaved their magic together. Three outright Championships and one shared in six glorious seasons together, as Bennett made the early retirement of Barry John not the apocalyptic event some in the Principality had feared. As for Edwards, you have to wonder whether his record 53 consecutive caps from debut will ever be matched by a Welshman.

SCOTLAND CLAIMED THE CALCUTTA CUP AND GRAND SLAM IN 1984 & 1990)

MARCH 19

Two of the most memorable international try hat-tricks were scored by players who started their careers brightly but were to go on to have contrasting fortunes... Chris Oti dotted down three times against Ireland in 1988 in just his second England Test. In the days when a black man wearing the Red Rose was a rare event, the Wasps wing delighted Twickenham so much that a section began singing Swing Low Sweet Chariot. The tune, which sprang from the cotton fields of America in the days of slavery, was seen by some as a derogatory gesture, but was quickly adopted as England's rugby anthem. As for Oti, injuries and the presence of Rory Underwood restricted his career to just 13 caps.

March 19 2000 is the day Brian O'Driscoll made the rugby world sit up and take notice... Paris in the spring was traditionally seen as a tough time to take on France, with their galaxy of talented backs frequently running riot in warm sunshine. However, Ireland had unearthed a gem in the 21-year-old O'Driscoll, who shocked the 80,000 crowd at Stade de France with a stunning exhibition of powerful, yet beguilingly silky running. Ireland won 27-25, their first victory against France for 17 years and first in Paris for 28 seasons.

MARCH 20

You have to keep your eye on the opposition, but this was even more imperative for a pair of remarkable men in the 1920 Calcutta Cup match. England flanker Tom Voyce faced up to Scotland prop Jock Wemyss, both men having lost the sight in one of their eyes during World War I. The match was played just over a year after the cessation of hostilities, England's victory ensured a three-way tie in the first post-war Championship, but the presence of two victims of the horrors of the so-called "war to end all wars" summed up the spirit of the time.

Feeling tired? Got that sluggish feeling? The 2004 Romania rugby team claimed that excuse for a 33-24 defeat by Russia in Krasnodar. The Romanians said they were nodding off before the game and struggled to stay awake during play. Samples taken from 12 of the squad revealed traces of a soporific called Phenothiazine and they pointed the finger at the Russians, urging the International Rugby Board to do something about it. With no proof of deliberate malpractice by the Russian federation there was little the IRB could do.

MARCH 21

The captain gets a large portion of the glory when his side wins the Grand Slam, sometimes overly so. That gripe cannot be pointed at France's 1981 leader, Jean-Pierre Rives. If there was ever a man who led by example it was Rives. Blond locks flowing, bloodied face coursed with desire and refusing to give in. There were some future French skippers in the side that beat England 16-12 at Twickenham – Serge Blanco, Pierre Berbizier and Philippe Dintrans – taking their initial steps to rugby greatness and Rives' influence must surely have rubbed off on them.

This was the day when Irish rugby finally threw off the mightiest of albatrosses from its back. A 61-year wait is a fair old trot, but as the purveyors of their national drink used to say "Good things come to those who wait" and how Ireland enjoyed its first Grand Slam since 1948. The title clincher in Cardiff was an epic... The crown was slipping away with just a few minutes to play, as Ireland mounted a ferocious attack on the Welsh line. The ball was shifted to Ronan O'Gara... this was his Jonny Wilkinson moment... and Munster's hero slotted a deft drop goal. Then, such drama as a penalty near halfway was awarded to Wales – could Stephen Jones deny them? The ball careered towards the posts and dropped agonisingly short – wow!!

MARCH 22

Nothing stirs French blood like Englishmen ranged up against them. Their first ever rugby meeting was at Parc des Princes in 1906. It didn't go well for the French, though... As is often the case when a newcomer mixes with the big boys they got pummelled, 35-8 – an absolute cricket score in those days. England fly-half Adrian Stoop was in his pomp and wing Arthur Hudson was a beneficiary, helping himself to four tries. It would be 21 years before the French would achieve their first win over the English.

It took France some time to be accepted as equal partners at the Five Nations table, a battle Italy are currently fighting in its Six Nations incarnation. If a day could be pinpointed that made the Five Nations really think about becoming six it was March 22 1997. Italy had already beaten Ireland in Dublin in January, when they met Grand Slam champions France in Grenoble. A 40-22 victory made it really feel like time to discuss expansion. Rome in March didn't seem like such a bad destination...

MARCH 23

A first Grand Slam, any Grand Slam, is a moment of raucous celebration. It was the case in 1968 when France climbed a mountain they have become very familiar with. However, the achievement was tinged with sadness... Two of the squad, Guy Boniface and Jean-Michel Capendeguy, had been killed in separate road accidents just before the tournament began – an unbelievable turn of events. So, as France won in Cardiff, memories were stirred of two ill-fated men.

The passing of Boniface and Capendeguy reminded rugby followers that there is a bigger picture than what goes on between 30 players on a field. That was very real in South Africa until the light of liberation shone through for its people with the eradication of apartheid. The formation of the South African Rugby Football Union in 1992 marked in stone that SA Rugby was no longer administered along racial lines as it unified the South African Rugby Board (Whites) and the Rugby Union (Coloureds). Many years on it's still beyond credulity that any distinction should have been made in the first place.

MARCH 24

In 1962, France visited Cardiff with European rugby apparently at its mercy. Unbeaten in the Five Nations for three years, with just draws against England denying them Grand Slams in the two previous seasons, the Cockerel was clearing its throat to proclaim a first clean sweep. Both Scotland and England had been beaten and, with the unfancied Irish to come in Paris, a win against Wales was seen as the final major hurdle. However, 20-year-old full-back Kel Coslett's penalty ruined the dream for another year. Coslett was never seen again in international rugby union, joining St Helens to start a 14-year RL career.

South Africa's World Cup triumph in 2007 was headlined by the dazzling running of Bryan Habana. Other key performers were Victor Matfield, Percy Montgomery, Schalk Burger and John Smit, but no-one did more to drive the Springboks to the pinnacle than scrum-half Fourie Du Preez, born on this day in 1982. Du Preez brought cunning and artistry to the team – a man who makes it happen for others with his speed of thought and action. It's as hard for a South African called Du Preez to brush off the weight of history attached to the name as it is for a Welshman called Edwards, but Fourie is now close to Frik's legendary status.

MARCH 25

Rugby has a utopian air about it when it is played well, people of all shapes and sizes coming together as a whole. Two performers who exemplified that philosophy were Barry John and Benoit Dauga, who both won their final caps in the 1972 Wales v France clash. John was the supreme rugby artist, using his ball skills and running ability to create opportunities while Dauga was one of the roundheads in the pack, putting his body on the line to earn possession and possessing the skills of an exceptional leader.

How Wales could have done with Barry John in 1990, the nadir of their fall from greatness. Wales fans retreated from Dublin the day after the disaster before as a demoralised bunch. They had seen the Dragons defeated by Ireland at Lansdowne Road, condemning them to a first-ever whitewashed season. It was a damning indictment of the Welsh Rugby Union, who had revelled in the success of the 1970s, but failed to ensure a legacy. Thankfully for Welsh rugby supporters, the regional system almost immediately bore fruit with two Grand Slams.

MARCH 26

What were you doing at the age of 18? I'm guessing not many are saying "beating the All Blacks twice" but that was exactly the feat achieved by a remarkable scrum-half. Haydn Tanner was in the 1935 Swansea and Wales teams that stunned New Zealand. The teenage prodigy became a highly respected international and on this day in 1949 brought the curtain down on a 25-cap career which would have been many more but for the intervention of World War II. Gareth Llewellyn is the only Welshman to have had a longer spread of years between debut and last cap.

Tanner was a player who successfully crossed the divide in Welsh rugby between east and west, winning 13 caps while with Swansea and 12 during his time with Cardiff. In the passionate hotbed of the valleys there were also perhaps even more bitter local rivalries, such as Swansea and Neath. The fact that the Ospreys has emerged from this age-old enmity as a success is a tribute to the Welsh regional structure. In 2005 they clinched their first Magners League title with a victory over Edinburgh at The Gnoll. Nowadays they play all their home games at the Liberty Stadium, ridding the prospect of die-hard Neath fans grudgingly cheering the home team at St Helens... anathema.

MARCH 27

This is when it all began... March 27 1871 at Raeburn Place in Edinburgh. Having answered a challenge issued by a group of Scottish players, a team representing England lost by one goal in the first ever international rugby match. A crowd of 4,000 saw Angus Buchanan credited with the first international try, but goals were the only means of scoring in those days so it was William Cross's conversion that won the match. Two further tries were recorded, one after what was said to be a 10-minute argument... Dr. HH Almond, the Scottish umpire, quoted as saying: "When an umpire is in doubt, I think he is justified in deciding against the side which makes the most noise. They are probably in the wrong."

If rugby has a WG Grace it has to be Adrian Stoop, born exactly 12 years after the first international match. A man recognised as having ideas before his time, fly-half Stoop was an innovator credited with developing the partnership between the players who now wear numbers 9 and 10 (in his day unnumbered and known as left and right half-backs). Stoop provided the canvas for the likes of Cliff Morgan, Barry John, Jonny Wilkinson and Dan Carter to exhibit their skills. His legend lives on at the Harlequins ground named in his honour. Stoop has achieved rugby immortality.

MARCH 28

In 1921, England achieved their third Grand Slam in four seasons, spread across both sides of World War I, when they beat France in Paris. Much of their success was derived from the magnificent half-back combination of WJA `Dave` Davies and Cecil "K" Kershaw. The were the first to integrate in the style professed by Adrian Stoop, and the opposition had little answer. The naval officers were never on the losing side when they played together for England.

If Davies and Kershaw were the heartbeat of one great side, then Mervyn Davies was at the epicentre of another. The moustachioed No.8, looking forever like some Mexican bandit from a spaghetti western, led Wales to consecutive Five Nations titles in 1975 and 76. However, shortly after that latter Grand Slam success, "Merv the swerve" was to suffer a near-death experience that ended his career. During a Welsh Cup semi-final between Swansea and Pontypool, Davies collapsed on the field with a brain haemorrhage. Happily, the great man recovered, although he was never seen in action on a rugby pitch again.

MARCH 29

Pat Sykes became the first Wasp capped by England, against France in 1948. If it's a surprise that one of England's foremost clubs took so long to provide the national team with a player, it should be noted that Wasps have a history of being left behind by others. Their representatives denied the club the honour of being a founder member of the RFU when they turned up at the wrong venue, at the wrong time and on the wrong day for the first meeting of the organisation in 1871.

Victory over Romania is pretty much taken for granted by the powerhouses of international rugby. Back in 1986, though, it was different. Bankrolled by the Ceaucescu regime, Romania was a rising force. Wales, Scotland and France had been beaten in Bucharest, while New Zealand had been held to just 14-6. So Scotland's 33-18 triumph at the National Stadium was a significant achievement, with Gavin Hastings scoring 25 points in just his fifth Test. As Hastings' star waxed, so Romania's waned. However, the passing of a brutal dictator and the demise of the national rugby team is probably a reasonable trade-off for most Romanians.

MARCH 30

In 1982 and 83, Ireland achieved outright or shared Five Nations titles, but were whitewashed in 1984. The Irish bounced back to have another shot at the Championship and Triple Crown in 1985 against England at Lansdowne Road. Brendan Mullin's try put them ahead, but seven minutes from time Ireland trailed 10-7. Up stepped Michael Kiernan to kick a penalty and, with the crowd in a frenzy, Kiernan calmly added a drop goal to ensure a sixth Triple Crown.

Eighteen years later, Ireland and England met again in Dublin, but this time it was a Grand Slam decider. The Irish had not assumed the mantle for 55 years and England had fallen at the final hurdle in three of the previous four seasons, so the pressure for both was immense. A matter of protocol summed this up... Martin Johnson would not take a backward step for anyone. Asked to move his team to the other side of the pitch before the pre-match presentation to the Irish President, Johnson refused. Cue angst from the Lansdowne crowd, but Johnson proved his point where it matters, leading England to a 42-6 demolition. The single-mindedness that brought World Cup glory later that year was there for all to see.

MARCH 31

The ravages of World War II left the sporting landscape bare in 1946. No full international rugby was played in the northern hemisphere, as sport found its place in people's priorities after six years of utter turmoil. Light relief for European rugby fans came from an expeditionary squad of New Zealand Army players, who concluded a five-month tour in Paris on this day. They were nick-named the "Khaki All Blacks" and fulfilled a total of 33 fixtures in Britain and France, losing just twice.

Being picked for the Lions is the greatest individual honour a British and Irish player can achieve. To have been deemed worthy to wear the famed red shirt, above the claims of so many others, is something to be proud of. So it was for Coventry flanker Peter Robbins in 1959. From joy to despair as, while playing for the Barbarians against Newport, Robbins broke his leg and missed the trip to Australia and New Zealand. He was overlooked for the 1962 Lions tour and never played international rugby again.

RUGBY
On This Day

APRIL

APRIL 1

Racial stereotypes are a regrettable thing... They linger on but in living memory we have never seen an England player in a bowler hat and pinstripe suit at Twickenham, a Scot with ginger hair and wearing a kilt inspecting the Murrayfield pitch or an Irishman in a green top hat and Leprechaun suit. However... There has been a Frenchman with a beret... Andre Behoteguy played 19 times for Les Bleus in the 1920s wearing the so-called national headgear, winning his last cap against England on, perhaps appropriately, April Fools Day 1929. There is no evidence to suggest that he was sporting a Garlic and Onion necklace as well...

No additional garments were required by one of the game's greatest performers, Gareth Edwards. The legendary scrum-half made his entrance into international rugby in 1967 against France in Paris at the age of 19, the first of 53 consecutive Wales caps. He was never dropped (how could they?) and was never forced to miss a game through injury. It was as if the rugby "gods" recognised that his talent must shine, while mere mortals were allowed to falter. Would he make an impact today? With his speed, strength, power and sublime pass there's little doubt that professional rugby would have rewarded him handsomely.

APRIL 2

Two great players from England's golden era after World War I appeared for the last time against France in 1923. Cyril Lowe and WJA "Dave" Davies concluded their exceptional careers with a Grand Slam triumph in Paris. Davies led the side, slotting a drop goal in a 12-3 win (the 20th victory of his 22-cap vigil) to seal England's 4th clean sweep in six seasons. Lowe failed to add to an English record 18 tries that stood until Rory Underwood appeared six decades later, but his strike rate from 25 Tests still stands favourably against most.

While Davies and Lowe found achieving Grand Slams a straightforward task, England's first professional sides found the task beyond them. Wales in 1999 and Ireland in 2001 did for them in the final game and in between was perhaps the most jarring of the lot – a hitherto winless Scotland side at Murrayfield. On a wet Edinburgh day, England lost the plot, with fly-half Duncan Hodge scoring all his side's points in a 19-13 win – Scotland's first over the Auld Enemy for 10 years. England still won the title, but doubts over their big match temperament were magnified.

APRIL 3

Rugby was the South African government's best sporting friend during the apartheid years. While all other major sports shunned the country, limited contact was maintained. No official international team played cricket against South Africa from April 1970 to November 1991, but the Springboks fulfilled 50 matches, the majority against full national teams, in that 21-year period of "isolation". Eight of those were against the "South American Jaguars". There were seven comfortable victories for the Boks but, in 1982, the Jaguars recorded their only win. One man was responsible – Hugo Porta scored all their points in a 21-12 success.

Argentina is, by a mighty distance, the best Hispanic rugby nation. No other Spanish-speaking nation has come anywhere near the semi-finals of the World Cup, as the Pumas did in 2007. Rugby has a foothold in Spain, but only as much as volleyball has in England or cricket in Denmark. However, in 2005, progress was made with the first Heineken Cup match to be held on the Iberian Peninsula. Biarritz, faced with hosting hordes of Munster fans in the quarter-finals, shifted the match across the border to Estadio Anoeta in San Sebastian – home of Real Sociedad. The move paid off – 32,000 saw the Gallic Basques reach the last four.

APRIL 4

An 18-year-old trotted on to the Twickenham pitch late on in England's 1998 match against Ireland who was to become his country's most celebrated player. Jonny Wilkinson was the youngest for 61 years to wear the Red Rose in a full international. Clive Woodward had spotted something special and was proved right. At the time of writing, Wilkinson's 1099 points for England and the Lions is unsurpassed and he also has his name against multiple World Cup, Six Nations and England records. For all that, though, he will always be remembered for what he did on a November night in Sydney back in 2003.

In 2001, the International Rugby Board enshrined sin bins into the laws of the game, following a 16-month experiment. Players had always left the pitch on a temporary basis to get stitches inserted, but now alleged miscreants get to rest on the sidelines for 10 minutes. Some referees get "yellow fever", while others adopt the age-old verbal warning and use the card seemingly as a last resort. Grounds reverberate to yells of "Off!! Off!! Off!!" whenever the whistle blows and an innocent-faced flanker emerges from the wrong side of a ruck. There's a bit of panto about it, but on balance the system works.

APRIL 5

A blow for equality was struck in Pontypool when Wales hosted England in the first ever Women's Home Nations International. The visitors won 22-4. Wales skipper Liza Burgess continued to be a stalwart of the women's game, eventually ending her career in the 2007 Six Nations – 20 years after that first international. Ieuan Evans also began his Test career in 1987, his lengthy Wales career coming to an end in 1998. It's hard to envisage Evans playing alongside the generation of Shane Williams, but that's what Burgess achieved, and being a forward makes her longevity all the more remarkable.

Ieuan Evans was not in the Wales team that took on France in the final match of the 1998 Five Nations, and he probably thinks just as well. The Dragons slipped to a 51-0 humbling, which at the time was a Championship record and still stands as the biggest Welsh defeat in a tournament now expanded to Six Nations. The venue was Wembley, used by Wales as a "home" ground while the Millennium Stadium was being built, and the result took France to back-to-back Grand Slams for the first time in their history.

APRIL 6

There have been plenty of perceived rugby villains. The sport provides varied opportunities for those with an eye for the dark side of life. A man who was, in wrestling parlance, someone opposition crowds "loved to hate" was All Black prop Richard Loe, born on this day in 1960. Loe won 49 caps and would have won a few more but for disciplinary issues that included a six-month ban for eye gouging. His rugged features and uncompromising approach earned him the nickname "The Enforcer".

Loe was never a contender for the Sevens game at the top level. Too many wide open spaces, I guess. However, his compatriots have proved skilled operators at the discipline. In 2007/08 the New Zealand team were virtually unstoppable. Wins on the IRB circuit in South Africa, Dubai, USA, Hong Kong and on home soil in Wellington created an unprecedented winning streak. They arrived in Adelaide for the Australian leg as the hottest of favourites, reached the final, but something of the spirit of the 1995 World Cup final seeped into their Springbok opposition and, for the first time in 48 matches, the All Blacks were beaten.

APRIL 7

Italian rugby has struggled to be a truly national sport. Pockets of fervour exist, mainly in the north, but generally the game is a pastime of the few. In 1958, as the Azzurri tried to make an impression from outside the established order, the Italian Federation took their marquee fixture against France to the self-styled capital of the south – Naples. The Neapolitans saw an 11-3 defeat for the hosts, and the sides returned to the city in 1966, but no fixture with such a profile has occurred there since.

It would be stretching a point to say that everything was conspiring against England achieving a Grand Slam at the dawn of the 21st century, but agricultural illness? In 2001, the "Foot and Mouth" crisis caused the planned Ireland-England fixture in Dublin to be postponed until the autumn, meaning perhaps the most in-form team in the history of the Championship missed the moment where their dominance was at its height. Wales, Italy and Scotland had all been pulverised and now France were put to the sword 48-19. Clive Woodward's team were in a rich vein but the summer break, and consequent build-up of pressure, appeared to sap their strength and another Grand Slam went begging in Dublin.

APRIL 8

Some players arrive on the international stage and immediately appear to be born to have been there. Michael Jones, born on April 8 1965, claimed the All Blacks' No.7 shirt for the 1987 World Cup and proceeded to be a key man in their eventual triumph. Quick, perceptive and with excellent handling skills, Jones is widely regarded as the greatest ever openside flanker. A man with devout Christian principles – he refused to play in the Sunday semi-final against Wales – Jones needed all his willpower to overcome a serious knee injury in 1989 and finished with 55 caps, a paltry tally for a man of his talent.

The game has changed... incontrovertibly in terms of the playing schedules of the top stars. The likes of Bryan Habana, Dan Carter, Brian O'Driscoll and Shane Williams only appear in international or top class club/provincial action. Rewind 20 years and you'll find a very different scene. No watertight contracts, no talk of "burn-out", players played when and for who they liked, as long as they showed an appropriate level of commitment. Rory Underwood was at his peak in 1989, but turned out for the RAF against The Navy. Four tries for the flying wing delighted his employers... The RAF of course. Rugby was his hobby.

APRIL 9

Much has changed but one institution clings on to its almost regal place within the rugby firmament – The Barbarians. The club was founded by William Percy Carpmael in 1890. His dream was for players from different clubs to come together on tour in an act of rugby sportsmanship. The status may have slipped since its heyday, when being picked for the Baa-baas against a touring side was almost like a Lions call-up, but players come from all corners of the world to wear the black and white hoops – oh, just bring your own socks.

The English and Welsh rugby fraternity have an interesting dynamic – seemingly can't live with them, can't live without them. For decades, Gloucester v Cardiff and Newport v Bristol were highlights of the season, and then there was of course the annual Five Nations dust-up. League rugby made the club side of the equation wane and eventually cease to exist, while European competition brought only an occasional fix. Both parties missed the regular trans-Severn rivalry and so the Anglo-Welsh Cup was born. In 2006, Wasps beat Llanelli Scarlets at Twickenham in its inaugural final.

APRIL 10

Post-war French rugby hero Jean Prat sums up the true sporting sense of the word "legend". He dragged the French team almost single-handed into the realms of competitiveness. Under his watch France claimed their first share of a Five Nations title in 1954 and he scored the winning try in their initial victory over the All Blacks that year. On April 20 1955 Prat won his last cap against Italy in Grenoble, a low key end for one of the seminal careers in French rugby history.

South African rugby creates flashpoints. Hot conditions, ancient enmities and "partisan" crowds often push players to the edge (and over). Fully 30 years before the sin bin was officially adopted, a bright spark in the Springbok refereeing cabal proposed the "cooler" to take the heat out of certain situations. The international authorities were not impressed but the South Africans were used to being isolated at the time, so went it alone. In 1975, Naas Ferreira sent two warring parties to the sideline for five minutes during a Pretoria Reserve League match – the first known use of any kind of "temporary suspension".

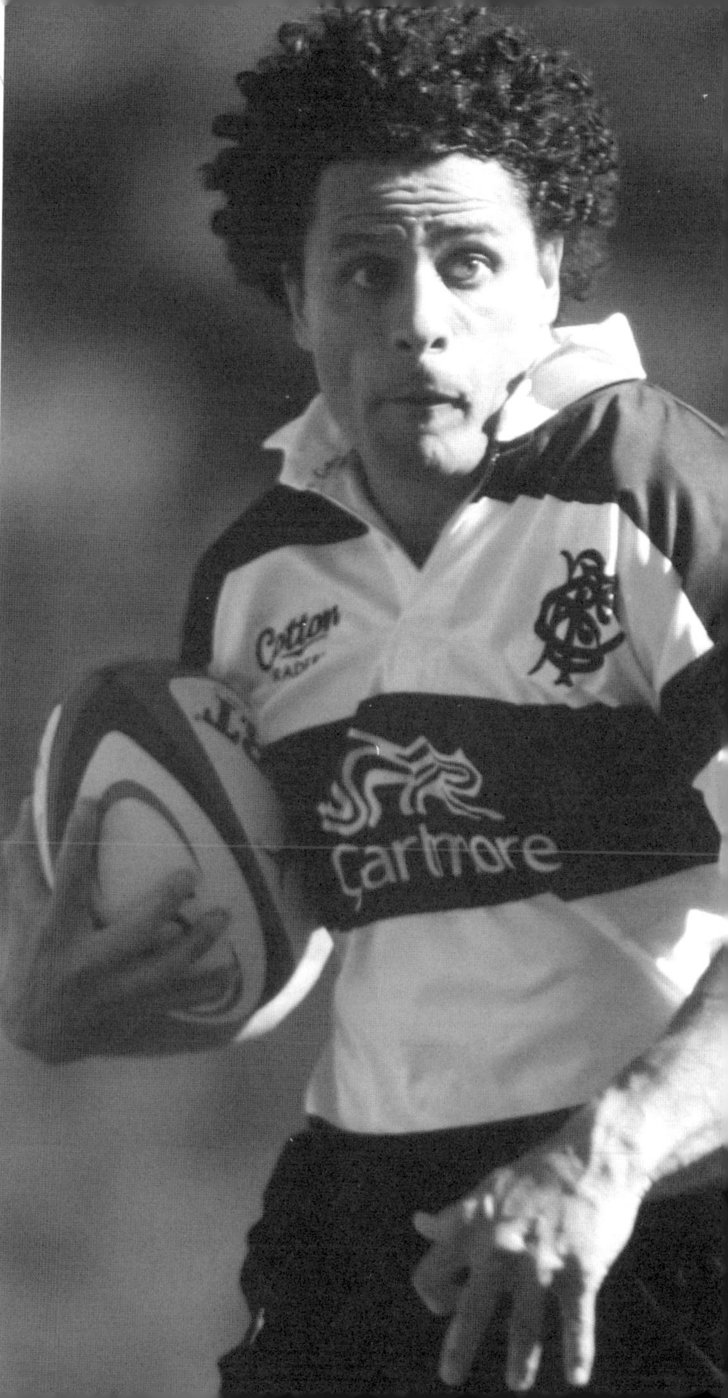

DOUG HOWLETT – STAR ALL BLACK IN THE FAMOUS BAA-BAAS SHIRT

APRIL 11

1950 was extremely notable for Wales full-back Lewis Jones, born on this day in 1931. He made his debut against England at the age of 18, while serving for the Royal Navy, starred in the first Welsh Grand Slam for 39 years and then something really extraordinary happened... Ireland full-back George Norton broke his arm on the Lions tour of New Zealand, Jones was whistled up as a replacement but there was not enough time for him to sail to the Antipodes (as the squad did in those days). Jones was flown the 12,000 miles – the first player to arrive on a tour by plane. The trek, via Los Angeles, took four-and-a-half days.

Wales played two seasons of Five Nations rugby at the old Wembley Stadium in 1998 and 1999, while their new Millennium Stadium citadel was being constructed. The abiding memory of that brief sojourn is Scott Gibbs' magical late try against England in 1999. The men in white, the "away" team on home soil, were edging towards the Grand Slam when suddenly Gibbs performed a jinking, mesmeric run to the line, handing Neil Jenkins a relatively straightforward conversion to win the game by a point. England were devastated and the party's probably still going on in the valleys.

APRIL 12

The first in a stream of 113 years of memories occurred in 1884 when Ireland's first international in Wales coincided with the initial Test match at Cardiff Arms Park. The Welsh match-winner on that first international occasion was Buller Staddan. It was young Buller (William James Staddan), making his debut, who slotted the crucial goal. He was backed up by tries from Tom Clapp and William Norton but, as all rugby historians know, those didn't count in those days. The Irish failed to register anything.

From Buller Staddan to Maurice Richards... For a Welshman to play in a 30-9 win against England at Cardiff Arms Park to clinch the Triple Crown and Five Nations title is special enough, but to score four tries... wow! The world was Richards' oyster, a 24-year-old playing in a back division alongside Gareth Edwards, Barry John, John Dawes and JPR Williams. Instead, Richards chose Salford and rugby league, where his exploits would be rewarded with brass in his pocket rather than just plaudits from a grateful nation. He was soon replaced on the Wales wing by another man who would have a brief flirtation with union fame before becoming a 13-a-side legend... John Bevan.

APRIL 13

When the Heineken Cup began in the Black Sea town of Constanta in 1995, there were plenty of prophets of doom. It would never work, they said. English and Scottish clubs also had their doubts, sitting out that first season. How wrong they all were... The tournament has been arguably the best thing to happen to the game in the professional era and on this day in 2003 it was appropriately Leicester Tigers and Munster, two of the foremost teams in the history of the event, who battled out a quarter-final at Welford Road – the 500th Heineken Cup match.

Snow and rugby are occasional bedfellows, but there's the few centimetres generally found in England once every 20 years and where you find the real stuff... Outside of Russia, Krasnoyarsk may not mean much to anyone, apart from long-haul airline pilots and avid students of sub-Six Nations European rugby, but the Siberian city is the "Mecca" of the game in the vast wilderness and has even hosted Ireland in a World Cup qualifier. In 2008, Georgia clinched the European Nations Cup with a quite literally hard fought 18-12 victory there. It's so cold you know, you have to engage in mass brawls just to keep warm...

APRIL 14

When Ireland and France faced each other at Lansdowne Road in 1973, the Five Nations table was in an intriguing state. England had four points from two wins, Scotland and Wales also had a 2 in the W column and the French... yep – two wins. The Irish were the odd ones out, with just a solitary triumph, but if they could get the better of the French it would create a unique, quintuple tie (this was in the days before points difference). Willie John McBride's men managed to edge to a 6-4 victory and history was made... The title was shared five ways or, if you are of a darker disposition, the Wooden Spoon was jointly held by all.

The fortunes of rugby in the United States have similarities to football (sorry, apologies to our American brethren, soccer). The female side of the sport has been traditionally far more successful than their male counterparts. In 1991, the "Sh-Eagles" won the first Women's World Cup, beating England in the final in Cardiff. The men have been regulars at the finals of their World Cup but most definitely play a walk-on part. In contrast, the women have consistently held their own, also getting to the final in 1994 and 1998.

APRIL 15

For that great France lock of the 1980s, Jean Condom, born on this day in 1960, it must have at first been a source of bemusement why legions of British and Irish rugby fans would snigger when his name was announced. Shouldn't they have more respect for a man who would play 61 times in the hard school of the Test match engine room, reached a World Cup final and was involved in a Grand Slam? Standing tall in the line-out, Condom could be relied upon as a safe option for his hooker to go to at all times.

The year was 1967 and step forward 18-year-old Keith Jarrett to write his name large in the history of Wales-England matches. He was a centre but was pitched in at full-back at the Arms Park... what a decision. Fielding a stray kick, Jarrett set off on a monumental gallop down the wing to score an unforgettable try. He scored 19 points in all as Wales swept to a 34-21 win – their only triumph of an otherwise humdrum campaign. But, as legend has it, the Welsh can forgive anything their team does as long as they beat the English.

APRIL 16

Ryan Constable had a generally unspectacular career. There was the one Wallaby cap in 1994, as a replacement against Ireland, before he quit Australia and headed to Saracens. His rugby legacy was created in the year 2000 at Bedford's humble Goldington Road ground, when Constable went try crazy. Just 3,067 were present to see the Aussie bag six tries to set a Premiership record that is likely to survive for some time. A number of players have got five, but Constable continues to stand alone as a six-shooter.

In 2008, just six months after guiding England to the World Cup final, Brian Ashton was informed by the RFU that his time was up as coach. Ashton had accepted the job when it seemed no-one else was willing to take it, amid the wreckage left by Andy Robinson's departure. He turned things around, suffered a disappointing Six Nations but ended it by thrashing Ireland 33-10. He was promised that he would not be sacked, despite certain players and coaches appearing to circle their wagons around him, but Martin Johnson proved irresistible to the RFU, opting for a national hero above a man who had got them out of a hole.

APRIL 17

A total of nearly 100 nations are members of the International Rugby Board. Germany are among that number (ranked perhaps surprisingly high in the mid-20s). However, delve deeper into German rugby and you'll find a rich heritage. In 1927 the German national team took on France in their first international match at Stade Colombes in Paris, many years before the more established Argentina and Italy made their bows. The Germans succumbed 30-5, but won the return fixture, a month later in Frankfurt, 17-16. That remains the highpoint of their rugby history.

In 1971, as part of lengthy centenary celebrations, the RFU organised a special match between England and an RFU President's XV. Unusually for such a fixture, the RFU decided to award caps, but there again you probably deserve a cap for facing the likes of Pierre Villepreux, Jo Maso, Colin Meads, Frik Du Preez, Ian Kirkpatrick and skipper Brian Lochore. The President's men who, Villepreux and Maso apart, were all from the southern hemisphere, ran in six tries in a facile 28-11 victory over an England team decidedly in the doldrums.

APRIL 18

The advent of the World Cup made the authorities ponder what to do with the Sevens format of the game. It was popular, but had never really been taken seriously at international level. In 1992, Murrayfield hosted the first Rugby World Cup Sevens tournament. As is often the way with parties, it's the guest that shows initial reluctance who steals the show. England dragged their feet, sending a youthful line-up including pups such as Lawrence Dallaglio and Matt Dawson, but the English stunned more seasoned operators of the abbreviated game to walk away with the cup.

Rob Andrew was always seen as a reliable pair of hands as a player. Frequently selected ahead of the more flamboyant Stuart Barnes, Andrew steered England through some troubled waters and to some notable triumphs before becoming Newcastle's player/coach. So when the RFU wanted to hire an elite director of rugby in 2006 they again opted for perceived pragmatism ahead of imagination, this time naming Andrew instead of Sir Clive Woodward. RFU chief executive Francis Baron said Andrew would form a "good team" with then England coach Andy Robinson... Robinson was dismissed within eight months.

APRIL 19

For decades, rugby union saw a steady trickle of players jump ship and accept big money offers from rugby league. Professionalism changed all that. Indeed, the procession began to turn in the opposite direction with defectors returning to the fold and league superstars, such as Jason Robinson, trying their hand at union. Scott Gibbs was the last major union player to switch, in 1994, just over a year before the rules were re-written. He joined St Helens with Swansea chairman Mike James quoted as saying: "Of all the players who have gone to rugby league, Scott is the first one I wouldn't want to see in the Swansea club again." Two years later Gibbs was back in South Wales, playing for the All Whites as a professional...

The first season of the Premiership was dominated by two clubs with lofty ambitions – Newcastle Falcons and Saracens. Bankrolled by Sir John Hall and Nigel Wray respectively, they had offered substantial first professional contracts to established stars, and the power of cash told... They met at Vicarage Road on April 19 1998, attracting a capacity 19,000 to see rugby in Watford. Sarries won by a point, and a single point also separated them at the end of the season, this time in Newcastle's favour.

APRIL 20

One of the big rivalries of the modern era has been Wasps v Leicester. They come from different points of the rugby compass; Wasps were, for many years, seen as almost second class citizens but began to develop into a real force in the game during the 1980s and have been mighty competitors in the professional age, despite relatively meagre support. Leicester, meanwhile, boast the largest membership, fan base and dedicated rugby stadium of any English club. They meet as equals on the pitch, though, and their biggest clash came in the 2007 Heineken Cup final at Twickenham. Wasps, as so often when it really counts, won.

Just six months after South Africa were crowned 2007 world champions, qualifying for the 2011 World Cup got underway – in the exotic location of Grand Cayman in the Caribbean. The Cayman Islands lost 12-39 to Trinidad & Tobago and bowed out of the Americas section a week later after also losing to Mexico and beating Jamaica. No chance to take on the All Blacks, Springboks, England and the rest for the islanders, who are a group of social players after all. Perhaps that's just as well... Every national team in rugby finds its own level, unlike football where mismatches such as Spain v San Marino do nothing for the game.

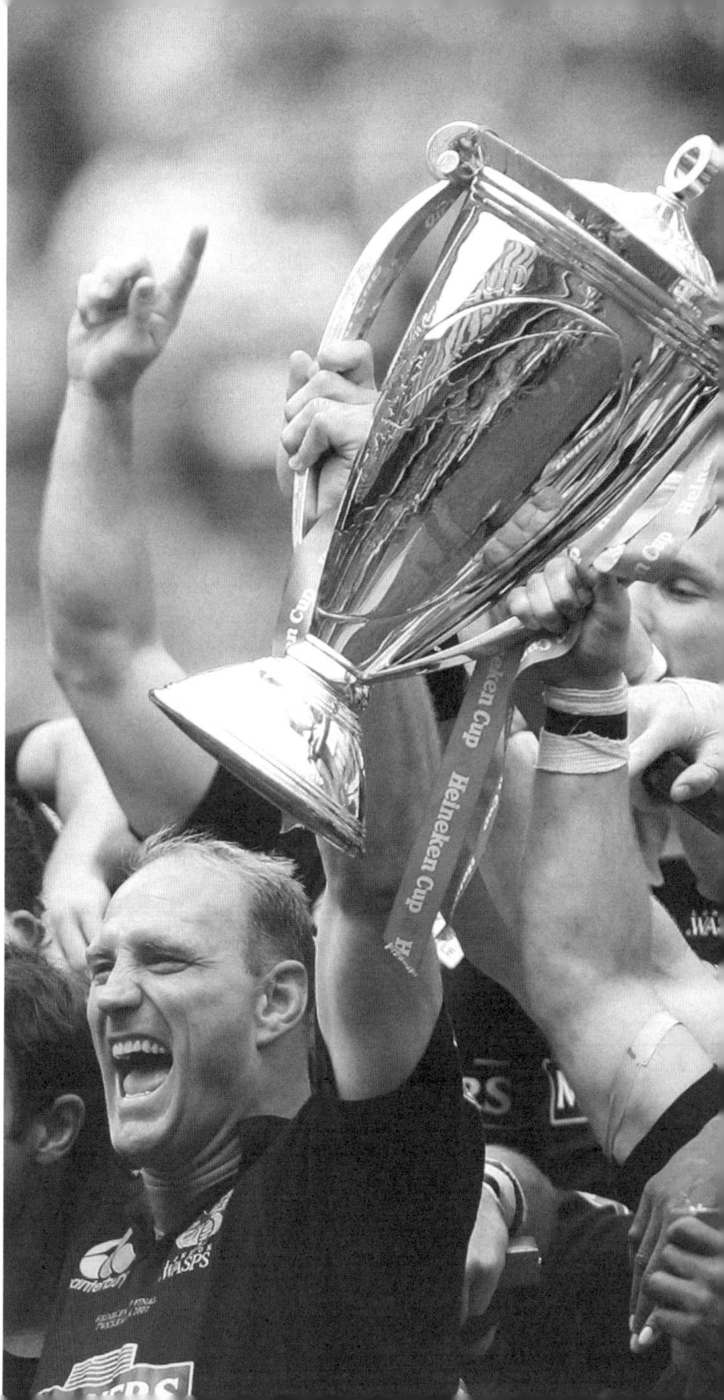

LAWRENCE DALLAGLIO & WASPS CELEBRATE EUROPEAN SUCCESS

APRIL 21

Llanelli Scarlets are the nearly men of the Heineken Cup. Yet to reach the final, three times they have faced English opposition in the semi-finals, and three times they have lost. Two of them were heartbreakers... Late penalties by Paul Grayson for Northampton in 2000 and Tim Stimpson for Leicester (via the crossbar) in 2002 denied the Scarlets. In 2007 they faced the Tigers again, but their time had gone... An ageing side lacking that little bit of star quality lost 33-17. They have a spanking new stadium, but have others across Europe with more cash left the West Walians behind?

Every four years comes a magical moment in the rugby spectrum – the naming of the Lions squad. Players, fans and journalists speculate on who will be included in the months leading up to the announcement and there are always shocks and surprises. In 2009, Paul O'Connell was confirmed as captain (when many supported Ireland Grand Slam skipper Brian O'Driscoll) and Riki Flutey was given the opportunity to become the first man to play for and against the Lions, having appeared for Wellington on the 2005 tour.

APRIL 22

Whoever plays in the Number 10 shirt is the playmaker of a rugby union team. There can be little debate about that, but there is about what you call them... Fly-half, out-half, stand-off, first five-eighth... they all amount to the same thing and the responsibility of the role makes a Test debut an even more nerve-racking occasion. How impressive, then, to score 28 points, even if it is against a so-called lesser nation. Andrew Mehrtens did that for New Zealand against Canada in 1995, the largest haul in a first international. However, barely had the ink dried in the record book than along came Mehrtens' understudy, Simon Culhane, with a whopping 45 points against Japan to take the mark.

Nelson Mandela presenting Francois Pienaar with the World Cup in 1995 after South Africa claimed the pot at the first attempt... The achievement is a landmark in rugby history but there was a sad story behind the scenes. Coach Kitch Christie had been battling leukaemia for many years. In March 1996, he was forced to leave the job and on this day in 1998 Christie died, leaving a grateful nation in his debt for taking the Springboks to the pinnacle of the game just nine months after taking on the onerous role.

APRIL 23

In 1988, the Irish put on a special match to celebrate 1,000 years of the city of Dublin. The choice of opposition on St George's Day was England, who selected a new captain for the occasion – John Orwin. His reign began with a 21-10 victory, but Orwin was dropped after the ensuing summer tour of Australia, a young upstart called Will Carling was named skipper and Orwin was never seen again in a full international. Orwin lifted the curious Millennium Trophy, a pot in the shape of a horned Viking helmet.

You don't necessarily need any kind of cup or trophy at stake for a Leinster v Munster fixture – but it helps... In 2006, a new chapter to the ancient rivalry between East and West was written when they met in a Heineken Cup semi-final at Lansdowne Road. There was only one team in it as Munster won 30-6. Three years later, Leinster got their own back in spades at Croke Park with a 25-6 victory – Leinster's biggest shellacking of the Munstermen in professional times and a foretaste of the ultimate triumph, against Leicester at Murrayfield four weeks later.

APRIL 24

While England's men struggled for years to find the formula that could win the World Cup, the women achieved the task at the second attempt in 1994. Okay, so the southern hemisphere was not present in Scotland (in particular the "Gal Blacks" from New Zealand) but you can only beat what's put in front of you and England smashed Russia, Scotland, Canada and France (scoring 134 points and conceding just 25) before defending champions USA gave them a game in the final (38-23).

The physical nature and intensity of rugby at the highest level frequently pushes players to the brink of, and a little beyond, the laws but there's no excuse for acts such as the reprehensible eye gouging. Dylan Hartley, a fine performer when he opts to play rugby, was cited for making contact with the visual equipment of Wasps' James Haskell and Jonny O'Connor while appearing ("playing" does not seem appropriate in this context) for Northampton and on April 24 2007 was found guilty and banned for six months – giving an indication of the seriousness of the incident. He missed possible selection for England's tour of South Africa and the World Cup.

APRIL 25

To get into the mindset needed to justify wearing the All Black shirt many New Zealanders appear to become obsessive, as if the world is against them. In 1992 their governing body gave them a chance not to bother having to imagine... This was for real, caps were awarded when they were faced with three matches against a World XV to celebrate the centenary of the New Zealand Rugby Union. With the series tied at 1-1, an All Blacks side boasting the likes of Sean Fitzpatrick, Michael Jones, Frank Bunce, Va'aiga Tuigamala and John Kirwan swept aside the world to win 26-15 at Eden Park.

Epic Heineken Cup matches... there have been quite a few, but one stands above the rest for skill, intensity and atmosphere. In 2004, Munster and London Wasps, arguably the two leading sides never to have won the trophy at that point, were drawn together in the semi-finals. Lansdowne Road was packed to the rafters with 40,000 red shirts, only broken by officials, hangers-on and a small knot of Wasps followers. What followed was a thunderous match, climaxed by gladiatorial Wasps hooker Trevor Leota plunging over in the corner to clinch a 37-32 victory four minutes from time... I get goose-bumps recalling it.

APRIL 26

Every sport needs innovation. Wavell Wakefield changed the way forward play was viewed in the 1920s and his work was taken a stage further by South African legend Hennie Muller three decades later, who died on this day in 1977 at the age of 55. Nicknamed "Die Windhond" (the greyhound), Muller used speed developed in his early career as a wing to revolutionise back row play. Muller pressurised the fly-half with his "in your face" style and his influence was key in a Springbok side that only lost once in his 13 Tests, including a Grand Slam tour of Britain and 4-0 whitewash of the All Blacks.

Muller was only a toddler when Test rugby appeared to bid farewell to one of South Africa's great sporting arenas – The Wanderers in Johannesburg. However, after a 56-year break and during those bleak apartheid years, the authorities staged a "Test" against the South American Jaguars at the cricketing citadel. It was akin to England opting to turn out at The Oval instead of Twickenham but would be seen as nothing exceptional in Australia where the SCG, MCG, Gabba and Adelaide Oval have all hosted big matches.

APRIL 27

Top rugby players don't mind being sent to Coventry... It's a traditional hotbed of the sport and gave the game one of its great entertainers – David Duckham. Its rugby club fell on hard times just as others were grasping the nettle that the game could become a major commercial sport, but the recent use of the football team's Ricoh Arena for big matches has brought thoughts that maybe big time rugby could come to the West Midlands city on a permanent basis. Munster have certainly enjoyed themselves there... In 2008, they won a Heineken Cup semi-final against Saracens, turning the Sky Blues' ground a very deep shade of red.

Dr Karl Mullen was very much a man of Leinster, but the whole of Ireland was united in respect when news came through of the death of the first man to lead the Irish to the Grand Slam. Mullen's team in 1948 were inspired by his leadership and genius of Jack Kyle at fly-half, but the gynaecologist would have found it hard to conceive that his country would take 61 years to climb to the top of the mountain for a second time. Thankfully, Mullen lived to see Brian O'Driscoll's side repeat the feat, just a month before his passing.

APRIL 28

A butcher from the Scottish borders created the worldwide phenomenon that is Sevens rugby... Ned Haig's brainwave was a sports tournament, including running races and a seven-a-side rugby competition, to boost funds for the Melrose club. In 1883, the "Melrose Sports" was born, with the hosts claiming the "Ladies of Melrose Cup" after a fiercely contested final against local rivals Gala. Haig died in 1939, shortly before the non-rugby festivities at the Sports were ditched and the event became the Melrose Sevens. A humble sports day has spawned an annual international circuit in places such as San Diego, Dubai, Hong Kong and Adelaide, and possible Olympic recognition. What a legacy...

Rugby was establishing itself in the 1880s. Five years after the birth of Sevens, another noble tradition began... the first British and Irish touring team. The destinations were Australia and New Zealand for a motley collection of mainly North of England-based players. On this day in 1888 that "British team" played effectively the first Lions match, beating Otago 8-3, and went on to fulfil 34 more fixtures against club and provincial opposition, losing just twice. However, the tour suffered tragedy halfway through when skipper Bob Seddon was tragically killed during a boating trip on the Hunter River in New South Wales.

APRIL 29

Top clubs are multi-million pound businesses, but for most of the 20th century the highest domestic accolade for an Englishman was playing in the County Championship. The tables started to turn in the club's favour in the 1980s, as league rugby placed performing for your club on a higher footing, quickly leading to top players abandoning the county set altogether. In 1989, Bath and Leicester embodied this change when they fought out the cup final in front of 59,000 at Twickenham – a world record for a club match and 30,000 more than attended the County climax four weeks earlier. Bath skipper Stuart Barnes scored the match-winning try two minutes from time to seal Bath's fifth cup triumph.

Leicester and Bath continued to go hammer and tongs at each other in the early 1990s, Bath holding sway with four league titles in a row from 1991-94. However, the Tigers were generally their sternest foe and, in 1995, Leicester skipper Dean Richards clasped his huge mitts around the league trophy, in front of an exultant Welford Road crowd, following a final day 17-3 victory over those fellow men of lettered shirts, Bristol.

APRIL 30

Sporting triumph and disaster, those two great "impostors", are familiar to all sports teams. For Harlequins, though, one of their greatest days is bracketed with their worst... In 1988, Quins produced a scintillating display to claim their first English Cup. Will Carling scored two tries, Andrew Harriman one, and dual New Zealand and England international Jamie Salmon kicked four of his side's six goals in a memorable 28-22 victory...

However, in 2005, tears were shed at The Stoop as Quins were relegated, after 18 unbroken seasons in the top flight, following a one-point defeat by Sale. Jeremy Staunton's late penalty, which could have saved them, slipped past the posts and Quins were condemned to mixing it with the likes of Sedgley Park and Cornish Pirates in 2005/6. Many viewed the calamity with glee, as Quins were said to have been involved in discussions to ensure that either there was no relegation or that the Premiership was expanded. Those overtures were dismissed, but they returned a year later as emphatic National League champions.

RUGBY
On This Day

MAY

MAY 1

There are losers, as well as winners, in "open" rugby... While the Six and Tri-Nations make their top players into wealthy professionals, the largely amateur "second tier" of Japan, USA, Canada, Fiji, Samoa and Tonga find that it is less than a level playing field. How to keep this vital section of the world game competitive with the elite? The answer put forward was the Epson Cup – a sort of Six Nations for the small fry. Japan beat Canada 23-21 in its initial fixture but, when the North Americans found playing A teams from the major nations in the Churchill Cup more appealing, the Epson ran out of ink. How to close the gap between the haves and the have-nots remains a crucial issue for the IRB.

To say that Argentina have ruled the rugby roost in South America would be as indisputable as declaring that there's a lot of ice in Antarctica. The Pumas have been competitive at the highest level without having any sort of meaningful local competition. Two examples were South American Championship matches against Paraguay in 2002 (a then world record 152 points and 24 tries) and leaving Venezuela utterly snookered with a score of 147-7 in 2004. The latter mismatch saw Fernando Higgs, remarkably, become the ninth Argentine to score five tries or more in an international.

MAY 2

A big day for Leicester Tigers fans... Twickenham was like a second home for their heroes between 1979 and 81, as the parochial world of English club rugby got to grips with the concept of competing for something tangible rather than just bragging rights. The cup had started with little fanfare in season 1971/72, but a big day out at Twickenham and to be recognised by the outside world (if not necessarily the rugby-playing masses) as the best team in the country, seeped into the consciousness of several progressive clubs. Leicester brought a sizeable travelling support to HQ to see Gosforth defeated 22-15, and their club become the first triple winners of the domestic cup.

Fast forward 18 years and the Tigers were sealing their first Premiership title. In a nice piece of symmetry, they did so by beating Newcastle Falcons – effectively the professional incarnation of the Gosforth club – who were champions the previous season. Kingston Park was hardly the same as the cauldron of Welford Road, but those from the East Midlands in the 5,000 crowd chanted "Toy-gers!! Toy-gers!!" with gusto.

MAY 3

There have been some dodgy venues for top club rugby but the most bizarre has to be Bramley Road in North London. This was where the homely Saracens club, turned almost overnight into a bustling commercial operation by Nigel Wray's millions, played their home games since World War II. A public open space with a small stand plonked in the middle, the remains left by the canine users of the park had to be removed before matches and the changing facilities were Sunday morning football standard. Things had to change and, in 1996, the last top flight match was played in Southgate before an initial move to Enfield FC and then onward and upwards to Watford.

Some were shocked, some were amused, some just shook their heads... A huge rugby match decided by a penalty shoot-out... After 80 minutes and extra time couldn't separate Cardiff Blues and Leicester Tigers in a 2009 Heineken Cup semi-final at the Millennium Stadium it was off to the 22-metre line and take your turns at kicking goals. It came down to a flanker and a number eight in "sudden death"... Martyn Williams, a magnificent openside, will now be remembered for missing from the kicking tee while to Leicester's Jordan Crane went the glory after his "swinger" managed to bisect the uprights.

MAY 4

Will Carling was the darling of English rugby fans. As the 1995 World Cup approached, Carling, who led the team from rock bottom in 1988 to within an ace of claiming the Webb Ellis Trophy in 1991 and to three Grand Slams, had a humorous, but ill-timed, snipe at the RFU committee, broadcast within a Channel 4 documentary called Fair Game. Carling said: "You do not need 57 old farts running rugby." The blazers didn't like it and moved with uncharacteristic haste to sack the errant England skipper. A "peasants' revolt" forced Carling's reinstatement within days.

Respect for the referee is a Holy Grail of rugby. Any sign of this being eroded is treated as a very serious issue. And so, in 1996, at the end of a dramatic English Cup final won by Bath with a late try, when Leicester flanker Neil Back pushed match official Steve Lander to the ground in apparent disgust, it created a right old hornet's nest. Back pleaded that he was pushing at "a body" and didn't realise it was the whistle-blower. The disciplinarians would have none of it and handed down a six-month ban. The sport's soul was cleansed.

MAY 5

Ronnie Poulton was the Shane Williams of the early 20th century. Blessed with speed, agility and an innate sense of a try-scoring opportunity, Poulton led England to the 1914 Grand Slam, scoring four tries against France. A year later he was dead, killed by a sniper in the World War I trenches – a tragic loss for the game. Poulton had also starred for Oxford at Varsity level, recording an extraordinary five touchdowns in the 1909 match when multiple try-scoring was a rare event. Shortly before his death, Poulton inherited a fortune from an uncle and added "Palmer" to his name in deference to his late biscuit baron relative.

When it comes to subjectivity, award ceremonies take the biscuit. Chris Robshaw was hailed as the Premiership's "Player of the Year" in 2009. Yet to be capped, he had done sterling service in Harlequins' march to the semi-finals from the blindside flank. But hang on, a big reason why he had not been picked by England was the presence of Tom Croft – outstanding as Leicester topped the table and progressed to the Heineken Cup final, plus probably being England's best player in the Six Nations. Croft must have wondered what he had to do...

MAY 6

In the late 1980s, Neath had a ferocious reputation stretching beyond Welsh club rugby. Coach Ron Waldron had turned the men from the Gnoll into a formidable unit and the 1988/89 season saw them notch world record tallies for points (1,917) and tries (345). Known as the "Welsh All Blacks" for more than just their kit, their 1989 Welsh Cup final victory over Llanelli was laced with controversy. The Welsh Rugby Union were dabbling with the sin-bin and referee Les Peard sent Neath No.8 Mark Jones to the cooler after he was caught stamping on Scarlets prop Laurence Delaney's head. Shouldn't that be a straight sending-off? Neath won 14-13, amid a tide of resentment from the Scarlets.

An important staging post for Italy on the march to fulfilling their dream of turning the Five Nations into Six... The 22-12 victory over Ireland in Treviso was the Azzurri's first win against one of the traditional rugby powers – the eight you have to impress to get anywhere in the game. Paolo Vaccari scored the only try, with Diego Dominguez adding 17 points from his trusty boot. This duo, plus scrum-half Alessandro Troncon, skipper Massimo Cuttitta, centre/scrum-half Ivan Francescato and Aussie-born lock Mark Giacheri were the mainstays of the team. It's this depth of quality Italy need to rediscover if they are to progress.

MAY 7

Will there ever be a club team who dominate the English game for such a sustained period as Bath did for a decade from the mid-1980s? Coach Jack Rowell brought together a group of ferociously competitive personalities and the chemistry worked. The 1994 cup final win against Leicester was not quite the end of an era (four more trophies would be won over the next same number of seasons) but Rowell was off to join England, while it was goodbye to half-back duo Stuart Barnes and Richard Hill. Bath won the league and cup double for the third time in six campaigns.

Rowell began his England tenure with a Grand Slam in 1995, a first-season feat equalled by Ireland boss Declan Kidney in 2009. The former Munster supremo was appointed Irish coach in 2008 – it was a "shoe-in". Kidney had developed Munster into the No.1 side in Europe, guiding them to four Heineken Cup finals, and had ended his association with the men in red by securing a second European crown. How about Kidney for Lions boss in 2013?

MAY 8

Two great rugby warriors were born on this day... In 1942, Benoit Dauga came into the world. French rugby has always been a union of flamboyant back play and hard-nosed action in the pack. Dauga was a supreme exponent of the latter. His efforts created the platform for the likes of Pierre Villepreux and Jean-Pierre Lux to weave their magic. Dauga was at the heart of a side that claimed three Five Nations titles, including one Grand Slam, from 1967-70. He finished with 60 caps in 1972 but was paralysed for a time due to a serious neck injury sustained in a club game in 1975. Happily, Dauga made a complete recovery.

Scottish rugby has a lot to thank David Sole for... The rugged prop, born in 1962 in the un-Caledonian setting of Aylesbury, led the Scots to the 1990 Grand Slam, masterminding an epic victory over the country of his birth in the Grand Slam decider. Sole welded his troops into an irresistible force that day. Playing in the all-conquering Bath side of the time strengthened his will-to-win, although club-mates Jeremy Guscott, Simon Halliday and Richard Hill must have regretted that steely competitiveness at Murrayfield.

MAY 9

Promotion and relegation... The prospect of going up a level, and the fear of descending down the ladder, adds vital interest to the narrative of a season. But when the door is slammed in your face, after you have unquestionably deserved your place, it leaves a bitter taste. Rotherham won the 2001/02 National League and looked set to join the elite. However, Premiership organisers said they failed to meet "entry criteria" based principally on their stadium. Rotherham agreed to ground-share with the town's Football League club but were rebuffed, despite Saracens and Wasps doing exactly that elsewhere.

Here's a victory for dogged determination and consistency... When asked to name the top points scorers in the history of the southern hemisphere's Super Rugby, Andrew Mehrtens, Matt Burke, Dan Carter and Percy Montgomery would undoubtedly feature, but how about Stirling Mortlock? The Wallaby and Brumbies centre is renowned as a tough-tackling, powerful runner. His prowess with the boot slips under the radar for most people, but he has accumulated points to such an extent that, in 2009, he surpassed Mehrtens as the most prolific scorer ever in Super Rugby, reaching 994 during the home win against the Blues.

MAY 10

The Kiwis love their heroes but there is a meritocracy in their country which dictates that no-one is "bigger than the game". In 1986, 28 of the 30 players named for the cancelled tour of South Africa the previous year took part in the New Zealand Cavaliers trip to the home of the apartheid regime. On this day they lost the first "Test" to the Springboks. There's no bigger NZ legend than Colin Meads, but when he agreed to coach the Cavaliers he was sacked as a National Selector. However, the authorities felt they couldn't afford to keep Meads out of the picture, so he was back in the mid-1990s as All Blacks manager.

Some pursue the limelight, others shun the trappings of fame. Manchester United's Paul Scholes is an example and another is former England flanker Richard Hill. Not for him dating a supermodel or pursuing a media career. Hill was so good, yet so unspectacular, always seeming to be in the right place at the right time, that his place among England's greatest players could be overlooked. Typically, he bowed out in 2008 with little fanfare at the end of a mid-table Saracens v Bristol game in Milton Keynes (Vicarage Road was unavailable).

MAY 11

When rugby union went professional the slate was wiped clean, all the old quarrels and enmities between league and union were, in theory, shunted aside. Few would have predicted, though, that things would move so quickly. In May 1996, champions from the rival codes, Bath and Wigan, played a two-match series (one game of league and one of 15s, predictably each won by the experts) and Wigan, the first RL team to play at Twickenham, won the Middlesex Sevens. Martin Offiah, Scott Quinnell and Va'aiga Tuigamala, Jason Robinson, Andy Farrell and Henry Paul were a real Sevens dream team.

The winter after Wigan's guest appearances saw Jason Robinson try his hand at the other code during the league close-season with Bath, a foretaste of his stunningly successful permanent switch to Sale. That first fully professional campaign in England saw the pressure of full-time rugby come to bear... Clubs wanted to join the top flight and the existing residents were equally desperate to stay there. A messy, and short-lived, compromise was promotion and relegation play-offs. Bristol beat Bedford 19-12 to remain in the elite, as the Premiership era began. The play-off concept disappeared three years later.

MAY 12

First impressions count they say, but the 1971 Lions disproved that theory. They began their tour, en route to New Zealand, against Queensland just 58 hours after arriving. A jet-lagged, lacklustre performance saw them slip to a 15-11 defeat. Queensland were not a great side at the time and their coach, former dual All Black and Australia international Des Connor, pronounced that it was the worst Lions squad ever to be sent to New Zealand. Connor's judgement was severely brought into question when John Dawes' men proceeded to win the series against the All Blacks 2-1 and laid waste to all the Provincial teams they faced. Oops!!

That achievement in 1971 was so significant because the All Blacks have been consistently just so good. They do things with utter conviction and don't hand out key roles lightly. You have to be made of the right stuff to be captain and the choice made in 2006 has definitely proved to be up to the mark. Richie McCaw was handed the highest accolade New Zealand sport has to offer on a permanent basis, having forced his way to the front of queue with a string of magnificent performances. He began with a 2-0 series victory over Ireland and led his team to three consecutive Tri-Nations titles, the only blip being the 2007 World Cup.

MAY 13

England made their first visit to Romania for a full Test match in 1989. Chris Oti scored four tries and debutant Simon Hodgkinson helped himself to 19 points, converting eight of the nine touchdowns, in a 58-3 triumph. Another first-timer by the name of Jeremy Guscott scored a hat-trick of tries, just two months before he was to make his Lions debut. England's dominance was such that even prop Jeff Probyn dived over the whitewash.

Rugby cuts across boundaries in Ireland. Three of the four provinces – Connacht, Leinster and Munster – exist wholly within the Irish Republic but Ulster is different... Tommy Bowe, who was named their Rugby Personality of the Year in 2005, is an example of a citizen of the Republic (born in Monaghan) who represented Ulster, gaining his chance to wear the green shirt of Ireland via playing with the Red Hand (a traditional symbol of British Northern Ireland) on his chest. Bowe, when quizzed about it, said that it didn't bother him: "If you're going to get offended... why play for Ulster," was his no-nonsense reply.

MAY 14

Where was the birthplace of New Zealand rugby... Auckland? Christchurch? Dunedin? Wrong on all counts... the first recorded match played in the hottest of rugby hotbeds was held in Nelson, when the newly formed club took on the local boys' secondary school, Nelson College, in 1870. It may have been where it all started, but Nelson is not one of the stronger NZ rugby regions. They have never been deemed strong enough to play the Lions on their own, seven times combining with Marlborough and all ending in defeat, and haven't appeared on the itinerary since 1977.

So, Nelson was not a destination for the last amateur Lions squad as they departed the UK in 1993. That side, led by Gavin Hastings, would fall to a 2-1 series defeat to the All Blacks and suffer ignominious losses to Otago, Auckland, Hawke's Bay and Waikato – strong sides, but a top international team should not be losing to them. History may not have been made on the pitch by Hastings' men, but at least they made their mark by the way they got there. Lions parties had arrived in the past by ship and plane, but those in 1993 were the first to travel in the comfort of "club class".

MAY 15

The major international rugby union fixture list is a pretty conservative beast – London, Edinburgh, Cardiff etc. have always been regular destinations. It's good to occasionally mix it up a bit and way back in 1927 France dipped their toes into the water outside the established circuit with a trip across the border to play in Frankfurt. Germany actually won 17-16 and it's a shame that Teutonic rugby didn't kick on. As one of the world's major financial cities, Frankfurt would appear to be made for Test rugby. Imagine all those bankers rolling up to an international, a la Twickenham or Stade de France...

Tucuman is hardly a rugby backwater (don't say that face-to-face to anyone from the Cuyo region unless you're as quick as Usain Bolt!) but in terms of remoteness to the rest of the big players in the rugby family, the town in north west Argentina takes some beating. In 1993, the Pumas played Japan at the Cancha de Atletico Stadium – the first major international to be held in Argentina outside Buenos Aires. The hosts won 30-27, and have gone on to beat Italy and Wales at the venue.

MAY 16

In 1998, the women's game finally got its act together and organised its first official World Cup. The USA and England had won the two previous "trial runs" but now everyone who was anyone in the sport was present in Amsterdam to celebrate a great leap forward. The tournament was won in emphatic style by New Zealand, playing at a skill level superior to most male teams around the globe. The Silver Ferns scored an astonishing 344 points across their five matches, conceding just 32.

If you're going to go out, go out with a bang... Richmond approached their final match of the 1998/99 season in administration. The ancient club had been seduced by the ambition of Ashley Levett to chase the Premiership dream when the game went professional, and had succeeded to reach the elite. But now, after two campaigns in the top flight, the money had run out and Levett could no longer support a team paying high wages and watched by meagre crowds. This was to be their last match before a three-way merger with London Irish and Scottish, but they departed in style with a 106-12 pounding of Bedford. The amateur club is trying to battle its way back up the leagues. Once bitten, twice shy?

MAY 17

A blisteringly hot day in 1998 proved to be the most significant in the history of rugby in the north east of England. Gloom had descended on Newcastle the day before, as the Magpies succumbed meekly to Arsenal in the FA Cup final but now, at The Stoop, Geordie sports fans, and the rugby fraternity in particular, celebrated seeing the Falcons claim the inaugural Premiership title with a convincing victory over Harlequins. Rob Andrew hoisted the trophy towards the clear blue sky – a new era had begun, or maybe not. The Premiership crown has yet to return to Kingston Park.

Five years on from Newcastle's singular triumph, the landscape had changed. For the first time a semi-final was co-opted into the schedule, leading to the initial Premiership final. Critics lined up to castigate the idea – how could a season-long competition be decided by one match? Wasps, who finished second in the league, took on table-toppers Gloucester at Twickenham. The gap of 15 points between the sides at the conclusion of the regular season was nullified, Gloucester were slammed 39-3 and Wasps became the first club to become champions after finishing second.

MAY 18

The campaign to reinstate rugby into the Olympics is gathering pace as I write, but some American rugby followers of a curmudgeonly disposition may want the application to fail... The USA were pretty handy (or at least keen to participate) in Olympic rugby, walking off with gold medals in both 1920 and 24 (the last staging of the sport at the five-ringed circus). Thus, the States are the reigning Olympic champions. The truth behind the tale is that they and France were the only entrants in 1920, while only Romania bothered to turn up alongside the French and the Americans four years later. Today marks the day when the USA retained their title, seeing off France in Paris.

A special date in the life of another Olympian... Nigel Walker, who was a semi-finalist in the sprint hurdles at the 1984 Games in Los Angeles, turned back to rugby (he was once selected for a Welsh Schools trial) after being overlooked for the 1992 Olympic track team. He made a quick impact in every respect, moving from Cardiff debut to international in six months and on this day in 1994 Walker joined legends Willie Llewellyn, Reggie Gibbs and Ieuan Evans as joint-holder of the Wales record for tries in a Test, with four in a World Cup qualifier against Portugal in Lisbon.

MAY 19

It was 2001 and Parc des Princes was full with Parisiens backing Stade Francais and a large contingent from Leicester Tigers – the Heineken Cup final had stepped up a gear. What a match... 27-all with two minutes left and then Diego Dominguez's drop goal appeared to have won it for Stade. However, Austin Healey's inspirational break created a try for Leon Lloyd and Tim Stimpson's conversion sealed an incredible 34-30 victory. The Tigers had won the Heineken for the first time and claimed an unprecedented treble – Premiership, Championship and European titles.

In terms of drama, the Super 14 equivalent of that 2001 Heineken Cup final was held in 2007. Bryan Habana made a stunning intervention to win the title for the Pretoria-based Bulls... With the siren denoting the last play of the match having sounded, Habana and his team-mates trailed The Sharks 13-19. The wing fielded a poor attempt to get the ball out of play by Francois Steyn and proceeded to carve his way to the posts, handing Derick Hougaard the chance to clinch the match with the last kick. Astounding...

MAY 20

In 2006, Munster finally laid claim to the Heineken Cup with victory over Biarritz at the Millennium Stadium. Of the 72,000 present that day, approximately 71,690 appeared to be wearing some form of red. It was like being at a mass political or evangelical rally with a rugby match going on in the middle. Inclement Cardiff weather led to the roof being closed and the concentrated noise from the red-shirted hordes was so loud that the TV gantry, where I was sat, was actually shaking. The Frenchmen didn't have a prayer and when the massive video screens displayed almost as many people gathered in Limerick, the wave of euphoria carried tired Munster limbs to a first title at the 11th attempt.

The Pacific Nations Cup... Sounds lovely, doesn't it? Swaying palm trees, the sea gently lapping the shore and very big men colliding into each other on a rugby field. The idea was for a competition to encourage the local talent in Fiji, Samoa and Tonga. What the organisers of the inaugural PN Cup in 2006 didn't bargain for was a monsoon hitting Apia on the day of the final. The players from local side Savai'i and Fiji Warriors performed manfully in the atrocious conditions, with the Samoans edging a gripping duel 10-5.

MAY 21

The Lions ventured to New Zealand in 1930 – the first British & Irish side to visit the "land of the long white cloud" for 22 years. The tourists' first match was against Wanganui and immediately controversy reared its head when the home side had the temerity to leave the field at half-time. This did not impress Lions manager James Baxter – who was from the old school even in those days. Baxter berated his hosts for breaching International Rugby Board rules... Seems all a little bit trivial now with it being accepted practice to go off rather than stand still, freeze and suck on some oranges at the break... Common sense, surely.

Not sure what Mr Baxter would have made of the concept of extra time... He would probably have been getting his "No.1s" on for the post-match dinner. In 2006, the European Challenge Cup (rugby's answer to football's Europa League) staged its final at the Twickenham Stoop and provided a spectacular match stretching beyond 100 minutes. James Forrester's kick and chase effort earned Gloucester a first European trophy by the epic score of 36-34 (AET) against London Irish.

MAY 22

The French had been organising a club tournament for 80 years before the first English Cup final was held. Gallic domestic rugby is basically the South and a few clubs from Paris and it's enough to come from the capital for your typical southerner, but when 15 Parisiens wearing bow ties and supping champagne at half-time are ranged against them, the blood boils nicely. Toulon, from the Cote d'Azur, put Racing Club in the shade at Parc des Princes in 1987 to secure their first title for 56 years... Much too long for Toulon, will Jonny Wilkinson help bring the glory days back?

It took football 58 years from the first international match to stage their first World Cup, cricket organised a world tournament just three years after the first One-Day International but on this day in 1987, 116 years after Scotland and England first played at Raeburn Place, rugby union finally got its own showpiece underway – and what a start... Hosts New Zealand thrashed Italy (no surprise there) but the highlight was one of the greatest tries ever seen in an international. John Kirwan ran from inside the All Blacks' 22 straight down the field to the other end, evading half the Azzurri team and, apparently, holding his breath all the way!!

MAY 23

Lawrence Dallaglio is a true titan of the game, unique among European players in that he has won every major honour there is. He has had his fair share of injuries and disappointments as well, arguably the most gut-wrenching of all came in 1999 when the News of the World claimed he had taken drugs on the Lions tour two years before. Dallaglio categorically denied the story and subsequent charges by the RFU were dropped. Dallaglio resigned as England captain the next day, ruling himself out of leading his country at the 1999 World Cup.

Happier times for Dallaglio five years later when he led Wasps to their first Heineken Cup triumph. Toulouse were the opposition and Twickenham was the venue. In a sensational finish, with the score 20-all, scrum-half Rob Howley chased his own kick more in hope than expectation with full-back Clement Poitrenaud in a perfect position to field the ball. However, Poitrenaud dallied, hoping the ball would run dead, and Howley pounced before the lackadaisical Frenchman could touch the ball down. Wasps won 27-20 thanks to Howley's thirst for an apparent lost cause.

MAY 24

All players want to make a name for themselves, but some unfortunates will always be remembered for a misdemeanour rather than outstanding performances... Former England prop Mike Burton, now a successful businessman, became the first England player to be sent off in a full international, when he was ejected at Ballymore after just three minutes of the second Test against Australia in 1975 for a high tackle. The match was coined "the battle of Brisbane" due to recurrent fights and the violence was such that the RFU decided not to suspend Burton.

The late Ray Gravell created many happy memories for Wales fans, but he was also one of the toughest centres ever to play the game – as a South African opponent found out on the 1980 Lions tour. Free State's De Wet Ras was expected to be in the Springbok squad for the Test series, but Gravell made sure he wasn't... A pulverising "tackle" broke Ras' jaw and he was out of contention for the forthcoming internationals. There was no malice aforethought from the Welshman; he just played the game very, very hard.

MAY 25

All Black legends Colin Meads and Wilson Whineray made their debuts on this day in 1957 against Australia in Sydney. For the next eight years they were to join forces in the New Zealand pack, with Meads going on for a further six seasons. They suffered just a handful of defeats together in all that time. Things didn't go quite so well for fellow first-timers that day, Terry Lineen and Frank McMullen. They were both dispensed with by the selectors following the 1960 series defeat in South Africa...

Meads and Whineray knew that the laws had to be bent on occasions to get that winning edge, as did another great forward – Neil Back. However, his high profile nudge at Peter Stringer as the half-back was about to feed a scrum at the end of the 2002 Heineken Cup final enraged Munster supporters. Leicester were trying to become the first side to retain the trophy, while the Irishmen were attempting to lay their hands on the prize for the first time. Back did rugby's version of Diego Maradona's "hand of God" to prevent Stringer from gaining quick ball in front of the Tigers' posts, with the English champions leading by a slender six-point margin. The spoils went to Leicester, while Munster skulked off in fury.

MAY 26

Wallaby rugby was a closed book to the indigenous Aborigine population until 1962, when Lloyd McDermott became the first of their number to pull on an Australia "jumper" in a Test. It was no easy ride for the newcomer, pitched in against the All Blacks, but he made a good enough impression. However, Australia were due to tour apartheid-ravaged South Africa and McDermott refused to go: "I didn't want to be an "honorary white"," he said. After just two caps, the fairytale was over. McDermott quit, joined rugby league and subsequently became his country's first Aboriginal barrister.

In 1995, Ivory Coast became the first West African team to reach the World Cup Finals. Their first match was a clash of rugby cultures, as the newcomers lined up against a member of the old guard – Scotland. Gavin Hastings and his men proceeded to teach the Ivorians a lesson, thrashing them 89-0 in Rustenburg. Hastings scored a European record 44 points. On the wing for IVC was the ill-fated Max Brito, who was to be paralysed as a result of a tackle in the game against Tonga later in the tournament.

MAY 27

At times it seems the northern and southern hemisphere are playing two different games of rugby. It's not a new phenomenon... In 1908, during the "Anglo-Welsh" tour, the issue was substitutions (or lack of them). During the defeat by Wellington, one of the home players was forced off due to injury. His captain asked if he could use a substitute, illegal under the laws at the time but commonly invoked under gentlemen's agreements in New Zealand. The Lions management were furious, and declined to play ball. The fact these so-called "guardians of the game" would allow wounded men to risk further injury says a lot...

After the big split in 1895, the area in and around Manchester was quickly considered a rugby league rather than union region. Sale were the traditional powerhouse but the proximity of St Helens, Salford, Swinton, Wigan and Warrington mitigated against them gaining the local profile of, say, Bristol, Leicester or Northampton. It could have gone either way when union went pro but, in Brian Kennedy, the Sharks had a friend with deep pockets and broadened their fan base with the move to Stockport. In 2006, Sale became the first team from the North West to win the Premiership, when they thrashed Leicester 45-20 in the final.

MAY 28

British & Irish Lions squads are selected with great fanfare, and much navel gazing about those who have "missed out". However, in reality, injuries and international air travel mean that many more than the chosen few get the Lions call. Home teams knowing that this is probably their first and last time to take on the famous tourists, are "physical" opponents. Take Manawatu in 1983... They won 25-18, but the Lions complained of being kicked, trampled and hit. Skipper Ciaran Fitzgerald, No.8 Iain Paxton and prop Graham Price all picked up nasty wounds, with the doctor saying the dressing room was like a battle scene.

Bill Beaumont, the 1980 Lions captain, knows all about the graft needed to perform in the pack at the highest level, but he was also a great servant to Lancashire. The County Championship no longer features top players, but, as a tribute to one of English rugby's greats, the tournament was renamed the Bill Beaumont Cup in 2007. The first final under the new name, appropriately, featured Lancashire, who were humbled 27-6 by Devon.

MAY 29

The 1974 Lions were very good. A 3-0 series score-line against the ever powerful Springboks says it all, but there were less challenging fixtures along the way... Rhodesia, Western Transvaal and Griqualand West were all put to the sword but nowhere near as much as South Western Districts felt steel on their necks. JJ Williams ran in a record six tries and England fly-half Alan Old, whose chances of Test action were negligible due to Phil Bennett, scored an unprecedented 37 points, largely through converting 15 of the 16 tries, in a 97-0 slaughter.

The 1980s saw Australian rugby union begin to make a mark, after decades of seeing most of its best talent go to league. There was the 1984 Grand Slam tour but, when England ventured Down Under in 1988, that team was breaking up after coach Alan Jones' departure. Opportunity knocked, particularly when two breakaway tries gave England a lead in the first Test. However, new Wallaby boss Bob Dwyer had the Nick Farr-Jones/Michael Lynagh half-back axis to rely on, Steve Cutler was still ruling the line-outs, with David Campese and Ian Williams potent finishers on the wings. Lynagh's boot and a Williams try, 22-16, thank you very much. England had still to win a Test against Australia in Wallaby land.

MAY 30

The amount of international rugby played in the professional era has militated against lengthy careers. When asked to play upward of 30 games a year, involving big collisions and physical demands, the body eventually says: "Enough!". That makes England and Wasps lock Simon Shaw something of a phenomenon... In 1994, as an amateur, 20-year-old Shaw arrived in South Africa as a replacement on England's tour for Martin Johnson. Remarkably, 15 years to the day later, as a pro, Shaw was back with the Lions, playing in the tour opener. Fellow 2009 Lion Leigh Halfpenny was literally a baby when Shaw started his career in 1990.

In 1996, Leicester Tigers made a massive signing... Bob Dwyer, who had guided Australia to the 1991 World Cup win, was hired as director of rugby – a huge statement of intent at the dawn of professionalism. The first season went well – Leicester reached the Heineken Cup final – but in his second campaign "player power" began to rear its head, with Austin Healey being the most high profile of those disaffected by Dwyer's methods. Healey was dropped from the squad, the board became disillusioned by the Australian and he was sacked, 21 months after his appointment. Tigers legend Dean Richards took over and the club won trophy after trophy before "Deano" also fell foul of Welford Road politics.

MAY 31

Consistent form, staying free of injury, a refusal to rest and maintaining a hunger for Test rugby... Those factors are rarely seen together for any great length of time. The man who managed the feat for the longest stretch has been former New Zealand captain Sean Fitzpatrick. The Auckland hooker played 63 Tests on the trot between November 1986 and May 1995, the last of which being the World Cup defeat of Wales. The sequence was broken when Fitzpatrick sat out the following match against Japan to be rested for the quarter-finals. Wallaby Joe Roff came within a match, but no-one else has got beyond 60 in a row.

Ireland, Scotland and Wales have always had a strong bond. In answer to the power of the English and French clubs, the trio set up the Celtic League. However, the alliance was fractured in 2005 when it emerged that the Welsh had agreed to play in the new Anglo-Welsh Cup competition in 2005/6 on Celtic League weekends. The Irish and Scottish chucked the Welsh out of the competition and threatened to set up their own two-nation tournament. A solution was found, pragmatism replaced anger – the Celts had to stick together.

RUGBY
On This Day

JUNE

JUNE 1

Great New Zealand full-back Don Clarke was a familiar foe for British and Irish teams in the 1950s and 60s. His steady kicking, toe-punting the ball regularly through the uprights, was a feature of international rugby at the time. The 1959 Lions had suffered at his hands (or rather foot) and, in 1963, it was the turn of England. Mike Weston's side were the first Red Rose outfit to tour New Zealand and, having lost the first Test with Clarke scoring 15 points, they were tied at 6-all with the All Blacks in the last minute of the second. However, Kiwi referee Pat Murphy awarded a penalty and Clarke condemned the English to another defeat.

The next New Zealand-England series held in the "Shaky Isles" was played in 1985, when England were at a very low ebb, having won just two matches over the previous three Five Nations tournaments. The inexperienced squad included future captain Mike Harrison, who was to make quite a name for himself on the tour. Debutant wing Harrison was christened "Burglar Bill" by the Kiwis after scoring interception tries in both matches in the series, as England slid to a predictable 2-0 defeat. Harrison was England's first World Cup skipper in 1987 before his brief fling with rugby stardom came to a halt in 1988.

JUNE 2

In 1984, England controversially agreed to tour South Africa, breaking the sporting boycott of the country during the apartheid era. The Springboks had not played any kind of Test match for two years (three if the South America Jaguars are discounted), so were desperate to prove their rugby was still of the highest quality. With many unable or unwilling to tour, captain (John) Scott had 10 uncapped men in his squad of 26 – lambs to the slaughter come to mind. The Boks ran riot in Port Elizabeth, majestic centre Danie Gerber pulling the strings in a 33-15 victory, following up with a hat-trick of tries in a 35-9 triumph a week later.

Wales wing Chris Czekaj was given the opportunity to cement a place in the team on the 2007 tour of Australia. The trip served as a warm-up for that year's World Cup. Sadly, during the second Test in Brisbane, Czekaj suffered a horrific accident, his right leg broken in five places, and feared that he would never play again. However, two years later, Czekaj returned to international rugby on the tour of North America.

JUNE 3

The 1970s was a curious decade for England. They made little impact in the Five Nations, winning just 11 of their 40 matches, but contrived to win in both New Zealand and South Africa... A year before beating the All Blacks in Auckland, and off the back of a Championship whitewash, John Pullin led a team including four debutants out in front of 66,000 at Johannesburg's Ellis Park. They faced a Springbok side unbeaten for almost two years. Two of those first-timers scored all England's points – a try by Alan Morley and five goals by Sam Doble – as the Red Rose bloomed to record an amazing 18-9 victory.

Pullin's men stood up to the Boks and there's an old rugby adage that if you don't do that in South Africa you will be punished. Canada appeared to take that on board in the 1995 World Cup, but their match in Port Elizabeth descended into an ugly spectacle. Irish referee David McHugh was at his wits' end, with violence erupting all around him, and felt compelled to send off SA hooker James Dalton and Canadian duo Rod Snow and Gareth Rees – the only time three players have been sent off in a major international.

JUNE 4

June 4 is connected with two record score-lines, although under somewhat different circumstances... In 1966, the Lions were 1-0 up in their series in Australia and headed to Brisbane for the second and final Test. Lang Park, the city's rugby league stadium, was the only viable option for the match, so everyone had to get special dispensation from the International Board to avoid "professionalising" themselves. Strange, but true... As for the match, the tourists scored a remarkable 25 points in 22 minutes in the first half, setting the platform for a 31-0 victory – a record win for the Lions against any international team.

In 1995, the All Blacks were not quite yet officially professional but it looked like pros v amateurs as they savaged Japan 145-17, a record for a World Cup match, in Bloemfontein. The occasion had a surreal feel to it, as the Japanese were actually enterprising counter-attackers but just couldn't create any platform up front. Simon Culhane scored a mammoth 45 points, superseding his colleague Andrew Mehrtens' mark for a debutant set just prior to the tournament, with Marc Ellis scoring six of his side's 21 tries. And they didn't even have Jonah Lomu in the team...

JUNE 5

Who is the greatest striker, batsman or athlete of all time? The big sporting questions that provoke heated debate... Add to the list fly-half, it's the principal position in a rugby team, the conductor of the orchestra, if you will. Many names are floated but one that always should appear is Mark Ella. Born on this day in 1959, Ella thrust himself into the spotlight in 1980, piloting the Wallabies to a first series victory over the All Blacks for 31 years, and ended his brief career by writing himself into rugby folklore on the 1984 Grand Slam tour, when he scored a try against each of the Home Nations.

Carisbrook, Dunedin is a long way to go for a game of rugby and has proved to be a devilishly difficult place for visiting teams to play at. In 1993, the Lions took on Otago at "The House of Pain" and that nickname took on an unfortunately accurate tone as the tourists ran up a full ledger of injuries. The two most notable being Martin Bayfield lying flat out for some time after being manhandled at a line-out before being carried off the field and Scott Hastings suffering a badly depressed cheekbone. The 37-24 defeat merely added a large dose of salt into many wounds.

JUNE 6

The archetypal image of rugby crowds is good humour and no need for the mass of police seen at major football grounds. Almost without exception this is true, but there has been the odd disturbance. In 1908, the Anglo-Welsh team (not officially accepted as "Lions" but treated as such in New Zealand), were taken apart by the All Blacks, 32-5, in the first "Test" at Dunedin. The story, though, was off the pitch as a mob, incensed by high ticket prices, tore down fences and entered the ground for free with the authorities unable to stop them.

The only trouble in the stands at Brisbane's Suncorp Stadium in 1998 was, for English ears, the guffawing of gloating Aussies... Clive Woodward took an under-strength squad on the hardest tour imaginable – one Test against Australia, two against the All Blacks and then the Springboks in Cape Town. Many of the triumphant Lions in South Africa the year before were resting, but the RFU had agreed the trip, so Woodward and co undertook their "tour of hell". The Wallabies put the rookies to the sword, inflicting England's heaviest defeat, 76-0.

JUNE 7

Never take a significant detour without checking ahead first... Ireland arranged to tour New Zealand for the first time in 1976 and the Irish, always up for the craic, decided they might have a dabble with Fiji on the way. They arrived in Suva to see if the Islanders were up for a game. There was just one tiny snag... Fiji were touring Australia at the time!! Back on the plane to NZ then and, once the All Blacks had probably stopped laughing, Ireland succumbed to an 11-3 defeat – a creditable result under the somewhat ridiculous circumstances and a ticking off for the administration department at the Irish Rugby Football Union.

Eleven years later, Ireland and Fiji were again playing matches in different countries Down Under, but this time it was wholly in the plan... The quarter-finals of the first World Cup saw Ireland, having finished second to Wales in their pool, forced to take on Australia in Sydney. The Wallabies ran out convincing 33-15 winners. Fiji, benefitting from South Africa's enforced absence, qualified for the last eight at Argentina's expense. However, Grand Slam champions France were far too strong and streetwise for the flamboyant Fijians at Eden Park, winning 31-16. It would be 20 years before Fiji would grace the last eight again.

JUNE 8

A date significant in Lions history... In the first Test of the 1968 series, South Africa recorded a fourth straight victory over the tourists for the first time, despite skipper Tom Kiernan scoring a then-record 17 points. Of wider significance, future Lions legend Mike Gibson became the first man to win a cap as a replacement, after Barry John broke his collarbone following a ferocious tackle from Springbok flanker Jan Ellis. It had taken 117 years for rugby's administrators to bring in a law that appears to be common sense.

Much happier times for the Lions in 1974 as Willie John McBride, winning a record 14th cap, guided his charges to a 12-3 triumph in the first Test on a quagmire of a pitch in Cape Town. South Africa had not lost a match to the Lions for 19 years and Newlands had not seen red, white, green and blue victorious in an international for 36 seasons. The try-less win wasn't pretty, but it set the ball rolling for an exceptional series and, in Pretoria and Port Elizabeth, the tries flooded in just as the rain had tippled down in the Cape.

JUNE 9

Tours traditionally gave world rugby's lesser lights a chance to take on the game's superstars. Hectic fixture lists makes those opportunities rarer these days but Wales visited Namibia in 1990, and were given two tough matches in Windhoek. On this day they won the second match 34-30. How the South Africans across the border would have loved the kudos of the 1987 World Cup third-placers visiting but, unlike the English in 1984, Wales were not going to break the boycott. Sadly for the Namibians, the return of their neighbours to the international fold coincided with their disappearance off the tour rota.

Canada is now a regular destination for England teams and in 2001, while Australia hosted the Lions (including a squadron of Englishmen), some Red Rose cadets were sent to Canada to play two Tests on England's first full tour of the country. Burnaby was the venue as young England fleeced the Canucks 59-20 to seal a 2-0 series victory. The trip was invaluable experience for future World Cup-winners Josh Lewsey, Ben Kay and Lewis Moody.

JUNE 10

The whole course of a Test series can be altered by one incident. Ireland fly-half Paul Dean was picked ahead of England's Rob Andrew for the Lions tour to Australia in 1989 but, in the first match against Western Australia, an injury forced Dean to leave the tour and Andrew was whistled up as his replacement. The change proved that the original selection was probably flawed, as Andrew was a key component in the Lions' 2-1 series victory. Perhaps Dean could have had a similar influence, we will never know, but Andrew replaced Craig Chalmers for the second and third Tests – both won by the Lions.

When South Africa rejoined the Test match fraternity in 1992, the ideal scenario was for a black player to be at the forefront of the Springbok team. Was it an impossible dream in a country where the indigenous people were persecuted for decades? Step forward Chester Williams. The "black pearl" made his debut in 1993, but missed the pool stage of the 1995 World Cup due to injury. He returned for the quarter-final against Samoa and immediately made his mark – four tries – and had the South African nation in his hand. The ultimate success followed two matches later – Nelson Mandela handing over the Webb Ellis Trophy to Francois Pienaar wearing a Springbok shirt – Chester must have been pinching himself...

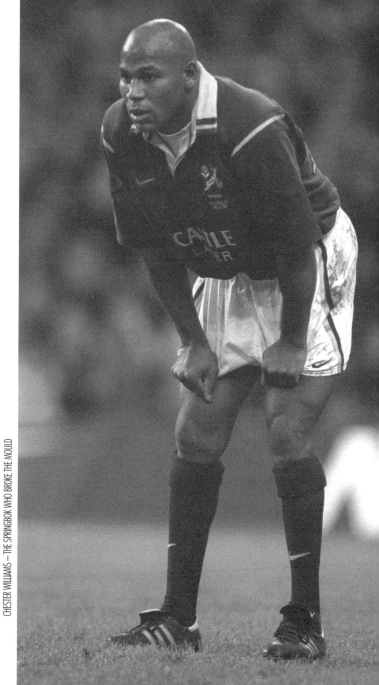

JUNE 11

The 1991 World Cup Final was a dagger to the heart of English rugby. It was all set up – France and Scotland had been seen off, just the last of the mortal enemies to be beaten in the grand climax at Twickenham in front of the Queen… But Australia were not going to be also-rans. Four years on, the two sides met in Cape Town in the 1995 quarter-final. Incredibly, there had been no full international between the two in the interim. It was close, 25-22 close, but Rob Andrew's drop goal was crucial and England had at last beaten the Aussies away from Twickenham… at the ninth attempt.

Andrew, despite all his achievements, would probably readily admit that he was not one of the game's great characters. For that added ingredient look no further than one of the surprise stars of the 1997 Lions tour of South Africa… John Bentley, who played for England before quitting for rugby league, returned to union in 1996 and earned selection for the Lions in the curious position of being a capped player (but not for nine years!!). "Bentos" made himself the heart and soul of that tour and played in the last two Tests when Ieuan Evans pulled up with a groin injury. He scored a hat-trick against Free State but his 70-metre try against Gauteng on June 11 was one of THE great Lions scores.

JUNE 12

Samoa reached successive World Cup quarter-finals in the 1990s and were suddenly in demand for tours. In 1999, France made a first official visit to Apia and there followed a "committed" Test match. Samoa centre George Leaupepe was sent off for throwing a punch and, two minutes later, team-mate Trevor Leota aimed a high tackle at Christian Califano, and he was off too. France scored two late tries to give the final score a hugely flattering look of 39-22.

Misdemeanours or not, it's a blessing the Russian police force were not on duty in Apia. Rugby is growing in strength in the world's largest country but obviously has some way to go… In 2006, more than 100 people were detained in Rostov-On-Don after police mistook a game of rugby for a mass brawl. Apparently, they had received a tip-off that things were "kicking off" at an empty sports ground. More than 70 officers found around 60 people watching what was claimed to be a fight between two criminal gangs.

JUNE 13

Explosive characters that don't toe the line are fascinating. Andy Haden made 117 appearances for the All Blacks (including 41 Tests), was the true successor to Colin Meads as the next great New Zealand lock, but was also the administrators' nemesis. He missed the first Test against Scotland on this day in 1981 after being banned for fighting in a club game, refused to tour Britain in 1983 as he wanted to promote a book and missed going to Australia in 1984 because the authorities wanted to investigate whether his off-field activities infringed his "amateur" status. They couldn't nail him, and the NZRU ended up employing him as a marketing adviser...

Two more larger-than-life personalities, arguably the most outrageously talented men to ever pick up a rugby ball, were involved in an amazing match in 1987... Serge Blanco and David Campese were pitted against each other in the World Cup semi-final. Campese became a world record holder with his 25th Test try (breaking Scot Ian Smith's 54-year-old mark) while Blanco concluded an epic move to score in the corner, clinching a 30-24 victory.

JUNE 14

Until the 1980s, there was no convention in rugby Test matches for the referee to be from a neutral country. Controversial decisions led to fingers being pointed, but what made the 1969 second Test between New Zealand and Wales curious was not a decision, but a celebration... When Fergie McCormick slotted a drop goal for the All Blacks, Kiwi ref Pat Murphy appeared to raise both his arms like a home fan would. Carwyn James, the 1971 Lions coach, did not forget the incident and a number of, in the Welsh view, "home town" calls by Murphy on that tour. So when Murphy was named as a prospective ref for the crucial final Test, James refused point blank to agree to the appointment.

More British stiff upper lip in the face of the Kiwis... If one passage of play provided a clue that England had the resolve to win the 2003 World Cup it was against New Zealand in Wellington. Opposing 13 for 10 minutes in the second half (Neil Back and Lawrence Dallaglio having been sent to the sin bin), home skipper Reuben Thorne opted for a succession of five-metre scrums against six forwards, plus centre Mike Tindall, but no amount of huffing and puffing could push them over. Back and Dallaglio returned and England edged a 15-13 victory.

JUNE 15

Some countries have a conveyor belt of world-class performers in the same position. Welsh fly-halves, All Black flankers, England locks, South African props... Normally, though, there is a short interregnum. For Australia, two of their greatest scrum-halves saw the end and the beginning of their careers coincide. John Hipwell replaced Ken Catchpole against New Zealand in 1968, the end of Catchpole's eight seasons as a Wallaby and the beginning of Hipwell's 14-year association with the green and gold. The Aussie No.9 tradition has been carried on by Nick Farr-Jones and George Gregan.

Cape Town is one of the great cities to visit on a rugby tour... Table mountain, the vineyards, the coastline... It's all lovely stuff and has been a popular staging post on trips to South Africa for over 100 years. The 1910 Lions certainly enjoyed themselves there, camped on the Cape for three weeks, including four consecutive matches at Newlands against the full range of Western Province teams. The first on the list was WP Country, who were beaten 9-3, before WP Colleges, WP Towns and eventually WP. They didn't seem to want to leave!!

JUNE 16

Mike Gibson was an almost perpetual presence in the Ireland back division for 15 years. His Test career came to a close after the second Test against Australia in Sydney, a match Ireland won to complete a 2-0 series victory. Gibson left the stage with a then-world record 81 caps, 69 wearing green and 12 for the Lions, having overtaken his old team-mate and fellow Ulsterman Willie John McBride. He went on five Lions tours, including the 1971 triumph against the All Blacks, playing alongside Barry John and skipper John Dawes... what a midfield combination that was.

Tonga was one of the great success stories of the 2007 World Cup. The Pacific Islanders, who had lived in the shadows of not only the Wallabies and All Blacks but also Fiji and Samoa, pushed both eventual finalists to the limit in the pool stage. The first seeds of the improvement were sown on this day in 1999, when the Tongans beat France 20-16 in Nuku'alofa – the first time they had beaten a major rugby nation at home. Exactly a year later New Zealand handed them a 102-0 thumping, but if (and it's a massive "if") Tonga can hold on to more of their talent they could be real competitors.

JUNE 17

JPR Williams was never one to shirk a challenge on the rugby field, whether fielding a high ball or even sprinting to take part in a mass brawl – JPR could be counted on. When Wales suffered an injury crisis on the 1978 tour to Australia, JPR was called upon to perform at openside flanker in the second Test. The Grand Slam champions lost 19-17, and with it the series, but JPR was not to blame. He gave a typically brave performance opposing one of the great Wallaby back rows – Tony Shaw, Greg Cornelsen and Mark Loane.

JPR would doubtless agree that reaching 100 caps in a sport as physically demanding as rugby union is quite an achievement. To not be content with that and march on into the distance is something else. George Gregan began his Test career when the sport was still officially amateur in 1994. He helped the Wallabies regain the World Cup in 1999, reached his personal century in 2004 and on June 17 2006, one day short of 12 years to the day since his debut, toppled Jason Leonard as the world's most capped player, when he came on as a replacement against the English in Melbourne. Gregan finished with 139 (20 more than Leonard), with just six as a replacement.

JUNE 18

"Sport and politics should never be mixed"... The late Llanelli and 1971 Lions coach Carwyn James stood in the 1970 General Election for the Welsh nationalists – Plaid Cymru. James garnered just 17% of the vote in the rugby-mad town where he coached its team to great success – 46% fewer than the winning candidate. Maybe a significant proportion of the Stradey Park faithful wanted the great Carwyn to stick to rugby...

England could have done with an act of Parliament to help them out in the 1995 World Cup semi-final, when they came up against a man Will Carling described as a "freak" – Jonah Lomu. The game had never seen such a specimen playing on the wing before, just 20-years-old, standing 6ft 5in, weighing 18 stone and... quick! Opposite number Tony Underwood was made to look like a seven-stone weakling as Lomu rampaged round, over and through him on his way to scoring four tries in the All Blacks' 45-29 romp. From every cloud... Underwood joined forces with Lomu to advertise for a pizza restaurant – so at least Underwood gained something from very public embarrassment.

JUNE 19

A rare dark day on the 1971 Lions tour of New Zealand... The tourists beat Canterbury 14-3, but in the process were beaten up, as some of the opposition went over the top in their aim to intimidate ahead of the first Test. Even the NZ media termed it "the game of shame". Sandy Carmichael suffered a multiple fracture to his cheekbone, Ray McLoughlin a broken thumb, Fergus Slattery had two teeth loosened and both John Pullin and Gareth Edwards were floored by sly punches. The Lions lost both their first-choice props amid the violence, but still managed to win the series 2-1.

It was not often that Neil Jenkins performed below-par... A total of 1090 points in 91 Tests tells you all you need to know. However, one of those rare occasions was for the Lions against Australia A in 2001. Nothing seemed to go right for Jenkins, and he had the indignity of being hauled off by his Wales and Lions coach Graham Henry just before the hour mark and replaced at fly-half by Austin Healey with the Lions 22-6 down. The tourists fought back but were beaten 28-25, their only defeat outside of the Test series on the whole trip.

JUNE 20

June 20 1987 was the day when the biggest rugby fixture was first staged... the Rugby World Cup Final. Eden Park was the venue as All Black captain David Kirk became the first player to triumphantly lift the Webb Ellis Trophy. Little did we know that, as preparations continue for a 2011 tournament that will also climax in Auckland, no NZ skipper has managed to claim the ultimate prize in rugby since. Tries from Kirk, Michael Jones and John Kirwan, allied to the relentless boot of Grant Fox, produced a 29-9 victory over a French team exhausted following their epic semi-final against Australia.

South Africans complained that the All Blacks were not true world champions in 1987, due to the absence of the Springboks. However, it should always be remembered exactly why they weren't there – apartheid. Six years previously, New Zealand hosted their traditional rivals for global supremacy, but the furore that tour caused strengthened the resolve of campaigners and led to an official rugby boycott lasting 10 years. One man who made a stand in 1981 was Bruce Robertson; the All Black centre played his last Test against Scotland, refusing to make himself available to play against South Africa.

JUNE 21

The 1930 Lions had the weight of history against them... New Zealand was a graveyard for the hopes of both the 1904 British and 1908 Anglo-Welsh teams. Neither won a match and New Zealand conceded just 11 points in the process. The four-Test series began in Dunedin with the "All Blacks" wearing white to prevent a colour clash with the then blue shirts worn by the Lions. Wing Ivor Jones scored a last minute try to inflict a 6-3 defeat on the hosts. New Zealand's unbeaten record against their former colonial masters had come to an end.

Just as the 1930 Lions were battling against the odds, so were their successors 67 years later – the first professional Lions. Martin Johnson's squad faced South Africa, the world champions, in a three-Test series, knowing that only one set of 20th century Lions before them had won a series there. They needed a good start... The man of the moment was Matt Dawson, only in the team due to an injury to Rob Howley, who conjured a piece of trickery that fooled the Springbok defence and led to a 35-16 victory in the first Test at Newlands.

JUNE 22

Where would rugby be without it's laws? The game often takes on the appearance of organised chaos and at least this document puts the "organised" into that phrase. It's often said that a whistle should follow every line-out, as none are 100 per cent to the letter of the law, but it's generally accepted that they are a framework from which the game can be interpreted. The men responsible were a trio of 19th century lawyers (now there's a surprise...) by the names of Rutter, Holmes and Maton. Their profession dictated why they are termed as "laws" and not "rules". Their work was ratified by the full RFU committee on June 22 1871.

Third place play-offs... Why do they exist? At the end of a World Cup, instead of disappearing to a beach somewhere, the beaten semi-finalists have to play essentially a meaningless match. In 1995, England, having been savaged by Jonah Lomu and the All Blacks, faced France in Pretoria. The players looked like they didn't want to be there, there was talk of pride being salvaged but no win would erase the humiliation inflicted in Cape Town. France celebrated Philippe Sella's 111th and last cap by winning 19-9 – a first Gallic win over the English for seven years.

JUNE 23

The sport was shaken to its foundations in 1995 when news broke of a deal between News Corporation and the South Africa, New Zealand and Australia rugby unions giving exclusive rights to show all official matches in those countries for 10 years. It was a triumph for Rupert Murdoch, as his bitter rival Kerry Packer had been negotiating to sign up 500 of the world's best players to appear in a professional "World Rugby Corporation". WRC failed to persuade the Springboks, urged by their union to remain loyal with claims that it would "match" anything Packer offered, and without the world champions there could be no viable WRC.

Whether professional or amateur, some in the southern hemisphere have an almost primeval need to inflict their will on the Lions by brutal means. Duncan McRae thought repeatedly punching Ronan O'Gara on the floor was a wise thing to do at a crucial stage of the New South Wales match. As the Irishman's face was made as red as his shirt, it came as no surprise that McRae was sent off. The Lions won 41-24, their determination to beat the Wallabies steeled and they won the first Test a week later.

JUNE 24

Australia played their first international match on this day in 1899, against Matthew Mullineux's "British team" in Sydney. This, the last 19th century "Lions" tour, was solely to Australia. The next time that happened was 90 years later. The Aussies showed that, despite Aussie Rules and the new kid on the block – rugby league – taking a hold, they had something to contribute, surprising the Brits 13-3. The Lions' only points were a try scored by the sole Welshman in the squad – Gwyn Nicholls – who was for many years renowned as the greatest centre ever to have played the game.

We told you so!! The shrill shriek of Afrikaners as South Africa won the World Cup at the first attempt in 1995. Avid Springbok fans decried both New Zealand (1987) and Australia (1991) as phoney world champions, because their green-shirted heroes were not permitted to take part. Joel Stransky's extra time drop goal settled the match and Francois Pienaar received the trophy from the one and only Nelson Mandela at an ecstatic Ellis Park. The only blot on the landscape was the claim by the defeated All Blacks that they had been poisoned.

JUNE 25

Summer rugby? It's gone down a storm in rugby league but, whenever the mercury level rises above 20°C, British union types seem to complain that it's just too hot. So what is "too hot"? Wales team doctor Rob Leyshon complained, in 1994, that conditions hovering above 38°C for his team's match against Samoa in Apia were "extraordinary and perhaps dangerous." Wales sliding to a humiliating 34-9 defeat possibly had something to do with it... Real danger was felt by Will Greenwood playing for the Lions against Free State in 2007, when he was knocked unconscious and almost slipped away from us.

Brian O'Driscoll's most dangerous time came in 2005, when the Lions captain suffered a tour-ending injury in the opening minutes of the first Lions Test against New Zealand. The controversy surrounding the most famous "tackle" ever made rumbles on to this day... Did opposing skipper Tana Umaga and hooker Kevan Mealamu deliberately drive O'Driscoll's head into the Christchurch turf in a dreaded "spear"? Sir Clive Woodward and his legion of staff and consultants certainly thought so, producing a lengthy video presentation to back them up, which was actually counter-productive. Nothing was proved or disproved.

JUNE 26

When Cardiff Arms Park was demolished in 1997 to make way for the Millennium Stadium, many doubted if the new ground could ever replace what had been lost. Perhaps the first match played at the new cathedral of Welsh rugby, on this day in 1999, made them think again... Wales had never beaten South Africa, the only major nation to avoid defeat by the Dragons. After 12 attempts, the best they had to show was a draw in 1970. Tries from Mark Taylor and Gareth Thomas, allied to seven successful Neil Jenkins kicks, did for the Springboks. The noise was terrific, it was just a shame only 27,000 turned up.

1999 was the year when not one, but two, great stadia were inaugurated. The Wallabies "welcomed" England to Stadium Australia, which was to be the main venue for the following year's Olympic Games. A crowd of 81,000 was attracted to a special game, which celebrated a centenary of Australian Test rugby. This was something different... Australia wore light blue shirts, with England performing in a darker hue, to replicate the kits worn when the Aussies took on the 1899 British team. As then, and the nine previous occasions England had been the opposition in Australia, the Wallabies were victorious.

JUNE 27

Wellington, New Zealand's capital, is exposed to Antarctic winds whistling up the Cook Strait. Not the ideal place to play rugby but it's where thousands of aficionados live – so to hell with the weather. The 1908 Anglo-Welsh team, 1-0 down in their three-match series, were sent to Athletic Park for the second Test on a typically foul day. It was 0-0 at half-time, the All Blacks edged ahead with a penalty and then Jack Jones was on his, well, "Jack Jones" as the only try scorer to level matters. Lions skipper Boxer Harding just had to slot the conversion to win the match. He missed from in front of the posts.

An epic in Pretoria decided the fate of the 2009 Lions. The first Test was a classic, but the second was different gravy as the Springboks claimed the series. At 25-all in the 80th minute, Ronan O'Gara's kick and chase ended with a penalty conceded 55 metres out, after his clumsy mid-air challenge on Fourie Du Preez. No problem at altitude for local hero Morne Steyn. But the Boks should have been permanently down to 14 after one minute, following Schalk Burger's despicable gouge on Luke Fitzgerald. A yellow card and subsequent eight-week ban was insufficient punishment.

JUNE 28

The Springbok captain is the figurehead of a squad with an intensity few can match. The players are brought up not to give a centimetre and to meet every physical and psychological challenge without flinching. It takes a lot for a public display of weakness but, although the scorecard tells a different story, the 1980 Lions followed their 1974 colleagues in making a South African doff his cap. Bill Beaumont's men went 3-0 down after a 10-12 defeat in Port Elizabeth, but opposing skipper Morne Du Plessis admitted that "the better team lost". Two weeks later, the Lions proved the point, winning the final Test 17-13.

In 1997, Martin Johnson led the Lions into battle in South Africa. This time the dreams of the 1980 amateurs were fulfilled by the first professionals. A tense second Test in Durban ended with the Lions edging the match 18-15 and taking an unassailable 2-0 lead. Scott Gibbs' inspirational team talk on the pitch, Neil Jenkins' assured goal-kicking and Jeremy Guscott dropping THAT goal as if it was a club friendly... The memories are as vivid now as if it happened last week. That's why Lions tours are so special.

JUNE 29

Throughout the 1970s and 80s, one man dominated Argentine rugby and dragged it towards being the power it is now – Hugo Porta. His consummate kicking game and speed off the mark made many observers rate him, at his peak, above the likes of Naas Botha, Phil Bennett, Jean-Pierre Romeu and Tony Ward, as the best fly-half in the world. In 1974 he really started to make people take notice; Porta amassed 23 points at the age of 22 against a powerful French team in Buenos Aires in a losing cause. By the time he retired, 16 years later, Argentina victories had become regular occurrences.

New Zealand sneaked a Bledisloe Cup encounter 10-9 in Auckland in 1985. The match marked the end of Andy Dalton's reign as All Black hooker. Dalton proved to be a test case in rugby's long-running (perhaps boring is the word) battle with itself over whether to adhere to strict guidelines on amateurism, or admit defeat and make the game open. An apparently innocent advert for a farming vehicle created a row about whether Dalton had used his position as an All Black to procure money and/or status through the ad. It's laughable now, but was treated with deadly seriousness then.

JUNE 30

Invercargill, the southernmost city in New Zealand, is a traditional stop on a Lions tour. Rugby Park is an outpost, but when 22,000 are packed in roaring on Southland against the cream of Britain and Ireland it becomes the heart of the rugby universe. The 1971 Lions, buoyant after winning the first Test in Dunedin, saw off their hosts 25-3. Every Lions tour needs a strong supporting cast and Alastair Biggar scored two of his side's tries. Mind you, when many roads in town are named after Scottish rivers, the tartan wing probably felt at home.

After losing 74-3 and 101-0 on their first full Test tour to South Africa, Italy would have been forgiven for a sense of trepidation when they stepped out at Port Elizabeth for a third dash at the Springboks away from home in 2001. They reached half-time in the unbelievably hopeful position of trailing 9-17. Could an historic upset be on the cards? It took just six minutes to dispel such thoughts. The Boks rattled in three tries and stretched away to win 60-14. The Azzurri have yet to end a Test within 19 points of South Africa.

RUGBY
On This Day

JULY

JULY 1

It's a surprise that Australia took 62 years to play a home rugby union Test outside of Sydney or Brisbane. There again, there's the curious geography of sport Down Under. In 1961, the Wallabies took on Fiji in Melbourne – but it might as well have been Manila or Mexico City for the interest shown by the locals. This was, and forever will be, the home of Aussie Rules. Union was having enough of a battle on the East coast, where rugby league had gained a grip, to contemplate taking on the VFL. It took another 33 years before Melbournians were treated to another Test. Now they get an annual fix, as the old barriers gradually come down.

Any news is good news to a skilled PR man. New Zealand Rugby Union chief executive Steve Tew claimed in 2009 that a Frenchman being assaulted in the nation's capital had turned out to be a positive story for his country. Mathieu Bastareaud had said he had been savaged by a gang outside his Wellington hotel on the evening following a Test against the All Blacks – creating worldwide bad headlines for NZ tourism. But he subsequently admitted he made it all up to cover supposed self-inflicted injuries while drunk. So that's alright then...

JULY 2

A really bad day for the 2005 Lions in New Zealand, they were savaged 48-18 as the All Blacks sealed an unbeatable 2-0 series lead in Wellington with their highest score in 34 matches against the best Britain and Ireland can muster. Humiliation was the word during the rounds of the bars in the capital, with most travelling fans blaming Sir Clive Woodward for dragging the good name of the Lions through the Kiwi mud with his doubtful selections and misguided handling of the media.

Does "Super rugby" work in the Southern Hemisphere? Tough questions were asked when news broke in 2009 that the New Zealand Rugby Union was taking over the Highlanders due to financial problems engulfing the franchise. Crowds had plummeted thanks to the economic downturn and a conspicuous lack of success, but when rugby is struggling to attract punters in Dunedin something is going seriously wrong. Perhaps the problem is identity, the Otago province has a powerful image, built over decades. Who are the Highlanders? The race to build new super teams has left a lot of fans cold.

JULY 3

Rugby followers are renowned for being a relatively conservative bunch, where the nagging hyperbole seen in football is rarely seen. So when a score is described as "the try from the end of the earth" it must have been pretty good. In 1994, France followed up their first Test victory with a 23-30 triumph against New Zealand in Auckland. It was the first time Les Bleus had beaten the All Blacks in consecutive Tests and their first ever series win against them. The highlight of this historic match was full-back Jean-Luc Sadourny finishing off a breathtaking 90-metre move, leading to that most glorious of descriptions.

Fiji, Samoa and Tonga have brought an extra dimension to the sport with a combination of skill, power, pace and a "physical" approach. However, could they compete in the professional age on their own terms, or would it be better to create their own version of the Lions? The three countries combined for the first time in an official Test match as the "Pacific Islands" in 2004, when they took on Australia at the Adelaide Oval. A 29-14 defeat was followed by further losses in New Zealand and South Africa, a first tour which was more like a baptism of fire. Trips to Europe in 2006 and 2008 ensued with only the Italians being beaten. All three nations saw success in the 2007 World Cup, so the jury is still out.

JULY 4

Scotland frequently get the proverbial nosebleed when they go south of the equator, or maybe it's just that they're not good enough. Either way, the Scots have beaten a Tri-Nations team only once away from Caledonia, in 1982 when Andy Irvine led his side to a 12-7 victory over Australia in Brisbane. The great full-back's Test career ended in defeat in the second Test. He finished as the world record points scorer with, by modern standards, a meagre tally of 273.

Irvine enjoyed more Test wins in a Lions shirt than Scotland's way down south and, because of the infrequency of opportunity to don the red jersey, there is no such thing as a "dead" Lions Test. Tell the 2009 vintage that their fantastic 28-9 victory in Johannesburg didn't mean anything and you'll get a curt reply. Some of that team will never play for the Lions again, but they were part of the famous touring side's first win anywhere for eight years and they equalled the 1974 squad's record score and win against the Springboks.

JULY 5

Can you imagine the 1971 Lions leaving behind Gareth Edwards and JPR Williams, or the 1997 squad making do without Martin Johnson and Scott Gibbs? In 1930 the selection of the British and Irish side was farcical as they journeyed to New Zealand without Wavell Wakefield and Ian Smith – two of the great players of the era – and lost 3-1. An example of the lack of that bit of class that could have made the difference was the second Test in Christchurch, despite Carl Aarvold's classy 40-metre try. The loss of scrumhalf Paul Murray to a dislocated shoulder was pivotal, and the tourists lost by an agonising margin of 13-10.

Newlands in Cape Town is one of the most evocative venues in world rugby and has a special place in Lions history. It's here where the 1974 and 1997 tourists discovered they had the resolve to be successful with first Test triumphs. The 1980 team failed in their Test series mission but took out their frustration with a stunning 37-6 trouncing of Western Province. It was their worst defeat for 84 years. Exquisite goal-kicking by Ollie Campbell and tries from Scots Andy Irvine and Bruce Hay, plus one from Clive Woodward, did for their hosts.

JULY 6

New Zealand and Australia launched a brave new world in Wellington in 1996 with the first Tri-Nations match. The Trans-Tasman rivals and South Africa had joined forces to create the tournament, a key component in a £360m 10-year deal with News Corporation. The All Blacks, sporting an exceptional team nothing less than legends, ran riot to record their biggest ever win over the Aussies, 43-6. A few weeks later they were crowned the inaugural (Grand Slam) Tri-Nations champions.

If citing commissioners had been around on the 1974 and 1980 Lions tours they would have had to regularly send messages to their families that they would be back late from the office. The referee was the sole arbiter in all respects in those days, and much was missed. Now we have video analysis. In 2009, the International Rugby Board felt the entire Springbok team were culpable and charged them with "misconduct" for a protest against the suspension of Bakkies Botha during the third Lions Test. White armbands with "Justice 4 Bakkies" scrawled on them were worn by all the players. Botha had been banned for a "dangerous charge" in the second match in Pretoria.

JULY 7

Japan licked their wounds for seven years after the biggest Test defeat of the amateur era, the 145-17 pummelling in the 1995 World Cup by New Zealand. On this day in 2002 they wiped their embarrassment from the record books with a 155-3 annihilation of Chinese Taipei in Tokyo – the biggest score and win by a major international team. Daisuke Ohata moved closer to David Campese's career mark with eight of the Cherry Blossoms' 23 tries, as virtually every attack ended in a score. How many would the All Blacks notch against Taipei? It's the stuff of nightmares...

They say they never come back...Tell that to Jonny Wilkinson who has been doing a passable impersonation of a "bad penny" for several years. In 2009, Wilkinson was named in the England squad, despite having not played a match for almost 10 months due to yet another injury, this time a dislocated knee. His appearance in Martin Johnson's line-up for the 2009/10 season was at the expense of the next most famous active England player – Danny Cipriani. The poster boy had fallen down the pecking order and on form, if not reputation, you could see why. There again, Wilkinson managed to dodge the bullet...

JULY 8

One day after his 24th birthday, with just one England cap to his name, Jeremy Guscott made his Lions debut in the second Test of the 1989 series in Australia. It was one of three key changes made by Ian McGeechan, with Rob Andrew at fly-half and Scott Hastings alongside Guscott. The tourists had lost the first match and were just 13-12 up in the dying minutes at Ballymore. Enter Guscott, with a deft kick ahead and pick-up, to hand Gavin Hastings a conversion. A week later, the Lions sealed their first series triumph anywhere for 15 years.

New Zealand have a fine record in the Tri-Nations, but if Jerry Collins was trying to make an ironic point about the ease with which they accumulate victories in the tournament he chose the wrong moment...Or maybe he was just caught short. The dressing room lavatories were not good enough for the All Black flanker just before the start of the 2006 series opener against Australia in Christchurch. In full view of the TV cameras, Collins urinated at the side of the pitch. Talk about releasing the tension...

JULY 9

Today in 1977 one of the great characters of the game made his last Test appearance – Sid Going. The Maori ace was an unmistakable figure at scrum-half, a fantastic All Black with, shall we say, a mature appearance. His duels with Gareth Edwards against Wales, the Lions and the Barbarians were legendary – the half-back version of Ali v Frazier. However, it was a Lions side without Edwards that effectively ended Going's Test career, winning the second Test 13-9 to level the series. Going was made a scapegoat and didn't return to the side.

It used to be so simple. A bloke wasn't picked to play if he wasn't playing well. Nowadays we sometimes have to navigate the stormy seas of employment law. As a legal challenge to the sacking of Wallaby wing Lote Tuqiri by the Australian Rugby Union was launched in 2009, his former Australia skipper Stirling Mortlock produced a flat bat to grace Lord's or the MCG when he declared that the players wanted "clarity" on why Tuqiri had been dismissed. Coach Robbie Deans backed the Union's stance but when the captain seemingly hadn't got a clue why one of his lieutenants had gone you have to ask questions about how the affair was handled.

JULY 10

Rugby has been populated by some hard men over the decades. Personalities who have looked fear in the eye and not blinked. These risk-takers just can't help themselves – they need that "edge" to perform mighty deeds. France prop Armand Vaquerin, capped 26 times during the 1970s, lived life to the full, even if the risks were too great. In 1993, he was drinking in a bar in his home town of Beziers when a game of Russian Roulette developed. Vaquerin lost the game, and his life. He was only 42.

One of the many whinges heard from footballers about referees is that they "don't understand the game" and "have never played at a decent level". Not true in rugby, where arguably the foremost whistle-blower in the world, Alain Rolland, played scrum-half for Ireland. Following in Rolland's footsteps is Saracens fly-half Glen Jackson, who was accepted into the inner sanctum of New Zealand referees in 2009, having completed his exams in England. The 2010 Heartland Championship (NZ's second tier competition) will see Sarries' record Premiership points scorer in charge.

JULY 11

Jean-Pierre Rives led from the front, putting his body on the line in the French cause during an eventful 59-cap career, but he took this to an extraordinary degree against Australia in 1981. Rives had dislocated his shoulder in the first Test of the two-match series but refused to desert his team for the decider at the Sydney Cricket Ground, playing heroically in obvious discomfort. However, against a Wallaby team inspired by half backs John Hipwell and Mark Ella, everyone needed to be 100% and a 24-14 score-line in the era of the four-point try was a conclusive margin.

Hipwell and Ella played at the SCG many times but never at the Melbourne Cricket Ground. That's a shame, because the thrill of playing for the Wallabies in front of 75,000 people at one of the greatest stadia in the world, and against the old enemy from across the Tasman – well, it's about as good as it gets for an Australian rugby union player. Throw in scoring all your side's points (more than anyone has achieved against the All Blacks), to win the game and we're talking dream land. It all happened at once for Matt Burke in 1998, when his haul of 24 inflicted New Zealand's first ever Tri-Nations defeat.

JULY 12

Lions tours don't come round very often. It's currently every four years, but in between the two World Wars the interval tended to be more like six. So imagine the desolation when you get injured in the very first match and your tour is over just as it's begun. It happened to Tom Holliday from Aspatria in Cumbria on the 1924 trip to South Africa. He was injured while playing at full-back against Western Province Town & Country, and that was that.

While Holliday would have given most things for at least one more game, his counterparts 73 years later would probably have gladly gone to the beach rather than drag themselves from Johannesburg to Sydney for the inaugural Cook Cup Test. As a piece of poor fixture scheduling it was genius...The 1997 Lions had just won a physically demanding series but heroes John Bentley, Matt Dawson, Lawrence Dallaglio, Richard Hill and Tim Rodber then had to join up with their Red Rose brethren to play the Wallabies seven days later. A relatively fresh Australia ran out easy 25-6 winners.

JULY 13

There's nothing like a party, particularly on a tour which seems to last for an eternity. The Lions of the amateur era wanted to enjoy life together almost as much as win rugby matches, although when they crossed the white line they were deadly serious. After losing the 1968 series with a narrow defeat in Cape Town, the tourists consoled themselves by letting their hair down at a hotel operated by 1938 Lion Jeff Reynolds. They ran up quite a bill, the "damage" allegedly running to nearly £1000, but tour manager David Brooks signed it off with a flourish: "Huh! It couldn't have been a very good party!"

The return journey in 1974 gave every British and Irish rugby fan an excuse for celebration. A 26-9 third Test victory clinched a first series win in South Africa for 78 years. JJ Williams scored two tries but the match is also remembered for a couple of massive brawls, as Willie John McBride's "take no prisoners" mantra was visited upon a Springbok side not averse to underhand tactics. The home side were soundly beaten 66-21 and 8-0 on tries scored over three Tests and as Danie Craven handed six new caps their blazers after the match, he said: "It hurts me to be giving you these... you have not earned them."

JULY 14

It's not just in the Ashes that the Australians get wound up by their colonial cousins. In 1989, a fractious Lions series came to a head in the build-up to the decider when Wallaby captain Nick Farr-Jones predicted "open warfare" after he claimed the tourists were too violent in the second Test. And it wasn't just the skipper, the Australian Rugby Union issued an incendiary press release, saying it would create a video "depicting certain incidents... believed to be prejudicial to the best interests of the game." The Aussies lost 19-18 to lose the series.

Fast forward 12 years and it was time for Aussie revenge on the "Poms". More ill-feeling in the prelude to another Sydney decider included Austin Healey dubbing opposition lock Justin Harrison "the Plank". The words came back to haunt, as Harrison claimed a crucial line-out against the throw late on as the Lions were pressing for victory. The Wallabies won 29-23 to claim a first-ever series win over the Lions and be the first side to defeat the famous tourists while also holding the World Cup.

JULY 15

A world record crowd of 109,874 at Sydney's brand new Stadium Australia saw the most stunning start to an international in history in 2000. The All Blacks scored three tries and were 24-0 up against the Wallabies after just five minutes. The then-world champions staged an exceptional comeback and, incredibly, the scores were level at half-time. Jeremy Paul's late try appeared to have handed the Aussies a record 11th straight Test win but then Jonah Lomu's rampaging run provided an epic conclusion. A fabulous match ended 39-35 to the visitors – a contender for the greatest Test in history.

Fighting is by no means unusual in a game of rugby, but one South African referee decided that things had gone too far in 2006 and called a match off. Stephen du Toit sent off a Collegians player early in the second half of an under-20 match against Harlequins in the Cape, sparking a free-for-all that ended with eight Quins players injured and a Collegian with a broken nose. Parents ran on to the field to break it up, but du Toit had had enough.

JULY 16

A sense of perspective should never be confused with apathy. Former England scrum-half Bernard Gadney, born on this day in 1916, was accused of not "wanting it" enough when he was misquoted ahead of the 1936 match against the All Blacks. Gadney led the side to a famous victory, having been reported as not caring whether they won or lost. Before his death in 2000, the Leicester Tiger rejected the notion: "The idea that we did not care if we lost is a load of rubbish," retorted Gadney. "We had to be civil in defeat. One should be able to have a beer with the opposition and congratulate them on their success."

Ah yes, meet those two "imposters" (victory and defeat) with equanimity... It's tough, though, when you've been crushed by the All Blacks. This is a bad day in the history of the Lions. In 1966, they lost the first Test 20-3 in Dunedin as New Zealand's plan to create second-phase possession through a "crash-ball" centre paid off spectacularly. It was the Lions' worst defeat by the All Blacks for 58 years. In 1983, they topped that with a 38-6 trouncing at Eden Park, Stu Wilson scoring a hat-trick of tries to become New Zealand's record try scorer. The 4-0 series whitewash set in train years of navel gazing about the future of the Lions.

JULY 17

We take numbers on shirts for granted. However, the initial generations of rugby players were brought up with no numbering. The first time the device was used was in 1897, when Queensland played the All Blacks, and it quickly spread to the full international game. However, as is their wont, Scotland dragged their heels...During the 1928 Calcutta Cup match, King George V allegedly asked former Scottish Rugby Union president James Aikman Smith why his team were not wearing numbers and was told "This, sir, is a rugby match, not a cattle sale". It was 1933 before the Thistle joined the fun.

Hawke's Bay didn't need identification aids in their mission to intimidate the 1971 Lions, but found that pure talent will always overcome brutality. The Test series was tied at 1-1, so Bay were keen to inflict scars (psychological and physical) on the tourists. However, Gerald Davies stunned the Napier crowd with four tries in a 25-6 victory. To lose was bad enough, to be humiliated another thing...Barry John showboated in retaliation, taunting would-be tacklers before clearing his lines.

JULY 18

They called Don Clarke "The Boot" for good reason. The toe-punter was rugby's first points machine in the 1950s and 60s, and almost single-handedly condemned the 1959 Lions to defeat. He was so good that following six goals in the 18-17 first Test victory there was much debate about whether the points system should be overhauled, as Clarke's kicks had cancelled out four Lions tries. At the time a penalty and a try were each worth three points, it would be 12 years before an extra point was awarded for a touchdown. Under current values, the Lions would have won 25-18 and would have been 16 points clear with 13 minutes left.

If the 1959 Lions were peeved, then followers of Treviso were furious in 2009 when their club was effectively banished from European competition amid political acrimony. Italy had decided they had to copy Ireland, Scotland and Wales and go for a more centralised approach. Only two Italian teams would compete in the Heineken Cup each season from 2010/11 – Roma and Viadana. Cue disgust from the direction of Venice, where the perennial champions believed they had a cast iron case. A row over autonomy for the club between the Federation president and his Treviso counterpart may have had something to do with it...

JULY 19

Two years after suffering World Cup final heartbreak at Ellis Park, the All Blacks got some consolation by sending South Africa to a thrilling Tri-Nations defeat in 1997 at the famous Johannesburg venue. Frank Bunce scored two tries as his side came back from a half-time deficit to record a 35-32 win, the first leg of a repeat Grand Slam.

Six years to the day further down the track and the All Blacks inflicted much greater misery on the Springboks with a record 52-16 hammering in Pretoria. Carlos Spencer was in his pomp on a sunny day on the high veldt, pulling the strings in a seven-try romp. The Boks were in a bad way, plunging into despair just a few months before the World Cup. Coach Rudi Straeuli's answer to the malaise was the shock tactic of Kamp Staaldraad, but the spectacle at Loftus Versfeld was probably even more humiliating than any naked route march through freezing cold water... Maybe...

JULY 20

The 1974 Lions, the famous "99" tour...Tourists who refused to take a backward step. During the Natal game, JPR Williams lost his composure after being tackled into touch by home skipper Tommy Bedford. Mistakenly believing he had deliberately kicked him, JPR set upon the flanker. Police restrained the Welshman and later on, when Bedford was flattened at a ruck, the crowd pelted whatever they could lay their hands on at the Lions. The match was stopped for 10 minutes while things calmed down. The Lions went on to win 34-6.

The first act in a legal saga saw Harlequins wing Tom Williams suspended for 12 months and his club fined £215,000 after being found guilty of cheating with fake blood during a 2009 Heineken Cup quarter-final against Leinster. Williams was replaced five minutes from time, with a supposed cut mouth. Nick Evans, who had been subbed himself earlier, came back on and had the chance to win the match with a drop goal, but failed. TV coverage showed Williams applied make-up so he could leave the field. Quins management were initially cleared, but Williams appealed and his ban was reduced to four months, Quins' fine was increased by £50,000 and Dean Richards, who had resigned as coach, was banned from all European rugby for three years as a murky cover-up unravelled.

JULY 21

A tale of two Aussies, former team-mates who are remembered on this day for very different reasons...Wendell Sailor made his name in rugby league; a powerhouse, free-scoring wing for the Brisbane Broncos and Australia. In his late 20s he wanted a new challenge and elected to make a sensational switch to rugby union. He won 37 Wallaby caps, including the 2003 World Cup final, but his career ended when he was banned for two years in 2006 after failing a drugs test. A metabolite of cocaine had been found in his system after a Super 14 match.

While Sailor went overboard, George Gregan kept his hand very firmly on the tiller for 13 years. The Zambian-born scrum-half appeared in his 48th and final Tri-Nations match in 2007, a 26-12 defeat by the All Blacks in Auckland. He had been a key figure in back-to-back Southern Hemisphere title-winning seasons in 2000 and 2001, before assuming the captaincy. He retired at the end of the 2007 World Cup as a Wallaby icon.

JULY 22

The early Lions tours (well, they weren't known as the Lions in those days, but we won't split hairs) were curious affairs. Some bizarre selections placed noted players alongside those of a calibre who would never get a place in the squad these days. Matthew Mullineux was picked to lead the 1899 tourists to Australia despite never having played or been considered for England. He wasn't even thought good enough to play for Cambridge in the Varsity Match. Mullineux played in the first Test defeat but wisely stood down for the second, allowing England's Frank Stout to skipper the Lions to an 11-0 win in Brisbane. The Lions won the series 3-1. Mullineux had correctly assessed that he should "get his coat".

A Monday night Test match was a radical step in 1991 but it didn't really matter what day of the week Australia played a Wales team who had just been thrashed by 71-8 by New South Wales – it was only going to end one way. So it did, 63-6, with the match notable for David Campese regaining the outright title of most prolific Test try scorer with his 38th. The Wallaby wing had only lost sole ownership of the accolade two days before, when Serge Blanco drew alongside.

JULY 23

Springbok prop Johan Le Roux was hungry to prove his worth in Test rugby in 1994. However, his burgeoning career came to a sensational full stop when he was caught making a meal out of Sean Fitzpatrick's ear during a Test match in Wellington. The match officials had missed it, but TV replays picked up a shadowy figure appearing to bite off more than it could chew and closer analysis pointed the finger at Le Roux. The 33-year-old was sent home in disgrace, banned for 18 months and didn't play for South Africa again.

Le Roux obviously wanted his own type of trophy, but legitimate international rugby prizes have been multiplying at a dizzying rate since the sport went professional. All of a sudden administrators and sponsors wanted something tangible for victorious captains to lift rather than just the age-old pride of victory. Australia and South Africa have been grappling for the Nelson Mandela Plate since 2000. In 2005, South Africa retained the bauble with the name of their greatest citizen on it with a 33-20 victory in Johannesburg.

JULY 24

The Springboks beat the All Blacks 16-7 in Durban in the first Test of a four-match series they won 3-1 that caused a blight to descend over events 8,000 miles away. The controversial tour had led to a mass African boycott of the Montreal Olympics, due to the Kiwis being present at the same time as their rugby team were playing in a country ravaged by apartheid. The irony was that New Zealand's star athlete, John Walker, saw his main competitor in the 1500 metres withdrawn from the Games – Tanzania's world record holder Filbert Bayi. Walker claimed Gold, one of only two won by the Kiwis in Canada.

Durban-born Andrew Mehrtens went on to become one of New Zealand's rugby heroes. One of the highlights of his 70-Test career was a 34-15 win over Australia in Auckland in 1999. The fly-half kicked a world record nine penalties, plus a conversion, in an unprecedented individual Tri-Nations haul of 29 points. His efforts were yet another blow to the solar plexus for the Wallabies at Eden Park – 13 years since their success at New Zealand's premier ground.

JULY 25

New Zealand's unremitting (1971 excepted) hold on British and Irish teams began in 1908, when the All Blacks sealed a series victory over the Anglo-Welsh tourists. There's a debate over whether this should be considered a "Lions series" but, whatever its status, three Tests were played making it New Zealand's first series against Europeans. After a home win and a draw the decider was played at Potter's Park – Auckland's first Test. Far from the rigorous preparations seen these days, AF Harding's visitors had been partying all week and were thrashed 29-0. The definition of a second Test hangover!

The All Blacks also enjoy a party, as Doug Howlett has proved in recent years (see Oct 29), but winning rugby matches will always be a serious business when you carry the weight of a nation's hopes. The team of the late 1960s had the broadest of shoulders, winning a world record 17 consecutive Tests from 1965-70. The sequence ended with defeat in Pretoria – the Springboks being the only team able to live with them during that period. The All Blacks conceded just 16 tries during those 17 wins, scoring 54.

JULY 26

Since 1995 the international calendar has not only been bloated but the venues get bigger and bigger. Stadium Australia, a redeveloped Twickenham, Croke Park – all have improved capacities and, ah yes, that must mean more money for the Unions. The Australians were one of the first to spot that the sudden need to pay the players meant extra cash was required. Thus, in 1997, the famous Melbourne Cricket Ground was requisitioned for a Bledisloe Cup match. The Wallabies lost 33-18 but the 90,000 crowd meant lots of lovely lolly. The MCG has since been used twice more.

Another coup for the ARU was the appointment of Robbie Deans as Wallaby coach. Deans had been the driving force behind the hugely successful Crusaders side and it was thought inevitable that he would become the new All Blacks supremo after their 2007 World Cup demise. Surprisingly, Graham Henry was kept in post and the Aussies spotted an opportunity to lure Deans across the Tasman. He faced up to his home country for the first time in Sydney in 2008 and a 34-19 victory produced much angst in the "Shaky Isles" – how could we let him go...and to them? Henry wreaked revenge three times later in the year but what if Deans were to craft a World Cup victory in 2011?

JULY 27

Jonah Lomu underwent a kidney transplant on this day in 2004 in Auckland. Nine years before he had terrorised defences (particularly England's) at the World Cup, and had won the last of 63 All Black caps on the European tour at the end of 2002. Lomu had been suffering with recurrent trouble from the organ for most of his rugby career, after being diagnosed with a rare disorder called nephritic syndrome in 1996. Quite remarkably, in June 2005, Lomu appeared in Martin Johnson's testimonial at Twickenham. In all respects, he is an extraordinary character.

The Southern Hemisphere carp about European clubs stealing talent but it's not all a one-way street. In 2009, Argentine superstar Juan Martin Hernandez agreed to leave Paris and Stade Francais to join the Sharks in Durban for 2010, having been trailed for years by Premiership clubs. If Argentina get their wish and are allowed to play in an annual tournament with Australia, New Zealand and South Africa, it could be the first of a procession of Pumas back south. That is unless the money is not good enough, of course.

JULY 28

The 1982 Falklands Conflict ended sporting relations between Argentina and Britain for the foreseeable future. Only the luck of the draw (1986 FIFA World Cup and the "Hand of God") pulled them together. In 1990, England finally returned to Buenos Aires, albeit with a weakened team, as the first British rugby team to play Argentina since the war in the South Atlantic. The match, won 25-12 by England, was also notable as the first of what was to be a world record haul of 114 caps for Jason Leonard.

England were awarded the 2015 World Cup after a tense vote in Dublin in 2009. The IRB Council sided 16-10 with the RFU's bid, with its seven club football grounds alongside Twickenham, Wembley and the two largest club rugby union-only stadia in the country – Welford Road and Kingsholm. The prospect of Old Trafford and Anfield staging matches is exciting and, once again, Wales wriggled their way into someone else's show, with the Millennium Stadium lined up to stage two quarter-finals. Superb venue, but if one country is awarded a tournament shouldn't it just use facilities in that nation? Ah, but Wales had a couple of crucial votes...Political expediency makes work for many hands.

JULY 29

We didn't know at the time (but, perhaps, had a fair idea) that the second Bledisloe Cup match in 1995 would be the last Test of the amateur era. Only the trophy and national pride was on the line – no contracts or win bonuses. Rumours of trust funds and under the table payments had been circulating for years, but this was it – officially the last time the stars would perform for "free". The old days went out with a bang, seven tries in a hard-fought 34-23 victory for the All Blacks to regain the Cup.

One of the goals of the new era was to drag the existing "second tier" nations to a more competitive level. The International Rugby Board are investing millions of dollars into trying to improve the standard in Canada and the USA, a key plank of which is the "North America 4". Billed as a chance to play in a "high intensity" competition, Canada West beat US Falcons in the inaugural final at Fred Beekman Park, Columbus in 2006. It's a noble concept, but the reality is that without high profile imported players the locals will not improve enough and no-one is going to watch. High intensity? Not quite.

JULY 30

The 1970s was the greatest decade in Lions history; the rampant back play of 1971 and the all-conquering 1974 squad. Follow that...the 1977 Lions couldn't. The tour, coached by 1971 captain John Dawes, didn't go half as well. By the time they arrived in Dunedin for the third Test of four, the Lions had lost one and drawn one. The pitch was so wet a helicopter was used in an attempt to dry it out, but the surface turned goal-kicking into a lottery. Even so, six misses out of seven was a poor effort, the Lions lost the match 19-7 and the series.

Rugby has glorious venues, but the odd rank one as well. In the mid-1980s, the SCG – home for so long of both the Wallabies and New South Wales – was becoming unfeasible as a regular venue. For the 1987 World Cup, the rickety Concord Oval was transformed into a modern, if small (20,000), stadium. It didn't feel like a major ground and lasted just one more season before the move to the more spectacular Sydney Football Stadium, next to the SCG. The last of eight Wallaby Tests held at Concord was a 30-9 Bledisloe Cup defeat on this day in 1988. It hasn't been lamented.

JULY 31

World War I was a brutal graveyard for so many talented sportsmen, sent to the front and never to return. Northampton's Edgar Mobbs, who played seven times for England, was killed while attacking a machine gun post at Ypres in 1917. Apparently he kicked a rugby ball ahead of him before he was shot – once a rugby man, always a rugby man. A match was created in his memory – East Midlands v the Barbarians – played each peacetime year from 1921 to 2007 at Franklin's Gardens, before the pressures of professional rugby made Bedford take up the mantle from 2008.

The third Test in 1971 was the most important Lions match for 16 years. Not since 1955 had a British & Irish squad stood on the threshold of avoiding a series defeat and the Lions had lost all their previous rubbers against the All Blacks. The Lions began strongly; Barry John's drop goal and two converted tries made the score 13-0 at half-time. The crowd got on the Kiwis' backs, but they fought like tigers with a Laurie Mains try giving them hope. The Lions were pinned on the defensive, assisted on one occasion by a stray dog obstructing centre Bruce Hunter, but held out for their biggest win over the All Blacks and, more importantly, could not be beaten in the series. The final Test was drawn – mission accomplished.

RUGBY
On This Day

AUGUST

AUGUST 1

New Zealand laid waste to their southern hemisphere rivals in the first two editions of the Tri-Nations, but they approached their penultimate match in 1998 against Australia having lost both their games – a remarkable turnaround. It had been 49 years since the All Blacks had lost three Tests in a row...surely it couldn't happen. Well, it did, the Wallabies winning by the misleadingly close score-line of 27-23, having dominated in Christchurch. It was a performance worthy of future world champions.

Yes, the Wallabies raised the Webb Ellis Trophy in 1999 and, having accomplished more in rugby than most, John Eales decided it was time to hang up his boots in 2001. They called him "Nobody" ("Nobody's perfect") but this guy was very special. Having achieved the final missing link on his cv – a series victory over the Lions – he announced that he would take the international stage for the last time at the end of the 2001 Tri-Nations. He led Australia to 41 wins in 55 matches as captain.

AUGUST 2

Throughout history Australians have been on their guard against Japan, yet the Wallabies were one of the first to recognise that the Cherry Blossoms from the "Land of the Rising Sun" deserved a full rugby Test match. It was 1975, 25 years before any of the British and Irish nations deemed it appropriate to hand out full caps outside of World Cups against the Japanese. A 37-7 victory was their reward.

Drifting on to the round ball for a moment, Tony Woodcock was a striker for Nottingham Forest in Brian Clough's remarkable team of the late 1970s. His rugby namesake is an All Black prop who also gets the curious surname on score-sheets from time-to-time. Woodcock scored two tries in a 39-10 victory over Australia in Auckland in 2008, a match that proved to be the catalyst for his side's march to another Tri-Nations title. The mobile prop has touched down three times in Tests at Eden Park – only nine men in history have scored more there.

AUGUST 3

An event occurred in 1880 that generations of rival fans and players may have wished never happened...All in the spirit of "friendly" rivalry, of course. Leicester Football Club was formed at the George Hotel in the city, when representatives of three clubs agreed to amalgamate to become the Tigers. Those pioneers would have smiled with satisfaction 121 years later, when Leicester became European champions. Well done to Leicester Societies, Leicester Amateur and the appropriately-named Leicester Alert for their foresight, as I'm sure those of you in Bath, Northampton, Munster and Toulouse would heartily agree!

Christian Cullen lit up the rugby firmament for six years. At his peak there can have been no more exciting full-back. He didn't have Serge Blanco's charisma, Bob Scott's positional sense or JPR's defence but Cullen was a thrilling sight, with the ability to side-step at near full pace. He scored 46 tries in just 58 Tests before debilitating knee injuries struck and ended his international career. His last Tri-Nations cap for the All Blacks was on this day in 2002, he finished with a record 16 tries in 24 TN games.

AUGUST 4

In 1914, nine days after the outbreak of World War I, the Rugby Football Union issued a fateful circular advising all players to join the armed forces. Dark times indeed...During the course of the following four years, over 100 international players would die during the conflict. A terrible toll that included 1905 New Zealand "Invincibles" skipper Dave Gallaher, England try machine Ronnie Poulton-Palmer and 1904 Lions captain David Bedell-Sivright.

In 1962, South Africa continued their remarkable record against the Lions, an 8-3 victory in the third Test confirming a sixth straight Springbok series triumph over the best from Britain and Ireland. The tourists had not won a series in the republic in the 20th century, but an Ulsterman making his Test debut in the red shirt that day was to change all that...Willie John McBride won the first of a record 17 caps and, 12 years later, he would go on to lead the Lions to rugby nirvana.

AUGUST 5

The 1966 Lions were seriously out-manoeuvred in New Zealand. They failed to cope with the abrasive style of Kiwi rugby and slumped to 4-0 series defeat, and four other losses to provincial opposition. Allegations of "dirty play" reached such a pitch that the Governor General, Bernard Fergusson (later Baron Ballantrae, no less), was called in to speak to the rival captains, Brian Lochore and Mike Campbell-Lamerton, on the eve of the second Test in Wellington to "remind them of their responsibilities". Campbell-Lamerton could not lead by example, though, as he was dropped after the first Test debacle.

They played in the same position, were both international captains, but the careers of Campbell-Lamerton and John Eales at the highest level could hardly have been different. While 1966 summed up the Scot's mediocre record, double World Cup winner Eales was simply awesome. None more so than against New Zealand in Wellington in 2000...At 21-23 down with just a few minutes remaining, Aussie dreams of a first Tri-Nations crown appeared to be sunk. But hang on, a penalty, up steps the skipper, chief line-out jumper and goal-kicker. He swings his elongated right leg, the ball soars and just manages to bisect the posts. The Wallabies win, beat South Africa three weeks later and claim the title.

AUGUST 6

There's a fine line between being a hero and a zero in rugby...And that line often involves injury. David Bedell-Sivright, as much of a handful on the pitch as his name is a mouthful, led the 1904 Lions to an unbeaten tour of Australia before embarking on a first full Test trip to New Zealand... Unfortunately, though, the Scottish forward was to see little action in the "Shaky Isles", breaking his leg in the first match against Canterbury. Sad, but there's simply no comparison to the horrors and fateful end he would meet in World War I.

A happier event in 1955, the date of one of the greatest matches ever played. South Africa and the Lions went hammer and tongs in their first Test in Johannesburg before a then-world record 95,000 crowd. The Lions scored five tries, with Jeff Butterfield and Cliff Morgan inspirational, but were hanging on at the end. Theunis Briers brought the assembled masses to a state of delirium with a late try, leaving Jack van der Schyff with a conversion to win the match. He missed, the Lions won 23-22 and the series would be drawn 2-2.

AUGUST 7

Rugby at the Olympics may well be the future, but in the mid 20th century it was very much a thing of the past. A player who managed to grab Olympic glory despite this was Wales wing Ken Jones, who won Silver in the sprint relay at the 1948 Games. The Brits finished behind the USA but were awarded Gold when the Americans were deemed to have messed up a baton change. However, three days later the appeal was successful and Jones had to exchange Gold for Silver, but he still rated the achievement higher than his Welsh and Lions caps.

While South Africa and Australia now compete as equals on the rugby pitch, back in 1971 it was very different. The Springboks had beaten the Wallabies 4-0 two years before and now went into the third and final Test of the reverse tour in Sydney 2-0 up. Rugby union was king on the high veldt while Down Under it struggled for a profile. The tourists duly won 18-6 and it was the last time Frik Du Preez was seen on the international stage – a lock who Carwyn James lauded as having "every one of the skills necessary to be the completely equipped forward."

AUGUST 8

What an adventure touring in the early part of the 20th century must have been. Months on a ship sailing to the other side of the world, where you would encounter a different way of life and climate, making new friends through the shared idyll of playing rugby. The first Australians to make the trek to Britain set off on this day in 1908. They were to lose heavily to Wales but could at least go home and boast that they had beaten the "Poms" 9-3.

There are far more ancient rivalries, but none match the intensity of New Zealand v South Africa. Both think of themselves as the traditional top dogs and their matches are summit meetings at world rugby's highest table. More often than not in the amateur era the home team won (the pre-professional All Blacks failed to win a series in Springbok land) but a rare example of an early NZ success came in Cape Town in 1970 when Brian Lochore led his charges to a 9-3 victory. The famous "Grizz" Wyllie made his debut on that day.

AUGUST 9

On a Lions tour of New Zealand just three or four matches are officially listed as "Tests". However, virtually all the encounters could be described as thus. From Northland to Southland, and Taranaki to Canterbury the provincial teams are highly motivated and skilled units desperate for prized scalps. The lyrically named Bay of Plenty may sound enticing but provided the 1977 Lions with tough opposition in their final skirmish with an NPC side, following 17 victories, in the gaseous environs of Rotorua. Tour skipper Phil Bennett kicked five penalties in a 23-16 win.

To achieve 90 points on the scoreboard in an 80-minute rugby match is quite something, but when that tally is shared 55-35 between two top teams it represents a superb spectacle. In 1997, the All Blacks and Springboks put on an exhibition at Eden Park involving 12 tries. Purists tutted but the rest of us marvelled. If this was professional rugby union give us more. New Zealand went on to achieve the southern Grand Slam and South Africa finished second, having scored 67 points over their two defeats against the champions. Hard luck, lads.

AUGUST 10

Legendary All Blacks captain Sean Fitzpatrick enjoyed a challenge. Just as well because, in 1996, having led his side to victory in the first Tri-Nations, he was faced with lifting a ridiculously big trophy. Something appeared to have gone wrong in the creation of rugby's newest bauble (rumour has it that the makers got their metric and imperials mixed up) and Fitzpatrick was left with a serious weight-lifting issue, having stretched every sinew to ensure a 29-18 win over the world champions.

Amid the raft of rugby league superstars trying their hand at union in the early days of professionalism was Iestyn Harris. Lauded as the man to lead Wales back to the pinnacle of European rugby, Harris signed for Cardiff in 2001 with much hoopla. Fast-tracked into the Wales team after just 200 minutes of union action, it was all too good to be true. He played in the 2003 World Cup but was back in league country a year later. His experience showed how difficult it is to adapt from one code to the other. Expected to be a Welsh Jason Robinson, he went the way of Henry Paul and Andy Farrell.

AUGUST 11

They call the Carisbrook ground in Dunedin the "House of Pain". Fanatical Otago fans and pumped-up New Zealand sides have traditionally made the place a "hell-hole" for visiting rugby teams. During the course of the entire 20th century, the All Blacks played 29 Tests there, losing just twice (on both occasions to the Lions). Australia were the victims on 10 occasions, so when the Wallabies ventured to the deep south in 2001 the sheer weight of history made them underdogs, even as world champions. Jonah Lomu celebrated his 50th cap with a try but 18 points from Matt Burke were crucial in an historic 23-15 away win.

While the City of Manchester Stadium is now the home of football superstars from around the world, in 2002 the brand new arena was the prime venue for the Commonwealth Games. It's second rugby sevens tournament took place at Eastlands, with New Zealand bidding to retain their title. It came down to a repeat of the 1998 final, the All Blacks v Fiji. The Fijians were 15-14 ahead but then the champions stepped up a gear with an incredible three tries in as many minutes to claim gold.

AUGUST 12

The last major act of rugby's first century was staged in Sydney on this day in 1899. In 86 years, the game had moved from an English schoolboy's high jinks to a British team taking on Australia 10,500 miles away. This was the fourth and final Test, with the British Isles (they weren't officially called Lions then) 2-1 up. Durham's Charlie Adamson scored 10 points as the "Poms" sealed a 13-0 win but the event was a far cry from Lions Tests of more recent vintage. Despite the Aussies having a chance to draw the series, just 7,000 spectators turned up at the SCG.

Between the two World Wars English cricket had Jack Hobbs, football fans marvelled at Dixie Dean and rugby aficionados would literally doff their caps to Wavell Wakefield, who died at the age of 85 in 1983. He led his country to three Grand Slams but his lasting legacy was the idea that forwards should do far more than just set-pieces. While the early part of the 20th century saw rugby played at a pedestrian pace, it was Wakefield's innovative ideas that spawned the more open style of play we see today.

AUGUST 13

For top players, touring is a very different pastime to the experience encountered by their predecessors. The pioneers from the Victorian era would barely recognise today's trips as tours at all. Professional athletes told what to eat, where to go, how to train and with limited opportunity to explore where they are. It was all very different in 1888 when playing rugby formed just part of the adventure for the first British tourists to Australia. Sadly, though, one of their excursions ended in tragedy when skipper Bob Seddon was drowned while sculling on the Hunter River.

In 1977, touring was still seen as a way to broaden the mind, but the more serious approach to the game, and the legacy of two wildly successful trips earlier that decade, put enormous pressure on Phil Bennett's Lions in New Zealand. It wasn't just the All Blacks who were out to get them, the media seemed hell-bent on disrupting their focus with lurid headlines about alleged misdemeanours of various kinds off the field. Even the weather was appalling. A 9-10 loss in Auckland sealed a 3-1 series defeat, Scotland scrum-half Dougie Morgan scoring all his side's points.

AUGUST 14

This day in 1971 was a landmark in British and Irish rugby history. New Zealand had never been beaten in a Test series by any side from those Isles, and only twice at home by anyone else. Wales had been humiliated two years before and now many of their stars went back for more in Lions colours. However, wins in Dunedin and Wellington, sandwiched by defeat in Christchurch, meant that John Dawes led his team on to Eden Park for the final Test safe in the knowledge that they could not be beaten. A dramatic match ended 14-all, the Lions had achieved what six previous and four subsequent squads failed to do.

Not many have got the better of the All Blacks on a regular basis, but a special talent who did was David Campese. "Campo" made his Test debut on this day in 1982 in the first of a three-Test Bledisloe Cup series in Christchurch. His big-match temperament shone through as he scored a try, the first of eight he would notch in 29 matches against New Zealand. He could not inspire Australia to victory, but did nine years later in a memorable World Cup semi-final in Dublin.

AUGUST 15

In 1992, just five months after the official abolition of segregation by colour in South African rugby, the ironically named All Blacks took on the Springboks in Johannesburg – South Africa's first post-apartheid Test match. It was a momentous day, New Zealand winning a terrific match 27-24, but for all the revelry in South Africans at last taking to the field as representatives of an inclusive system it was still an all-white team against the All Blacks. It would take many years for the creation of a Springbok side more representative of its nation.

The new South Africa's appearance on the scene directly led to the founding of the Tri-Nations tournament four years later. New Zealand won the first two titles, but in 1998 turned up in Durban for their final match in the amazing position of played three, lost three. A whitewash was unthinkable and, leading 23-5 with just 11 minutes left, it appeared to be impossible. However, the world champions staged an incredible comeback, two converted tries the prelude to James Dalton's late winner. The All Blacks lost 23-24 and were winless wooden spoonists – staggering.

AUGUST 16

Visiting teams always find it tough in South Africa. The climate and altitude are often debilitating factors and that's even before you consider the skill, power and fury of the Springboks. France ventured to "Afrique du Sud" for the first time in 1958, aware that nine consecutive overseas squads had failed to achieve a series win there since the 1896 British tourists. There was all to play for in the second and final Test in Johannesburg, the first match having been drawn. Lucien Mias inspired his side to a 9-5 win at Ellis Park. France had truly arrived on the world stage, and would win their first Five Nations the following year.

Fathers take pride when their children excel at anything. In the sporting context, there's also a curious dynamic for most...to see them become brilliant, you have to accept being bettered by your offspring...often hard to take. Time will tell if Owen Farrell will ever be accepted as having surpassed his dad, Andy, but the Farrells made their mark in history as the first father and son to appear in the same first-class rugby match, when Owen replaced Andy during a pre-season game against Australia's Western Force in 2008.

AUGUST 17

Japanese rugby has always appeared to have been viewed as a curiosity rather than a serious competitor by the leading nations. The "big eight" would field non-cap XVs but it wasn't until 1973 that Japan played its first official Test against one of the big boys – France. Two years later another landmark was reached when Australia provided the opposition for Japan's first series. Beaten 37-7 in Sydney, a slight improvement was achieved in Brisbane on this day in 1975 but 50-25 was a reflection of a gulf that still exists between the world powers and the perennially out-muscled Cherry Blossoms.

Great tries seep into people's memories but, occasionally, a tackle makes just as big an impression...It was the 1994 Bledisloe Cup match at Sydney Football Stadium. With the final whistle imminent, and his side trailing 16-20, New Zealand wing Jeff Wilson embarked on a stunning 30-metre run to the corner. With the line at his mercy he prepared to dive and, then, like a bolt from the blue, George Gregan flung himself at the blonde All Black, knocking the ball out of Wilson's hands. Australia regained the cup and Gregan had created a piece of folklore at the dawn of his world record-breaking Wallaby career.

AUGUST 18

Don Clarke is responsible, a cynic would say guilty, of turning kicking goals into an art form. Until the great New Zealand full-back came along in the 1950s, a consistently successful goal-kicker was an unknown species. On this day in 1956, the man from Waikato stepped out in Christchurch for his All Black debut against South Africa. The series was one-all, with two to play. Clarke kicked a conversion and two penalties in both matches as the series was won 3-1 and went on to become the first man to reach 200 Test points. The All Blacks only lost four times with him in the team, Clarke was rugby's first points machine.

After his retirement, Clarke's New Zealand points record stood for over 20 years until another kicking metronome called Grant Fox came along. Fox played in some stunning teams but he was the man who turned possession and territorial dominance into something tangible, and was a major reason why the All Blacks went over three years unbeaten between 1987 and 1990. The run finally came to an end in Wellington, when Australia gained a consolation 21-9 win at the end of a three-match series.

AUGUST 19

There's something about South Africa against New Zealand at Ellis Park. In the amateur era there was a series of tight, gripping matches between the nations at the gladiatorial arena in Johannesburg, culminating in the extra time World Cup final in 1995. While the Tri-Nations has seen three spell-binding try fests, chief among which was the 10-try, 86-point meeting on this day in year 2000. Christian Cullen scored two tries to become the first Kiwi to notch 40 Test tries and the All Blacks finished with 40 points away from home...and lost by six.

The only consolation for Cullen and his chums were a couple of bonus points for losing by a margin within seven points and scoring four tries. The bonus system was developed in the southern hemisphere and finally arrived in England for the start of the 2000/01 season. No longer could teams just accept defeat, even if victory was an impossibility there was a chance of capturing a crucial point or two as a reward for plugging on until the end. Initial reluctance in some quarters gave way to acceptance...Apart from the Six Nations Championship, which steadfastly operates the old-fashioned two points for a win.

AUGUST 20

A Lions series has often provided the backdrop for the making of a superstar. Back in 1955, 20-year-old Northern Transvaal wing Tom van Vollenhoven made his Test debut for the Springboks against the British & Irish. A first Test defeat heaped masses of pressure on the home side for the second in Cape Town, but in van Vollenhoven they had a special talent. He scored a hat-trick of tries in a 25-9 rout. A further try came in the final Test win at Port Elizabeth which levelled the series, but his expected vintage career lasted only one more year before he was lured by St Helens to rugby league. He became an RL legend.

North Africa is not noted as a rugby hot-bed. The Moroccan national team has come close to qualifying for the World Cup on a few occasions, but by far the most significant rugby-related happening to occur in the region was the birth of 1997 France Grand Slam-winning captain Abdelatif Benazzi in Oujda in 1968. Benazzi met up with a French fourth division club in Czechoslovakia, while touring with Morocco in the late 1980s, who advised him to go to France...The rest is 78 caps worth of history.

AUGUST 21

South Africa and Australia are two of the most successful rugby nations. However, it could be claimed that both have not reached their potential due to selection issues. While, for a century, the Springboks excluded most of the population of their country on racial grounds, Australia were weakened by the impact of rival sports depriving them of a vast array of talent. The statistics suggest that the Wallabies suffered more, with only one series win (1965) in the apartheid era. In 1993, a 19-12 victory in Sydney sealed just a second Aussie series triumph over their long-haul visitors from the other side of the Indian Ocean.

By 2004, South Africa was at long last beginning to include black and coloured players on merit. The Springboks' second Tri-Nations title was won in gripping circumstances, a 23-19 final day win over Australia meant that for the first time all three nations finished on two wins. It all came down to bonus points, with the Springboks one ahead of the Wallabies. It nearly went wrong for the Boks...They were 23-7 up with 15 minutes to go, Australia fought back and nearly grabbed the spoils at the death.

AUGUST 22

It's intriguing comparing players from different eras and nationalities, but how much emphasis goes on who you play for, and with? Does playing in a champion team drag someone up to another level, or can you stand out in a struggling outfit? Agustin Pichot, born on this day in 1964, is undoubtedly Argentina's greatest scrum-half. A flamboyant character who attracted attention with his flowing locks and all-action style. Would he have been considered one of the all-time greats if he was French or Australian? No-one knows, but if he had been born 15 years earlier and played with Hugo Porta – wow, that would have been something.

International rugby can be a roller-coaster. We can't all be Gareth Edwards or John Eales and travel seamlessly from one triumph to another. Nick Mallett had rescued South Africa from the oblivion of home defeats by the Lions and South Africa and coached the Springboks to a first Tri-Nations title in 1998, when they beat Australia 29-15 at Ellis Park. Two years later, he was gone, ousted by a heady brew of player discontent, fan bewilderment and antagonising his bosses through criticism of ticket prices. The job's hard enough without that.

AUGUST 23

Rugby took its first tentative foothold in South Africa in 1862. It was, naturally, the white population that took on this "foreign" concept of two groups of men in an intense physical battle to gain territory as if it came naturally...which, to the Afrikaners, it did. The very ordered nature of South African society in the middle of the 19th century was neatly summed up by the combatants in the first recorded match at Green Point Common in Cape Town...The Civilians v The Military.

In August 2003, England were in the unaccustomed position of being recognised as the best team in the world. Clive Woodward had built a team with a relentless will-to-win, and skill levels to match. It led to a very un-English level of self-belief, so much so that Woodward decided to field a virtual second XV against a pretty much full-strength Wales at the Millennium Stadium. Was it arrogance? Sabre-rattling? Or, as Woodward would claim, an attempt to test the strength in depth of his squad? Whatever, the Welsh were not impressed when their men were put to the sword 43-9 by England's "stiffs".

AUGUST 24

Any actor will tell you that dress rehearsals don't always match up to the real thing. There are little tweaks that need to be made and, in any case, often best to keep the "powder dry" for the big performance. New Zealand played Australia in 1991, knowing that they would, in all probability, meet next in the World Cup semi-finals. Eden Park saw a try-less 6-3 victory for the All Blacks. Two months later, Dublin hosted the same teams and was treated to a fantastic spectacle, with the Wallabies running out 16-6 victors. Falling before the final, when favourites, was to become a familiar World Cup story for New Zealand.

In 1996, after 68 years of trying, the All Blacks at last ticked their final box. An epic 33-26 second Test victory in Pretoria earned a first series triumph in South Africa. Even without the unavailable Jonah Lomu, that team must be rated as one of the greatest ever. Christian Cullen had burst on to the scene, Jeff Wilson scored two superb tries, Frank Bunce and Walter Little in midfield, Justin Marshall, a formidable front five and what a back row – Michael Jones, Josh Kronfeld and Zinzan Brooke. The latter scored one of his trademark drop goals.

AUGUST 25

The 1962 Lions travelled to South Africa to face the nucleus of the previous year's Grand Slam Springboks, but with the encouragement that their predecessors in 1955 had achieved a drawn series. A draw and two narrow defeats burst their bubble but there was still the final match in Bloemfontein...Could the Lions avoid the ignominy of being just the second squad to be nilled in a four-match series in South Africa? Er, no... The Lions were totally outplayed, with home fly-half Keith Oxlee scoring a record 16 points in a 34-14 trouncing.

How often is genius tempered by assorted "baggage"? Fiji wing Rupeni Caucaunibuca astounded the rugby world with his feats in Super rugby and was a star of the 2003 World Cup. So quick, so strong, so agile, so hard to tackle and...so hard to manage. In 2005, "Caucau" was banned from playing for Fiji for 12 months after the governing body lost patience with his erratic off-field behaviour. He failed to report for a trip to Samoa, then turned up at the airport but didn't board the plane when his wife developed a toothache, just after he was told that he would have to pay for the cost of her flight to Apia.

AUGUST 26

Lions tours are now big business wherever the famous touring team go. However, this was not the case in Australia just after World War II. The 1950 Lions went to Wallaby land as a bit of an afterthought, following a 3-0 series defeat in New Zealand. They found the standard of play across the Tasman nothing like as tough, and sealed a 2-0 triumph with what was then their biggest Test score, 24-3. The match was a curiosity rather than a must-see for an Aussie sporting public more interested in other matters, evidenced by a crowd double the size watching a domestic rugby league match on an adjoining ground.

This was the day, in 1995, when rugby union changed forever with the most important announcement in the history of the sport – rugby union was going professional. It was enough to make the sport's elders cough and splutter...After years of attempting to stem a tide of dis-satisfaction with archaic regulations that denied the top stars to earn any money from their skill and dedication, while others in rival sports became very wealthy, International Rugby Board chairman Vernon Pugh uttered the fateful words: Rugby Union was to become an "open" game.

AUGUST 27

In 1910, South Africa were established as a leading force in the game. The Lions lost the first Test and now had to win in Port Elizabeth to prevent a second straight series defeat to the Springboks. Enter England's Cherry Pillman, a loose forward picked at fly-half for this key match. Pillman utterly dominated proceedings as the Lions won 8-3. Opposition captain Billy Millar paid a glowing tribute: "My memories of this game are all dwarfed by Pillman's brilliance." The Lions lost their full-back to injury early in the deciding third Test and even Pillman couldn't prevent 14 (no replacements in those days) from succumbing.

Another Englishman who earned the hard-earned respect of the Springboks was centre Jeff Butterfield on the 1955 Lions tour. Butterfield scored three tries during the drawn four-Test series, but none were better than a supreme effort against Northern Transvaal. With the score at 11-all in the final few minutes, Butterfield received a loose pass in the Lions' 25-yard area, tricked the onrushing Blue Bulls and sprinted to score an amazing individual try. Even the great wing Tom van Vollenhoven couldn't catch him. The massed crowd at Loftus Versfeld were left in stunned admiration.

AUGUST 28

Rugby is given its name by the school where William Webb Ellis is alleged to have first picked up a ball and ran with it. Rugby School was the driving force behind the organisation of the new sport in the mid-19th century, but it was as late as 22 years after Webb Ellis when three pupils wrote the first set of rules. Messrs Arnold, Shirley and Hutchins issued 37 clauses to be adhered to, including "no cap or jersey must be used without the permission of the head of house" and "no protective iron nails or plates on the soles or heels of boots".

In 1999, Pool A of the World Cup was staged in Scotland. Murrayfield, obviously, was used but the Scots wanted to reach out beyond the traditional powerbase of their sport. So, the home of the country's football team, Hampden Park, was chosen to host matches. As a rehearsal, Scotland played Romania at the famous stadium and won at their leisure, 60-19. Of greater historical significance, this was the first Scotland international played in Glasgow for 93 years. The World Cup would see South Africa take on Uruguay at Hampden, but Scotland have only played there once since.

AUGUST 29

After years of prevarication and argument, on this day in 1895 rugby league was effectively born when 22 clubs from Lancashire and Yorkshire decided to split from the Rugby Football Union and create the Northern Rugby Football Union. Players in the north had complained of losing earnings through their rugby activities, and had allegedly been given payments as compensation, incurring the wrath of the RFU. At a meeting in Huddersfield, the likes of Wigan, St Helens, Leeds and Bradford enshrined the principle of "broken time" in the new organisation's constitution. In 1923, the NRFU became the Rugby League.

League has been a significant drain on the talent base of England and Australia, but New Zealand has been largely unaffected. The evocative power of the All Blacks shirt was enough to dissuade most from switching codes. Back in the 1960s, why wouldn't you want to play in a team led by Wilson Whineray with Colin Meads as his right-hand man and Don Clarke kicking the goals? Their team recorded a world record 17 straight Tests undefeated. The run was ended by Australia in 1964. It was the end of an era – Clarke's last cap.

AUGUST 30

Joe Warbrick could be called the father of New Zealand rugby. He toured Australia in 1884 with the first Kiwi representative team, was the inspiration (as selector, coach and captain) of the 1888 New Zealand Natives side – the first to tour the Northern Hemisphere, wear an All Black shirt with a silver fern emblem and perform the Haka. On this day in 1903 he was tragically killed when a geyser in Rotorua erupted unexpectedly while he was leading a tour group. The All Blacks had played their first official Test just 15 days before. It was as if Warbrick's work had been done, and what a legacy he has left.

It would be interesting to hear Warbrick's view on Clive Woodward's methods. Perhaps they would have got on, after all both were innovators in their different eras. Woodward chose this day in 2003 to send England out in revolutionary skin-tight shirts against France in Marseille. Having achieved a European record 14 straight Test wins, they were hunting the world mark of 17 as they prepared for the World Cup. Defeat by one point ended the run, but the shirts stayed and a variation is used by all major teams now.

AUGUST 31

France played some sublime rugby in the 1980s – two Grand Slams and a World Cup final defeat during that period seems a paltry return for the joy Les Bleus brought the sport. Much of the credit must be given to the incomparable Serge Blanco. Born on this day in 1958 in the very un-rugby territory of Caracas, he moved to France as a child and amassed 93 caps in a glittering career, laced with spectacular tries from his frequent, elegant forays into opposition territory. Blanco was a special player, many were quicker or tougher but few had his star quality.

Romanian rugby has never had anyone close to Blanco in the style department. Their brief spell of success was built on a powerful pack, and money from the corrupt Ceaucescu regime. The last of the Oaks' four Test wins over the Home Nations happened 20 months after the overthrow of the dictator, when they beat Scotland 18-12 in 1991. The money was drying up, as the new Romanian government had other more pressing concerns than rugby, and the game withered. No international British or Irish side has played a Test in the country since.

RUGBY
On This Day

SEPTEMBER

SEPTEMBER 1

Between the two World Wars South Africa and New Zealand established themselves as the pre-eminent powers in the world game. Their first series was drawn in 1921 while, in 1928, the Springboks staged the return and led 2-1 going into the fourth and final Test. The All Blacks were unfairly hampered by the absence of their Maori players, including legendary full-back George Nepia, as the South African regime would not accept "non-whites" in the tour squad. The visitors punished the racists with a 13-5 victory in Cape Town.

Australia's emergence alongside the All Blacks and Springboks has made the Tri-Nations the highest quality annual international tournament in world rugby. Too often, though, the Wallabies have failed to deliver, with just two titles won back-to-back at the start of the new Millennium. 2001 was a vintage year for the Aussies; they had won a Lions series for the first time and now needed to beat the All Blacks in the TN decider. At the end of a titanic match, their hopes were slipping away at 22-26 down but then Toutai Kefu dramatically plunged over and the cup was retained. All this and John Eales retiring – quite a night in Sydney.

SEPTEMBER 2

No-one wants to be caught out by the opposition knowing their tactics. Danie Craven, the figurehead of Springbok rugby for so many years, was paranoid about the 1955 Lions discovering his secrets and went to extraordinary lengths on the eve of the third Test. Worried that the foreign press would leak to the tourists, he insisted that the Boks trained in the evening to avoid prying eyes. The session was dubbed the "moonlight sonata", but the Lions still won 9-6.

All good things come to an end. Clive Woodward took six years to cajole England up the mountain to Grand Slam and World Cup glory, but then a rash of retirements and injuries contributed to a poor 2004 Six Nations. In the background were political tensions between the coach, the RFU and figures within the Premiership, which eventually led to Woodward resigning on this day in 2004. "I went into the same meetings with the same faces and heard the same things. I wanted more and we have ended up with less," was his parting shot.

SEPTEMBER 3

Professional rugby players prepare for matches with military precision. The threat of extreme weather is approached with rigorous physiological conditioning and even then the elements can prove to be too debilitating. The 1938 Lions had no such science on their side and when encountered with a temperature registering 34 degrees in Port Elizabeth they were at a severe disadvantage. Even the Springboks were unused to playing in such heat. The final score of the "tropical Test" was 19-3...Sammy Walker's Lions were burned in the furnace.

In hot conditions what is required is a regular supply of liquid. The mercury didn't reach 34 in Harpenden, Hertfordshire for the National Pub Sevens in 2006, but there were plentiful refreshments – just in case...The occasion was notable for the appearance of Andy Gomarsall in the winning team, Camberley's White Hart Marauders. Having been released by Worcester, Gomarsall was playing social rugby but Harlequins offered him a way back into the Premiership, a superb season earned him a place in England's 2007 World Cup squad and he played in the final – pub team to World Cup final in a year!!

SEPTEMBER 4

A rugby tradition ushered out in the homogenous professional age is Leicester Tigers sporting letters on their shirts. In 1926, for the match against Bath at Welford Road, the Leicester forwards were sent out alphabetically so that the crowd could distinguish the players in the morass of scrums, rucks and mauls. At first it wasn't felt necessary for the backs, standing isolated, to wear such identification but a year later they joined in. Bristol followed the Tigers in adopting letters, but the clubs used different systems, leading to confusion when they met.

After rugby bade farewell to the Olympic Games in 1924, the two had very little to do with each other until 1976 brought a political row with huge repercussions. The New Zealand Rugby Union controversially agreed to the All Blacks touring South Africa shortly after the Soweto uprising. There was worldwide opposition to the move, and nearly 30 African countries took the ultimate step of boycotting the 1976 Olympics in protest at New Zealand's presence. South Africa won the third Test in Cape Town on September 4 and claimed the series two weeks later.

SEPTEMBER 5

Newlands in Cape Town is one of the world's great rugby grounds. Nestled at the foot of Table Mountain, it provides a stunning setting. In 1891, it was inaugurated as a Test match venue for the final Test of the first South Africa v Lions series and continues to be the only venue in either South Africa or New Zealand to have staged the climax to a series in which the cream of Britain and Ireland have whitewashed the opposition.

Who would be a rugby referee? There are all those laws and interpretations, players trying to push legality to the limit in order to get an edge over the opposition and a home crowd raucously bemoaning any decision that goes against their heroes. And then they change something without telling you...Bertie Smith, an Irishman, was appointed for the Bath v Wasps season-opener in 1998 and asserted his authority by sending two players to the sin-bin in the opening stages. The only thing was he brandished a yellow card, which had been replaced in the Premiership that summer by a white. "No-one told me", said Smith.

SEPTEMBER 6

South Africa sealed their fourth straight home series triumph over Australia with an 11-3 victory in Cape Town in 1969. The Wallabies have yet to win an away series against the Springboks and are never likely to, now the Tri-Nations has taken over. It was to be the last time for a generation that the Springboks would host the Aussies. Later that year the turbulent tour of Europe ensured that only occasional contact with the outside rugby world would be made until 1992.

While South Africa spent most of the 1970s and 80s on the outside looking in, Australia went on a gradual upward curve. The Bledisloe Cup rivalry with New Zealand intensified as, from being whipping boys, the Wallabies began to stand toe-to-toe with the All Blacks. September 6 1986 was a landmark in this progression. Tries from David Campese and Andrew Leeds and 14 points from Michael Lynagh produced a 22-9 win in Auckland to seal a 2-1 series victory – just the second ever by an Australian side in New Zealand and the first for 37 years.

SEPTEMBER 7

The men who would go on to deliver the World Cup for England were named in the squad bound for Australia on this day in 2003. For three stalwarts during Clive Woodward's reign the day was one of the most disappointing of their careers...Austin Healey, Graham Rowntree and Simon Shaw all missed out on selection. Woodward rationalised his choice to pick Mike Catt ahead of Healey on the grounds of experience at fly-half, but described leaving out the two forwards as "the hardest decisions I've had to make in six years as head coach."

England mounted a turbulent, but ultimately impressive, attempt to defend the World Cup in France in 2007, losing in the final to South Africa. A fascinating tournament began with a shock, as Argentina beat the hosts at Stade de France. Ignacio Corleto's glory run to the corner was the crucial score in a 17-12 victory that marked the Pumas as live contenders. They would go on to finish third, beating France once again in the newly-coined "Bronze Medal Match", the first ever World Cup semi-finalists from outside the Six and Tri-Nations.

SEPTEMBER 8

Opunake, on the west coast of New Zealand's North Island, had just one claim to fame before the late 1970s...the birthplace of triple Olympic Gold medallist Peter Snell. However, in 1978, another son of the small town in Taranaki made his name – Graham Mourie. Born on this day in 1952, Mourie led the All Blacks to their first ever Grand Slam tour of the UK and Ireland, having been appointed captain of his country after just two caps. He finished his career having played 21 Tests, 19 as captain.

Not all international captains sit as calmly in the metaphorical hot seat as Mourie...Phil Vickery led England's defence of the World Cup in 2007 but got himself into a right pickle in the first match against the United States. Lens regularly hosts top French football and Vickery's attempted "tackle" on USA centre Paul Emerick would have earned a free kick and ticking off in that sport, a blatant trip. The match officials failed to spot it and Vickery went unpunished until being cited post-match. He received a two-match ban, lucky under the circumstances, and went on to play in the final.

SEPTEMBER 9

In 1978, this was a truly remarkable day in the life of Australia flanker Greg Cornelsen. The bearded wonder from Sydney stunned the All Blacks with four tries in a 30-16 Wallaby victory at Eden Park, an Australian record and the first forward in the history of the sport to score a quadruple in a Test match. Cornelsen's down-to-earth manner (his nickname was EMS – Every Mother's Son) made him shave off his trademark whiskers in the dressing room post-match, as he apparently didn't fancy being approached in the street by well-wishers.

There is little danger of the Portugal team being mobbed in the Algarve or Lisbon, such is their low profile at home, but 2007 brought a monumental occasion in the history of rugby in that country. "The Wolves" made their Rugby World Cup finals debut against Scotland in St Etienne, putting up a creditable performance in a 10-56 defeat. The honour of scoring their first try at the elite level went to wing Pedro Carvalho. After the expected 100-point drubbing by the All Blacks, the Iberians held Italy to 31-5 and only lost by four points to Romania.

SEPTEMBER 10

Media coverage of international rugby is now all-consuming. The world is kept up-to-date with Test matches as the action happens. Back in 1938 there was no live coverage of the Lions tour to South Africa and, with the Springboks having completed two easy victories and 13-3 up at half-time in the final Test, staff at a London news agency waited for the "wire" to bring bad news from Cape Town. Instead it read: SA 16-21 Lions. Surely it was a mistake...So the score was reversed to the expected outcome. But the Lions had mounted a courageous comeback to beat the Boks...Ye of little faith.

Live televised rugby is now everywhere, but it wasn't until 1994 that an English domestic league match was shown in its entirety. Bath v Bristol was the fixture and Stuart Barnes, just retired to take up a job with Sky Sports, presented the coverage. A few minutes before transmission Barnes was told a problem would mean his carefully rehearsed script would have to be ripped up and he would have to improvise on his debut in front of the cameras. A tough start to what has become a distinguished broadcasting career.

SEPTEMBER 11

Hugo Porta was born on this day in 1951 and would prove to be the single most important individual to any of the major rugby powers. In fact, if it wasn't for Porta would Argentina have been accepted as such? There has to be a doubt, so vital was the fly-half to the Pumas progressing from rugby outpost to leader of the non-Six and Tri-Nations pack and World Cup semi-finalists. He scored 593 points in a career spread over 19 years, and made those around him, and generations to come, believe they could compete with the big boys.

In 1982, there could have been a shift in the balance of power in the Southern Hemisphere. With South Africa banished following the controversial series in New Zealand the year before, Australia had a chance to assert themselves. They had beaten the All Blacks in Australia in 1980 and now they went to the final Test in Auckland at one-all, 24 years since a Wallaby team had been in such a position in the "Shaky Isles". What they didn't bank on was Allan Hewson's record 26 points in a 33-18 humbling.

SEPTEMBER 12

In terms of international rugby trophies, the Bledisloe Cup is only beaten in longevity by the Calcutta Cup. Australia and New Zealand have been playing against each other since 1903, but it wasn't until 1931 that something tangible was put at stake. Lord Bledisloe, the Governor-General of New Zealand at the time, donated the stout bauble and the All Blacks, as was their wont in those days, saw off their Trans-Tasman rivals 20-13 in Auckland to become the first to hold the BC.

Nothing fazes most props but one of their number had the embarrassment of being felled by some cooking material during a Test match in 1981... South Africa toured New Zealand against a backdrop of anger. The repulsive apartheid system was in control in their homeland and many thought it inappropriate for the Springboks to be part of the international rugby community. Passions ran high before the final Test in Auckland and a light aircraft hovered over Eden Park unleashing "flour bombs" on the players. Gary Knight took a direct hit, was knocked over by the impact and needed some treatment. Which I guess goes to show that "plane" flour is certainly not self-raising.

SEPTEMBER 13

Argentina's current standing as one of the top half dozen countries in the world makes it seem incongruous that the British and Irish used to refuse to award caps when they played them. Ireland ventured to Buenos Aires for the first time in 1970, losing both "Tests" (the first of which was on this day), but it wasn't until 30 years later that the IRFU deemed a trip to South America an "official tour". Such snooty behaviour did no favours and gave extra spice to Argentina knocking the Irish out of the World Cup in both 1999 and 2007.

Perhaps it was the legacy of the troubled 2001 Lions tour, but New Zealand coach Graham Henry gave the appearance of being paranoid as his team prepared for the 2008 Tri-Nations decider in Brisbane. The All Blacks accused a cameraman from an Australian TV station of being a Wallaby "spy", filming a closed training session – an allegation similar to one reportedly raised by the Kiwis just before facing England at Twickenham in 2005. In the end Henry's charges won 28-24 to secure a ninth southern crown. With Dan Carter on top form, who needs to worry about espionage?

SEPTEMBER 14

It is hard to believe that as recently as 1966 the Lions tour lasted for a staggering five months. Mike Campbell-Lamerton's squad played 33 matches in Australia and New Zealand, beating the Wallabies but losing 4-0 to the All Blacks and being turned over by four provincial sides. Then, for some bizarre reason, the organisers thought it would be a jolly wheeze to play a couple of games in Canada. The move back-fired...the weary Lions lost 3-8 to British Columbia in Vancouver before just managing to see off the national side in Toronto.

Now, to one of the most embarrassing nights in English rugby history... The pride of being world champions had ebbed away during four years of limited success, and a poor opening to the 2007 World Cup against the United States left England staring at a South Africa side who had put 50 points on them in consecutive Tests the previous June. The portents were not good, but this was a pitiful display. Humiliated 36-0, just the third professional England team to fail to score, it was a modern day miracle that they recovered to make the final.

SEPTEMBER 15

This is an England result which, even nearly 40 years on, makes you do a double-take. Having achieved an unlikely victory over South Africa in Johannesburg the year before, John Pullin led his country on a tour of Fiji and New Zealand in 1973. The Fijians were desperately unlucky to lose 12-13 in Suva and then three NZ provinces defeated Pullin's men to make the solitary Test against the All Blacks appear hopeless. However, tries by Tony Neary, Peter Squires and Stack Stevens secured a 16-10 victory at Eden Park – the first time New Zealand had been beaten at home by one of the British or Irish national teams.

The dressing room is special for any sporting team. It's a dramatic place where issues are sorted out and team spirit is supposed to be engendered. France allowed a broadcaster to film inside their sanctum during the 2007 World Cup, but the players became tetchy after the opening night defeat by Argentina gave them literally nowhere to hide. A compromise was reached whereby TF1 continued to shoot, but pictures would not be shown until after the tournament. The pressure of the World Cup, hey...

SEPTEMBER 16

The development of women's rugby across the globe marches on at a pace. It's heartening to see Canada and the United States compete in the upper echelon alongside traditional rugby powers such as New Zealand and England. And something appears to be stirring in central Asia, where Kazakhstan are showing that the image of subservient women portrayed by Borat is not up to the mark. Just ask the South Africans who, in the 2006 World Cup play-offs, were humiliated 36-0 by the Kazakhstanis. You could say it was an Almaty thrashing...

Time will tell if Kazakhstan becomes a powerhouse in women's rugby. First impressions can be deceptive...Gloucester recruited rugby league try machine Lesley Vainikolo in 2007 and the Tongan-born Kiwi international ran in five tries on debut against Leeds. Having qualified by residency for England, his pace and power brushed aside doubts about his positional play and skills in the eyes of Brian Ashton, who handed him four starts in the 2008 Six Nations. Martin Johnson is not such a fan and immediately left the "Volcano" out of his England squad

SEPTEMBER 17

New Zealand have handed out many severe thrashings over the years. The All Black way is to show no mercy and they are joined in that psyche by the Springboks. Having both developed the sport to such a pitch that the founding fathers from Europe could not compete, the two jostled for unofficial global supremacy until South Africa were cast asunder by apartheid. The 1949 All Blacks went into the final Test in Port Elizabeth 3-0 down and suffered the indignity of a whitewash. Basil Kenyon's Boks had claimed the pinnacle of world rugby in emphatic fashion.

Happier times for Kiwis in 2006 as the "Black Ferns" successfully defended the Women's World Cup with a 25-17 final victory over England. Amiria Marsh scored a cup-clinching injury time try after a valiant English effort in Edmonton, Canada. A third successive title was a superb way for skipper Farah Palmer to call it a day, although fellow retiree Donna Kennedy could claim superiority in one respect over Palmer. The 5th place play-off defeat by the USA was a world record 95th cap for the Scot.

SEPTEMBER 18

If you want to uncover a lasting legacy look no further than "Flying Scotsman" Ian Smith, who died on this day in 1972. Smith was the most devastating finisher of the first century of international rugby, passing away holding the accolade of leading Test match try scorer, almost 40 years after his last cap for Scotland. A stunning 24 tries in just 34 Tests made Smith the "Bradman of rugby" for many years, statistically untouchable. It wasn't until David Campese came along that his mark was surpassed, 15 years after his death.

Smith's place in the record books is beyond dispute, but his compatriot Colin Mair missed out on his place in the sun when his feat of scoring 30 points against Japan for Scotland in 1977 was ruled not legitimate, as the Scottish Rugby Union did not award caps. If Mair had slotted his nine conversions and four penalties against the same opposition ten years later he would have been lauded as a world record holder. As it was he fell behind Andy Irvine and Bruce Hay in the queue for the blue No.15 shirt and never won that cherished cap.

SEPTEMBER 19

A full-back takes a clearance and begins to motor downfield. With the defence massed ahead of him, the safe option is to launch a high, spiralling kick and hope that either himself or a team-mate can get underneath it in enemy territory, or at least pressurise an opponent into making a handling error. A simple, and perhaps over-used tactic, it was first developed in the west of Ireland, where one of the Limerick-based clubs employed it with great success. To all rugby men of a certain age, the high kick will always be referred to as a "Garryowen" in honour of the club founded on this day in 1884.

Welsh rugby has got its act together in recent years with the creation of four regional teams to centralise the available talent. Something had to be done after a result in the first round of the 1998/99 Heineken Cup showed the gulf in class between the top clubs in France and the Principality. Ebbw Vale had been runners-up in the Welsh Cup the previous spring but were put to the sword in Toulouse, losing by a record 108-16. Vale still compete in the Welsh league but their days of tangling with the aristocrats have been condemned to the past.

SEPTEMBER 20

The natives were restless in 1893, the Northern natives that is. At a special general meeting of the Rugby Football Union at the Palace Hotel in Westminster a motion was raised by representatives from Yorkshire calling for the RFU to allow players to receive "compensation for bona fide loss of time". The arch amateurs from the South would have nothing to do with that and marshalled their forces to defeat the move by 282 votes to 136. The seeds of revolt had been sown, though, and two years later the "Northern Rugby Football Union" (aka Rugby League) was born.

Professionalism opened up possibilities closed off to the Victorian players. Matt Dawson used his rugby fame in 2004 to earn himself a slot as a team captain on the BBC's *A Question of Sport*. The only thing was the inconvenience of an England squad session when he was due to record some of the shows. Dawson opted for TV instead of the team and was dropped by then coach Andy Robinson, who issued the stinging message: "The door is still open for a return at some point, should his (Dawson's) priorities change." They eventually made up and Dawson played for two years under Robinson.

SEPTEMBER 21

Less than a month into "open" rugby, the floodgates opened when Rob Andrew agreed to end his days as an amateur at Wasps and join second division Newcastle Gosforth club as a professional. Sir John Hall's dream was to create a rugby behemoth in the North East and, just as he built his football empire around Kevin Keegan, he chose Andrew as his oval ball ambassador. The player/director of rugby recruited trusted lieutenants from Wasps (Dean Ryan, Steve Bates and Nick Popplewell) before shopping in Scotland (Doddie Weir, Gary Armstrong and George Graham) and Wigan (Va'aiga Tuigamala) among other places. It took just three years for Andrew to secure the English title for Sir John.

When Ireland lined up for the anthems on September 21 2002, maybe "Ireland's Call" should have been substituted for the occasion by "It's a long way to Tipperary". As part of the "punishment" for failing to make the World Cup quarter-finals in 1999, the Irish were consigned to the qualifying competition for 2003 and were sent to the Siberian outpost of Krasnoyarsk to face Russia. The job was done, four tries to nil and 35-3.

SEPTEMBER 22

Top class Australian rugby union had, for a century, been almost entirely staged in New South Wales and Queensland. Then, along came the hugely successful ACT Brumbies and Canberra was put on the union map. Another gesture of acceptance that the capital was a new rugby centre came with the first Wallaby Test to be held there. Tonga were the visitors for a World Cup qualifier, dismissed 74-0 with Jason Little scoring four of Australia's 12 tries, and having Joe Sitoa sent off for stamping barely minutes after coming on as a replacement – the 40th man to be dismissed in Test rugby.

September 22 is far from being a purely dark day in Tongan rugby history. In 2007, the Sea Eagles flew spectacularly high when they almost beat the team that would go on to become world champions. With just over 20 minutes to go Tonga were locked at 10-all with South Africa in Lens. Three Springbok tries appeared to have settled the issue but back came the men from the Pacific with thrilling touchdowns from Sukanaivalu Hufanga and Viliame Vaki taking them to within five points. The sides scored a penalty apiece and shook hands at 30-25 to the Boks before holding an impromptu joint prayer session on the pitch.

SEPTEMBER 23

Welsh club rugby has always been a competitive environment. The 1970s saw many of the great stars of the game appearing for the likes of Cardiff, Llanelli, Newport and Swansea, and a merit table system had been in use for many seasons but it wasn't until this day in 1990 that league rugby officially began in the Principality. Even more spice was added to the traditional valley ding-dongs with the all blacks from Neath triumphant in the end.

Scotland have been trying to beat New Zealand for over 100 years but have yet to manage it. Despite securing home advantage in a World Cup staged in France (try explaining that one to the Americans!), and forcing the "All Blacks" to wear grey shirts, the tartan braves whimpered to a 40-0 hammering at Murrayfield. Doug Howlett scored two of his side's six tries to make him the all-time leading try scorer for his country ahead of Christian Cullen. Kiwis must wish all New Zealand's World Cup matches could be against the overawed Scots.

SEPTEMBER 24

The first official Australian rugby union tour of the UK began in September 1908. Rather than the "Australian team" the players wanted to be known by a suitable name, so they held a vote and decided on Wallabies. A Gloucester newspaper was the first publication to use the phrase in print and the following day skipper Herbert Moran revealed that other suggestions were rabbits, kangaroos and Wallaroos. "We all agreed that any name would be preferable to rabbits," Moran told a London paper. "Wallabies won by a couple of votes."

When the going gets tough, the Boks get going...Trailing 2-1 in a four-Test series against the Lions in 1955, defeat in Port Elizabeth would have been no laughing matter for South Africa captain Stephen Fry – who would have gone down as the first Springbok skipper for 59 years to lose any Test series (home or away). Having weathered a torrid first half trailing just 3-5, Fry's men stormed out for the second period with the famed Bokke spirit propelling them to a 22-8 victory. A series illuminated by the likes of Jeff Butterfield, Cliff Morgan, Tom van Vollenhoven and Clive Ulyate, ended all-square with rugby honour going to both sides.

SEPTEMBER 25

If you can put the abhorrent treatment of most of their population to one side, South African rugby provided its country with a host of successes before the world said enough, sort your domestic affairs out before we will play you again. The modern Springboks, much as the All Blacks, have a massive legacy to uphold. In 1937, for the first time South Africa was acknowledged as the best team in the world when, five years after a Grand Slam tour of the UK and Ireland, the Boks beat both Australia (2-0) and New Zealand (2-1) in Test series away from home. Today was the day the final Test was won in Auckland, 17-6.

To be chosen to skipper your country is one of the proudest achievements for any sportsman. Wales centre Nigel Davies became the 107th Welshman to earn the accolade when he led the Dragons against France in Cardiff in 1996. A thrilling match ended 40-33 to Les Bleus...and that was that for Davies, not just for captaincy, but apparently his Test career until he was recalled for the visit of England the following March. That ended in another defeat, his 16th in his 29th and last match for Wales.

SEPTEMBER 26

The 1999 World Cup had an expanded qualification system. Only official host Wales and the top three from 1995 (South Africa, New Zealand and France) were exempt. Australia were forced into a rather pointless exercise, hosting a four-team group with the top three guaranteed a place in the finals. Samoa gave them a decent work-out, only losing 25-13, but the Wallabies had already qualified after easy wins over Fiji and Tonga. The Samoans and Fijians joined them, while Tonga went on to win a "repechage" to also qualify. So what was the point?

The microscopic nature of the medical support available to major international rugby teams appears to leave nothing to chance. Players are tested, monitored and watched to ensure they are at peak condition. Occasionally something extraordinary happens...Ireland hooker Simon Best had to be rushed to hospital in Bordeaux after suffering a loss of feeling on his right side as he prepared for a crucial World Cup match against Argentina. An irregular heartbeat was diagnosed and five months later Best sadly had to retire at the age of 30.

SEPTEMBER 27

A decision with massive consequences for English rugby was made in 2000 when Clive Woodward announced that Martin Johnson would become England captain on a long-term basis. The Leicester lock had already led his country 12 times, but all of those occasions were as a stand-in when others were not available. Woodward now chose the man who would go on to lift the World Cup in three years of unprecedented success. He was a victorious skipper in 26 out of 27 Tests after the appointment, France in 2002 being the only defeat.

Political intrigue is never away from the Springboks and, symptomatic of the contrasting fortunes of South Africa and England in 2000, while the Red Rose camp was setting down a marker by handing Johnson the captaincy the Boks lost their coach when Nick Mallett resigned. Mallett was raked over the coals at a disciplinary hearing, after criticising the price of tickets for his team's home games. A side issue had claimed the scalp of a great coach, who guided South Africa to their first Tri-Nations title in 1998.

SEPTEMBER 28

International teams against club sides are a thing of the past in these days of whistle-stop tours and concerns about "burn-out". These were traditionally magical occasions when stalwarts, who never got to the highest level, and aspiring youngsters would tangle with rugby superstars in front of partisan local crowds. In 1935, Swansea became the first club to beat each of the Southern Hemisphere "big three", when they added the scalp of New Zealand to those of Australia (1908) and South Africa (1912), winning 11-3. Five of that team went on to beat the All Blacks in Wales colours later on the tour.

Any side – international, provincial or representative – wants to dictate proceedings. So the East Africa side that took on the Lions in 1955 had just the man when they selected future Ugandan leader Idi Amin in the squad. Amin presided over the deaths of allegedly 400,000 people and deported anyone of Asian descent living in his country during an eight-year reign of terror in the 1970s. Amin didn't see action against the tourists, as East Africa succumbed 61-0, but the British foreign office was happy to describe him around that time as: "A splendid type and a fine rugby player."

SEPTEMBER 29

One of the classic World Cup matches was played in Nantes in 2007, when Fiji sent Wales spinning out at the pool stage with an incredible 38-34 victory, involving nine tries. Prop Graham Dewes clinched a quarter-final clash with South Africa, the Fijians' first last-eight appearance in the 15-a-side world tournament for 20 years. It had looked good for Wales when Martyn Williams dived over with seven minutes to go but the tactical error of playing open, high-risk rugby against one of the best counter-attacking teams in the game came back to haunt them.

No such histrionics in Bordeaux, as Australia beat Canada 37-6 to complete an unblemished record in Pool B of the 2007 World Cup. The Wallabies, looking in good shape, would take on England in Marseilles in their quarter-final and were expected to meet their familiar foes, New Zealand, in a repeat of the 2003 semi-final. The beauty of a tournament, though, is the swing of momentum that can occur when an untested team takes on a side who have had some thorough work-outs. Both were not to make it through.

SEPTEMBER 30

Argentina have been the England football team's nemesis a few times over the years and the Pumas from that country have been the same to the Ireland rugby side in the World Cup. The Argentines have been responsible for both occasions when the Irish have failed to reach the quarter-finals. First in the 1999 play-offs and then, in 2007, the Pumas dashed the Triple Crown winners' dreams with a comprehensive 30-15 victory. Another bonus for the blue and whites was avoiding New Zealand in the last eight, as worthy pool winners.

The walking (well, sometimes walking) disaster zone Jonny Wilkinson notched up yet another major injury when the 2003 World Cup hero suffered a dislocated knee in 2008, in just his fourth match after returning from a six-month break (maybe not the right word) for shoulder surgery. The misfortune occurred in Newcastle's Premiership match against Gloucester – his 14th injury in the best part of five years – and was to prove to be his last ever appearance for the Falcons. At the end of the 2008/09 season he announced that he was leaving the North East of England for Toulon in the South of France.

RUGBY
On This Day

OCTOBER

OCTOBER 1

Italy's matches against Romania have failed to rock the rugby world over the years but, in 1994, their World Cup qualifier was given added global significance when a world record was equalled in Catania. Diego Dominguez scored all his side's points from penalties in a 24-6 victory that sealed their place in South Africa the following year, matching fellow "mule" Neil Jenkins' feat against Canada in 2003. The vagaries of the rugby record book dictated that an Italian could not be deemed to hold a world record until they joined the Six Nations in 2000. By then, Dominguez's tally had been surpassed anyway.

Another man to have made his name with the boot was Argentina fly-half Gonzalo Quesada. His text book style and calm temperament was never more in evidence than against Wales in the opening match of the 1999 World Cup. Quesada kicked six penalties in a 23-18 defeat that had Welsh nerves twitching right until the final whistle. They were the first six of a record 31 penalties for the Puma, as his country marched to the quarter-finals for the first time.

OCTOBER 2

Just when you thought professional rugby might churn out hundreds of dedicated automatons along came Keith Wood. The former Ireland captain, nicknamed "Fester" because his bald pate and doughty build brought similarities with the uncle from The Addams Family, brought passion by the bucket-load. During the 1999 World Cup he equalled an Irish record with four tries against the USA at Lansdowne Road. No Irish back had ever scored as many in a Test match, but a fellow forward had... Brian Robinson picked up a quadruple, also in a World Cup match in Dublin, against Zimbabwe eight years before.

Whenever Spain and Uruguay meet there's sure to be plenty of Hispanic fervour. You think of a sunny day in Montevideo, or perhaps Madrid, Seville or Valencia...but Galashiels? The small Scottish borders town, famous for textiles rather than tortillas, was the curious choice of venue for both countries' World Cup finals debut in 1999. Almost 4,000 turned up to see the Uruguayans win 27-15. A great spectacle, but surely a more impressive stage could have been found for a landmark occasion in the history of two emerging rugby nations?

OCTOBER 3

The Haka – is it a treasured part of the fabric of world rugby, or an unnecessary psychological advantage for the All Blacks? It can polarise opinion, but the pre-match ritual is without doubt a spectacle. It was first performed by the New Zealand Natives tourists in 1888, before their opening match against Surrey at Richmond. British crowds loved it, although aficionados claim the "Ake Ake Kia Kaha" cry they are described as using is not the same as the current one performed by New Zealand.

More trailblazers from the Southern Hemisphere...an official South Africa team played on a foreign field representing a non-racially aligned administration for the first time in 1992. No Springbok side had played away from home since 1981, a tour of New Zealand which had united opinion that it was not appropriate for them to perform internationally while there was no sign of apartheid being dismantled. The France Espoirs were their first opponents, at Parc Lescure in Bordeaux. There was little sign of any vintage Bok play, though...They lost 17-24.

OCTOBER 4

Some Chelsea fans may squirm at the prospect but their beloved Stamford Bridge has been used as a rugby ground. In 1905, just a month after the Blues played their first ever match, the Bridge was the venue for New Zealand's tour match against Middlesex. Dave Gallaher's impressive unit, who revolutionised how the game was played, totally outclassed the opposition 34-0 at a stadium which at that point had been used for almost 30 years mainly for athletics.

If a World Cup had been played in 1905 it would have been a massive shock if Gallaher didn't lift it. It was 82 years later that an idea which now seems so obvious was first staged. That was very much a warts and all, hastily arranged prototype, the 1991 edition was the real deal (unless you're South African). The magic of the new tournament cast its spell when Llanelli's evocative Stradey Park had the honour of hosting the first World Cup match ever staged in Wales and its first full international for 98 years, Australia v Argentina.

OCTOBER 5

The 1991 World Cup included possibly the unlikeliest English venue for a major international match – Cross Green, Otley. The players from Italy and the USA must have wondered if this was really the most important tournament their sport has to offer when they turned up at the homely 5,000 capacity stadium, scene of a famous North of England win over the All Blacks in 1979. With there being no appetite to use the county's rugby league or football stadia, Otley was the best Yorkshire could offer. Italy won 30-9.

Some players can be legends for their clubs or provinces but just don't "train on" to become international stars. An example is Ulster fly-half David Humphreys, who was one of the pivotal personalities in the early years of the Heineken Cup. In 2001, Humphreys scored a competition record 37 points against Wasps, two years after inspiring the Red Hand gang to become the first Irish Rugby Union province crowned European champions. Yet for Ireland, despite over 500 points in 72 caps, he so often failed to convince.

OCTOBER 6

For a country populated by less than 200,000 people, Samoa (or Western Samoa as it was called then) created a massive global stir in 1991 when its rugby team defeated Wales in the World Cup. The Samoans were making their debut in the big event and were not fancied to trouble the Dragons in Cardiff. However, aided by the referee incorrectly awarding a try in their favour, Samoa's sprinkling of future legends (Brian Lima, Frank Bunce, Stephen Bachop and Pat Lam) crafted a 16-13 triumph to spread gloom in the Principality. It was the first time one of the big guns had been defeated in a World Cup match.

A truly magical day in the 2007 World Cup...First, unfancied world champions England saw off bitter rivals Australia in Marseilles. The match was won up front as a reticent Aussie eight was blown to smithereens by the power-packed scrummaging of Andrew Sheridan and his cohorts, while Jonny Wilkinson (in a short interlude of fitness) kicked four penalties in a 12-10 victory. Later, in Cardiff, it was 1999 revisited as France shocked New Zealand. This time it was a quarter rather than a semi-final. The Kiwis whinged about poor refereeing but this under-achievement on the biggest stage is becoming a sad habit.

OCTOBER 7

The cliché "flying machine" has been used to describe many a speedy winger over the years. In 1891 the original was born, and his achievements still raise an eyebrow. Cyril Nelson Lowe arrived in Holbeach, Lincolnshire but this boy was not born to sail the seas. Lowe's destiny was to fly, as a wartime fighter pilot in the RAF and on the wing for England. A remarkable 18 tries in just 25 Tests is a strike rate the envy of all but a few.

Fists flew when Danny Cipriani and Josh Lewsey tangled at Wasps' training ground in West London in 2008. Such a spat occurs at many rugby training sessions – it's a sport of aggression. Cipriani's high profile in the tabloids, due to his relationship with Kelly Brook, made a mountain out of a molehill with the pair plastered over the front pages. It might have added a few on to the gate for the following weekend's Heineken Cup opener against Castres, though, where Cipriani and Lewsey publicly made up.

OCTOBER 8

It's the Springboks' gain that rugby league has never really caught on in South Africa. While the unions in England, Australia and Wales have been shorn of great talents over the years, the 13-a-side code has rarely dipped its toe into the pool of talent on the high veldt and blissful coastline at the foot of Africa. One exception was Tom van Vollenhoven, who signed for St Helens in 1957. The great wing from Bethlehem in the Free State was a deity to the Bokke fans, scoring four tries in just seven Tests. He went on to become an RL legend on Merseyside.

Like van Vollenhoven, Va'aiga Tuigamala was a mouthful to say but a joy to behold on the rugby pitch...Unless you happened to be an opposition wing. The Samoan bulldozer first came to prominence in the 1991 World Cup, with a try-scoring debut for the All Blacks against the USA at Kingsholm. The legend of "Inga the winger" was born, a sort of template for Jonah Lomu to follow...Go round them, sure, but isn't it more fun to go through them?

OCTOBER 9

When you think of rugby union in a political context, it's hard to overlook the ranks of the well-heeled public school educated elite who pack into the likes of Twickenham and Murrayfield for major matches. A wide variety of people enjoy the sport but the connotation of a "toff's game" lives on. For every "hooray Henry", there's an army of regular folk, and even the odd revolutionary, who love their rugby. The most famous rebel of the lot used to be a handy scrum-half...Che Guevara, who died on this day in 1967. He eventually chose fighting for victory at the Bay of Pigs rather than digging balls out of rucks and mauls.

The high water mark for North American rugby...Canada beat Romania 19-11 in the 1991 World Cup to seal qualification for the quarter-finals – the first side from their continent to make the last eight. That legacy, set by the likes of Gareth Rees and Al Charron, has not been carried through by subsequent generations of Canucks. Professionalism led to a steady decline in its rugby, as the vast majority of its top players remained amateurs. The 2007 World Cup was the first not to see a Canadian victory.

OCTOBER 10

The British honours system is a real can of worms to most people. Whether you agree with the principle or not, some of the recipients of awards range from the bizarre to the tenuous to the sheer ridiculous. If there is a place for such arbitrary gongs in a supposedly meritocratic country then one of the less controversial was handed out in 2008 when Bill Beaumont became a "commander of the British Empire". The 1980 England Grand Slam and Lions captain turned administrator is one of the most respected figures in the game.

Gavin Henson may need to mend a few bridges before he is invited to see The Queen. The Welsh spice boy just can't help making the headlines. While Beaumont was taking light refreshments at the Palace, Henson was given a very public dressing down by his club, two days after missing a training session. It appears that Henson did not take criticism of his performance against Harlequins the previous weekend well and went into a brief, self-imposed exile. No player is bigger than the team, Gav.

OCTOBER 11

In this book we have followed the circuitous route taken by the United States around England during the 1991 World Cup. After stepping out at Otley and Gloucester, on this day they reached their final destination, as the first USA team to appear in a full Twickenham Test. A 37-9 defeat and a ticket home was to be expected but the occasion will always be special, particularly for veteran, Glasgow-born full-back Ray Nelson, who scored a try on his last appearance for the Eagles.

While Italy mount an annual battle to win a match in the Six Nations they are all too often also placed, like rabbits blinking in the headlights of an articulated lorry, before the awesome power of the All Blacks. When they entered the roof covered arena in Melbourne for a 2003 World Cup match, it was against the historical background of six defeats out of six against New Zealand and 50 points conceded on five of those occasions. Foreboding doesn't do it justice. It was 70 this time... Oh well, 31 less than in 1999.

OCTOBER 12

The "Ginger Monster"... That's what they called Wales points machine Neil Jenkins, in recognition of his auburn locks and the fear he put into the opposition when he sized up a penalty or conversion. On this day in 1994, in a "World Cup qualifier" (both had already achieved the deed), against Italy he scored 24 points to equal his own Welsh record in an international and overhauled Paul Thorburn to became his country's all-time highest points scorer at 308. Wales would benefit by over 700 more before Jenkins called it a day

In 2003, England began the campaign that would end in World Cup glory when they took on Georgia for the first time. It was a clash of rugby cultures... The nation that invented the sport and has more players than anyone else against a passionate "new" country with just eight pitches, 300 players and one scrum machine. It ended 84-6, but the Georgians had shown that they had natural potential, particularly at set-piece time. Now, where can we get hold of another scrum machine?

OCTOBER 13

Now, to one of the most remarkable stories ever told about a rugby team, or any team for that matter...On October 13 1972, a plane carrying Uruguayan players from the Old Christians Club in Montevideo on its way to Chile for a tour crashed in the Andes. After three months of unimaginable suffering, stranded in the mountains, five of the team and 11 of the other family and friends were rescued – the other 29 on the plane had succumbed. The story inspired a book and then a film called *Alive*. Exactly a year after the crash, the players represented Uruguay in the South American Championship. You couldn't make it up...

France has plenty of reasons to curse Jonny Wilkinson over the years...153 to be precise, spread over 11 Tests which have seen Les Bleus on the wrong end of the score-line eight times. No wonder Toulon wanted him on their side! Wilkinson ruined French dreams in the 2007 World Cup semi-final with two penalties and a drop goal, allied to a Josh Lewsey try. Raphael Ibanez could not replicate what his football counterpart Didier Deschamps achieved and lead France to victory in "their" World Cup.

OCTOBER 14

In 1978, Argentina's football team were crowned world champions and their rugby side was beginning to show some promise, thanks to inspirational fly-half Hugo Porta. However, the British and Irish refused to grant the Pumas a full international. The match at Twickenham played on this day that year was to all intents and purposes a proper international, except to the RFU. The Pumas held the high and mighty to a 13-all draw and who could blame them for thinking that international rugby was an unnecessarily uneven playing field. Their time would come...

The one-man wrecking ball (aka Jonah Lomu) created history in 1999 when he scored the last of his two tries in the 101-3 demolition of Italy. The score nudged his career World Cup try tally to 12, breaking Rory Underwood's record. All this achieved in just eight matches, with only Wales and South Africa (famously in the 1995 final) able to keep him out. He achieved the feat in Huddersfield, the birthplace of rugby league – the sport that made several attempts to lure him away without success.

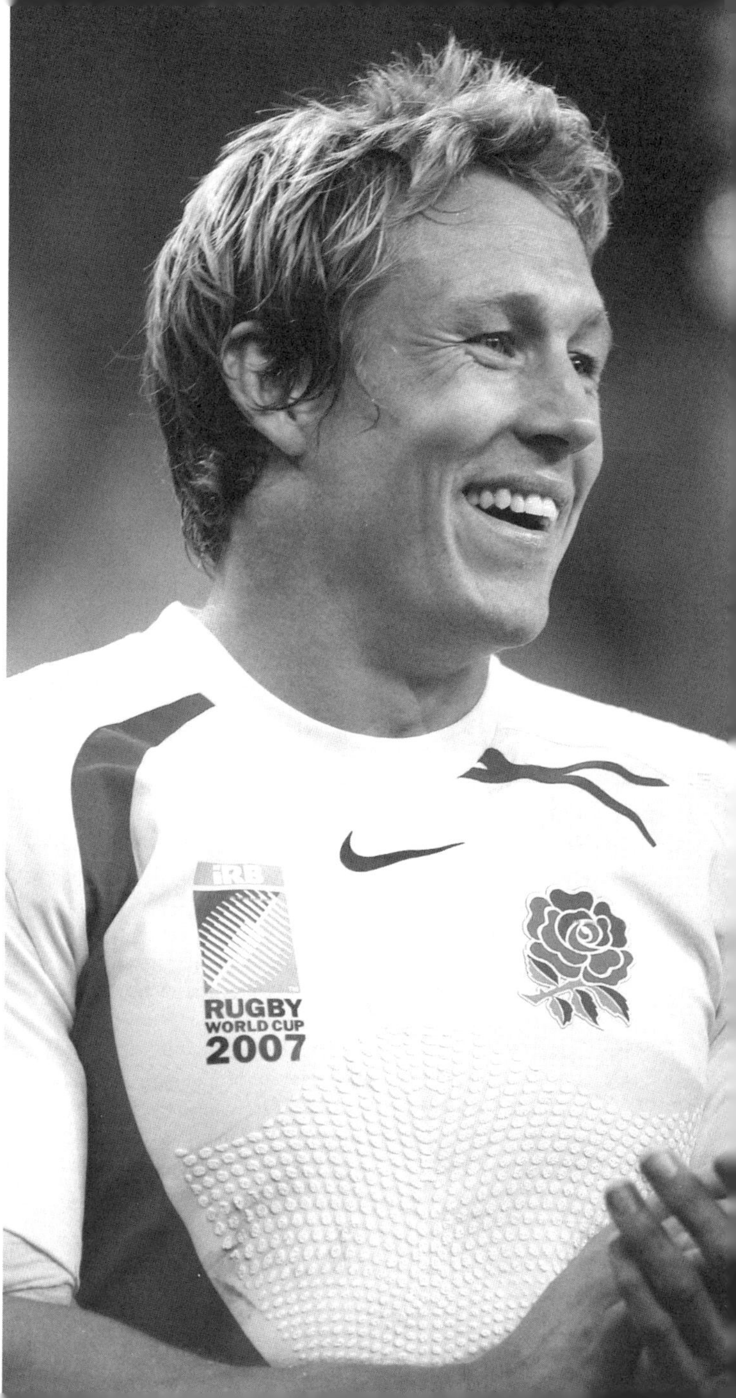

JONNY WILKINSON - KICKED FRANCE OUT OF THEIR OWN WORLD CUP

OCTOBER 15

Despite rugby being a pursuit which provides a better than even chance of injury, several medics have not been able to resist the thrill of competing at the highest level. JPR Williams, Mick Molloy and Jonathan Webb are three examples, former South Africa centre Brendan Venter is another. Venter gave his fellow practitioners some work when he (unintentionally he claimed) raked his studs across Uruguay flanker Martin Panizza's head during the 1999 World Cup. Venter was the 50th man to be sent off in a Test. His appeal was rejected.

Unsavoury incidents are not what Max Guazzini is in rugby for. The French media mogul took over Stade Francais in 1992, when they were a struggling third division side, and transformed the Parisien outfit into one of Europe's leading clubs. Guazzini gambled when he moved a 2005 league game against Toulouse from the 12,000 capacity Jean Bouin to Stade de France. How it paid off, with almost 80,000 turning up. More "left field" thinking followed with Stade trotting out in a garish pink and blue shirt sporting a floral design.

OCTOBER 16

Ieuan Evans was a speedy operator, but he was never quicker off the mark than against Japan in 1993, when he scored a try after a mere 45 seconds. Apparently this was the fastest touchdown ever recorded by a Welshman, although stop watches may not have been primed in the 19th century. Japan No.8 Hirofumi Ouchi needed all the calmness developed from his training to become a Buddhist monk to cope with this very sudden mishap.

You have to feel sorry for referees at scrum time in some matches. Continual resets put them under severe pressure to make a decision to resolve the issue, and they can never be right in everyone's eyes. Fiji led France 19-13 with just over 10 minutes to go in the 1999 World Cup, but then Les Bleus turned on the squeeze in a succession of five-metre scrums. Kiwi ref Paddy O'Brien ordered nine resets, before yellow carding two Fijians and awarding a penalty try. Fiji were sunk 28-19, with skipper and hooker Greg Smith offering the following: "I know more than the referee does, and feel that we were robbed."

OCTOBER 17

The 1999 Wales victory over England at Wembley has gone into rugby folklore, but that was not the first time England turned out under the Twin Towers, as they were then. Back in 1992, while Twickenham had the builders in, the RFU moved the home fixture against Canada to North West London. The "venue of legends" became the venue of line-outs for a day. Northampton's Ian Hunter, a man who would be tortured by injuries later in his career, celebrated his debut with two tries in a 26-13 victory, which also featured fellow new caps Victor Ubogu and Tony Underwood.

A momentous day for all South African rugby fans in 1992, as legendary fly-half Naas Botha led the Springboks out in Lyons for their first away Test match since the country was re-admitted to world sport. And what a way to mark the occasion...Centre genius Danie Gerber and wing James Small scored tries in a 20-15 win. Bring on the world, said the Boks...Only to be humbled by France in the second Test and England at Twickenham..

OCTOBER 18

Perth was the venue for England's first big test of the 2003 World Cup campaign – South Africa. Much had changed since the Springboks knocked Clive Woodward's men out of the 1999 World Cup and England were clear favourites. They didn't back that up on the field and were grateful to an opportunist, charge down try from Will Greenwood and Jonny Wilkinson's steady boot to ensure a 25-6 victory. Mission one – avoiding New Zealand in the quarter-finals had been surely achieved.

Verbal abuse of a referee is a serious crime in rugby union, and New Zealand whistle-blower Steve Walsh found out in 2005 that the punishment is just as severe if an official somehow thinks that mouthing off to a player is the right thing to do. Walsh was banned by the International Rugby Board for four months after being found guilty of clashing verbally with Shane Horgan during the Taranaki v Lions match.

OCTOBER 19

At the age of 25, Wales fly-half David Watkins had achieved many things in rugby union. He had won the Five Nations and a Triple Crown, captained his country and been the Lions fly-half on the 1966 tour. All of which left him with a decision to make in 1967...More of the (unpaid) same or brass in his pocket from signing a rugby league contract? He chose the latter: "I was paid £16,000 tax free – you could buy four houses for that," said Watkins.

Another No.10 on the move was Rob Andrew in 1995. Lured to the North East by Sir John Hall's ambitious plans for the Newcastle Gosforth club, Andrew left Wasps and took trusty lieutenants Dean Ryan, Steve Bates and Nick Popplewell with him. It all left an unsatisfactory taste for Wasps, but such player movements would become a reality in the professional age. Andrew reinvigorated rugby in the North East and the title was won in 1998. However, only a cup win came after those heady days. While Wasps climbed the mountain to glory four times in the league and three times in the cup during Andrew's 11 years on Tyneside.

OCTOBER 20

The ineptitude of some decisions made by administrators staggers you. In the 1999 World Cup there were 20 teams in five pools of four. The winners qualified for the last eight, but how should the other three places be decided? Rather than the best three runners-up, the second-placed and best third-placed country took part in play-offs midweek before the quarter-finals. The three winners were all soundly beaten, having had considerably less rest than their opponents. It was ridiculous, and the flawed play-off concept was ditched for 2003.

The 2007 World Cup final in Paris brought the inadequacies of the 1999 event into sharp relief. England, who would surely have been destined for elimination eight years before after coming second in their pool, managed to battle to the final. In the climax they met the team who had beaten them 36-0 in the pool stage – South Africa. The match turned on a controversial decision by Aussie video ref Stuart Dickinson to disallow Mark Cueto's "try" on less than clear-cut evidence. The Springboks joined Australia as twice winners of the Webb Ellis Trophy.

OCTOBER 21

Many have played rugby at the highest level, some have shown admirable excellence but relatively few have truly entertained. David Campese, born on this day in 1962, was one of those few. His mum hailed from County Cork and his dad from a village between Venice and Padua. Their Australian-born son would become the most prolific try scorer in Test rugby and be dubbed the "Bradman of rugby" by his long-time national coach Alan Jones. For an Australian, there can be no higher sporting tribute.

Another fantastic wing, without the cunning of Campese but certainly not lacking for pace, was named the International Rugby Board's World Player of the Year in 2007 – Bryan Habana. The day before he had received an even more valuable honour, a World Cup winners' medal, after matching Jonah Lomu's record eight tries in one tournament as South Africa secured global glory. Habana was so quick that he put up a respectable effort in a handicap race against a cheetah in a promotional event.

OCTOBER 22

Floodlit rugby union is a relatively new phenomenon. The major international grounds persevered without artificial illumination for decades before the demands of television drove the administrators to install bulbs for ever later winter kick-offs. Therefore, it may come as a surprise that the first recorded match under lights took place in 1878...did they really have electricity then? The historic game was a Lancashire derby between Broughton and Swinton at the Yew Street ground in Salford. Apparently, play was possible due to two lights suspended from 30-foot poles.

The standard of light for that 1878 match was possibly only slightly less than that provided by the famous "candles" at The Rec in Bath, until an upgrade in the Premiership era. As such, the key match against Leicester in 1994 was played in daylight. The two clubs were head and shoulders above the rest in League One and so, just two months into the season, it was viewed as almost a title decider. There were some bizarre circumstances...Tigers wing Steve Hackney had booked a holiday and, in the amateur era, Leicester could not force him to cancel while Tony Underwood missed the kick-off held up in traffic. Reserve scrum-half Jamie Hamilton was pressed into service on the wing...and scored the match-winning try.

OCTOBER 23

The 1993 All Blacks were the last amateur full New Zealand team to tour the UK, a trip that was also the last hurrah for English divisional teams taking on the tourists. London went out with a bang at Twickenham, the match attracting a record crowd of 56,000. The throng went away with memories of a stunning All Black performance in a 39-12 victory. Stephen Bachop and Jeff Wilson both scored two tries in a free-flowing exhibition, but a month later England were to inflict a surprise defeat on the tourists.

Coach Graham Henry was dubbed the "great redeemer" in Wales after instilling belief in a previously bedraggled national side. Ten straight wins up to and during the 1999 World Cup made the nation also believe, until they got turned over by Samoa. Suddenly, confidence took a jolt – not the ideal scenario for a quarter-final against Australia. Wales had not beaten the Wallabies for 12 years and the sequence continued. Wales were outclassed 24-9, no Millennium Stadium final for them.

OCTOBER 24

It's often been said that there must be a factory producing world-class fly-halves hidden in the Welsh valleys. Well, October 24 is a red letter day for that mythical production line with both Phil Bennett and Jonathan Davies being born, 14 years apart. Bennett, although supremely gifted, was almost understated in his approach, while Davies loved the big stage and acted like the conductor of an orchestra. Bennett edges it... He played in a fabulous era for Wales but to take over the mantle from Barry John so seamlessly was the mark of a great player.

The skill required to kick a drop goal is not to be underestimated. In virtually every game of rugby, from the lowest league to the Test arena, we see a fluffed attempt at the half-volley. How remarkable, then, to score five in one match, and in a World Cup quarter-final at that. South Africa fly-half Jannie de Beer literally dropped England out of the tournament in Paris with a sensational exhibition. No-one had scored more than three in a Test before. England were utterly demoralised by the end of the match.

OCTOBER 25

Australia raised more question marks about whether the really small fry should be allowed in the World Cup finals when they annihilated Namibia 142-0 in 2003. Appropriately, it was a cricket score at the famous Adelaide Oval, with Australia notching a World Cup record 22 tries. Mat Rogers, with an immense 42 points, and Chris Latham's five tries were also Australian World Cup records. A slaughter of the innocents in South Australia, Adelaide's first-ever Test match of the rugby variety.

Before independence, under the name South West Africa, Namibia hardened their skills in the Currie Cup. Not many foreigners have experienced South Africa's premier domestic tournament, one of the few being former France fly-half Frederic Michalak. The Gallic maestro was a member of the victorious Natal side in 2008 and it was on this day that the Sharks beat Pretoria's Blue Bulls 14-9 to claim a first Currie Cup title since 1996. Michalak had been involved in both South African and French championship sides.

OCTOBER 26

It's curious how two matches between the same countries, at the same venue, just 19 months apart can stir differing reactions. Scotland's 1990 Grand Slam decider victory over England is recalled through misty eyes, yet the Red Rose triumph over the thistle in the 1991 World Cup semi-final – a match at the very least on a par in terms of status and most probably a notch higher – gets very little coverage from winners and losers alike. Revenge was sweet for Will Carling and his men, but Australia were to crush their dreams in the final.

Tactical substitutions are de rigeur these days. The demands of modern rugby mean it's nigh on impossible for 15 men to play at full pelt for 80 minutes, fresh legs and minds have to be utilised from the bench. Mostly the changes run smoothly but, in the 2003 World Cup, England got themselves in a right pickle when, briefly, 16 men in white were on the pitch against Samoa. They were fined by the organisers and the Australian media made a meal of it in an unsubtle attempt to unsettle Clive Woodward's team...It didn't succeed.

OCTOBER 27

It's been a day for getting the abacus out in Asian rugby over the years... In 1994, Hong Kong beat Singapore 164-13 – an unofficial world record (to get the proper mark Hong Kong would need a seat on the International Rugby Board Executive Council). While, four years later, Japan slaughtered Chinese Taipei 134-6. Asia must currently be rated as the weakest of the six continents, there are just too many mis-matches. Three times Japan have scored 130+ against the Taiwanese.

The unsatisfactory nature of the Asian rugby fixture list has been a hindrance to Japan's development. In 2003, the Japanese bowed out of the World Cup win-less when fellow strugglers the USA beat them in Gosford, New South Wales. The result meant that the Americans had finally won a World Cup finals match after 10 straight defeats, dating back to the 1987 tournament when they played all their matches in Australia.

OCTOBER 28

David Campese established himself as a genius of a rugby player when he masterminded Australia's gripping 1991 World Cup semi-final victory over New Zealand in Dublin. First, a bewitching cross-field run had the All Black defence gasping and then, just before half-time, he collected Michael Lynagh's perfect chip and sprinted for the line. Assessing that a duo of Kiwis were descending upon him, and that Tim Horan was rushing up in support, Campese executed a staggering pass over his shoulder to his team-mate, who galloped to the line. The world champions lost their crown, beaten 16-6.

The part-Italian Campese would have been delighted to see Overmach Parma pull off a shock victory over the Dragons in 2006 to provide Italy with, for the first time, three teams in the Heineken Cup. Stadio Sergio Lanfranchi became the 76th different ground to host top class European rugby when Biarritz visited. A 50-7 defeat did not amuse the vast majority of the 1,200 present and another fearful hammering by Northampton persuaded all bar a few hundred to see Border Reivers. Shame, Overmach actually won that one.

OCTOBER 29

Canada have rarely set the birch on fire but consistency has been their watch-word at World Cups. For one of rugby's minnows, the Canucks have a respectable record. They have played in all six tournaments, reaching the quarter-finals in 1991 and against Tonga in 2003 maintained a record of winning at least one match at each World Cup. Sadly, that proud boast ended in 2007.

Grizzled veterans of international rugby tours will tell you that a large group of young (or young-ish) men together a long way from home will get up to "high jinks" from time to time – all in the name of "team spirit". Be careful, though...Intense media scrutiny, heightened awareness of members of the public about a potential "story" and mobile communication all mean modern players have to rein in that urge to let their hair down. All Black wing Doug Howlett was arrested in 2007 after a drunken attempt at hurdling parked cars at a London hotel. Police decided not to press charges.

OCTOBER 30

Hands up who thinks they know the most dramatic drop goal in World Cup history. Okay, Jonny Wilkinson's in 2003 maybe, but it can't be indisputable. There's Joel Stransky in the 1995 final and there were two candidates in the 1999 Australia-South Africa semi. First, Jannie de Beer slotted in the closing moments to send the action into extra time and then Stephen Larkham struck an immense 49-metre three-pointer with six minutes to go to bring Twickenham to its collective feet. Matt Burke's penalty sealed a 27-21 victory.

From two rugby heavyweights battering each other to a flyweight contest that was actually a landmark for the way Rugby World Cup handles its "lesser" matches. Romania v Namibia in the last round of pool matches was always, unless you're from those countries, a match that would have nothing riding on it. The Australians saw an opportunity, though. Break new ground by taking an international rugby match to Tasmania, encourage locals to support one of the teams according to where they lived and what do you get...15,000 turning up to watch.

OCTOBER 31

When you launch a new tournament that you hope will become a prestige event you want to make a statement...surely. Well, the massive success story that is the Heineken Cup began not in Cardiff, Dublin, Paris or any of the other great rugby locations but, bizarrely, in Constanta – a small Black Sea port in Romania – in 1995. Quite why the organisers decided this was a good idea is a mystery, but at least the opponents for local club Farul were favourites Toulouse. A crowd of 3,000 saw a 54-10 win for the French giants.

In 1999, just a day after what we thought would go down as the World Cup's most eventful semi-final, we had to think again...It was all going so well for New Zealand against France. Two sensational Jonah Lomu tries were the highlights as the All Blacks built a seemingly impregnable 24-10 lead at Twickenham. However, France chipped away with drop goals and penalties and then Christophe Dominici scooted in for a try. France led, and went on to record an unbelievable 43-31 victory.

RUGBY
On This Day

NOVEMBER

NOVEMBER 1

He wasn't there to see it, but William Webb Ellis would have been a proud man in 1923 when many of the greatest players of the time played a match to commemorate 100 years since the Rugby Schoolboy had allegedly "took the ball into his arms and ran with it" to invent one of the world's great sports. A combined England-Wales team beat their Scottish and Irish counterparts 21-16 at "The Close", Rugby School (Webb Ellis' old stamping ground) in front of 2,000 spectators.

Australia and New Zealand have played each other more times than any pair of countries, but the 132nd meeting in 2008 broke new ground... With limited growth potential in Oceania, the Tasman rivals decided to venture into Asia – the world's biggest market – to stage a Bledisloe Cup match in Hong Kong, famous for the annual Sevens but had never staged a full international before. The All Blacks won 19-14 in front of almost 40,000 people, so this was a rare occasion when the result seemed almost secondary.

NOVEMBER 2

Another in the litany of dates where Hugo Porta has almost single-handedly guided Argentina to a glory...This occasion was not a win, but the second Test against New Zealand in Buenos Aires in 1985 proved that with the fly-half maestro in their ranks the Pumas could mix it with anyone. Porta slotted four penalties and would have equalled a world record with his three drop goals had his country been recognised as one of the big fish. His 21 points was the sum total of Argentina's scoring, but was good enough to earn a draw.

There's no room in rugby for sentiment, the so-called "moral victory" means nothing – it's the numbers on the score-sheet that count. England approached the 1991 World Cup final against Australia berated for their forward-orientated style, but no-one expected them to turn their backs on a formula that had brought a Grand Slam and vital World Cup wins over France and Scotland away from home. They threw the ball around and should have had a try but for a knock-on by David Campese. Referee Derek Bevan ruled that penalty rather than penalty try was the correct decision, Australia held out for a 12-6 victory and England's gamble had backfired.

NOVEMBER 3

It's difficult to pinpoint times that have "changed the game" but one of rugby's eureka moments was the autumn of 1984, when Australia's marvellous Grand Slam team were touring the UK. On this day they began the epic journey to a first Wallaby clean sweep by beating England 19-3. It had been 17 years since the green and gold ruled the roost at Twickenham and Mark Ella – a genius of a fly-half – scored the first of his record four consecutive touchdowns on a Grand Slam tour.

Argentina were at last granted a full Twickenham Test in 1990. It didn't go well...England were still smouldering after losing the Grand Slam decider to Scotland and then in Buenos Aires, so took out their frustrations on a callow Pumas side. Among the visitors was an 18-year-old prop called Federico Mendez. He was to make an impression, laying out huge England lock Paul Ackford with a punch any heavyweight boxer would have envied.

NOVEMBER 4

Rory Underwood was the darling of the Twickenham crowd during a 12-year England career. The fresh-faced RAF pilot could finish with the best of them. A stellar date for Underwood came in 1989 when Fiji were ripped apart 58-23. The Leicester man scored five of his side's 10 tries against what eventually amounted to 13 men after two Fijians were sent off. Underwood's achievement equalled an 82-year-old England record for tries in a Test and was over 10% of his final career tally of 49 – a mark set to stand for a good while yet.

On the day Underwood was boosting his try average, Australia were clinching a first Test win in France for 18 years and introducing to the world a youthful centre partnership that would be at the core of their future success. Tim Horan and Jason Little were teenagers thrown together in Strasbourg to face the French, opposed in midfield by Philippe Sella and Franck Mesnel. The young Aussies showed great maturity to outplay their vaunted opponents, with Horan's two tries key to a wondrous Wallaby victory.

NOVEMBER 5

The 1980s...A decade of hope for England, after the first Red Rose Grand Slam for 23 years in 1980, had descended into disarray culminating in meek elimination at the 1987 World Cup and a desperately disappointing Australia tour in 1988. Something had to be done and manager Geoff Cooke plucked Will Carling, a 22-year-old centre from an Army background with just seven caps to his name, from the ranks. His first assignment was Australia at Twickenham and what a start it was. England won 28-19. The initial liberated style tightened up as the years ticked by but this was a new era, and Twickenham loved it.

Another of the game's most successful captains reached a landmark on this day in 2005. When George Gregan led Australia against France in Marseilles he broke Jason Leonard's treasured world record for most caps – in a sport as physically demanding as rugby union surely the blue riband of statistical highs. Gregan was to play 19 more Tests before declaring, to raise the bar to 139. Whether anyone's body and form can stand the numbing seasons it would take to reach Gregan's mark is questionable.

NOVEMBER 6

Unless you're Australian (and some have to be), the 1999 World Cup final was a bit of an anti-climax. Rugby fans had been treated to a pair of majestic semi-finals, chock full of wonderful skill and drama, but the Wallabies and France failed to deliver a spectacle to match the stunning setting of the Millennium Stadium. A goal-kicking fest ensued and we had to wait until the second half for two perfunctory Australian tries that sealed a 35-12 victory. John Eales and his mates were worthy winners, no question, with a mighty defence that conceded just one try in six matches.

Brian O'Driscoll took his first step along an often tortuous road to rugby nirvana when he was appointed Ireland captain in 2002. The majestic centre was just 23, but Eddie O'Sullivan knew that he would be a fixture in any Irish side for the foreseeable future and elected to build a team around him. Triple Crowns were claimed, but six years later there was still no Grand Slam. O'Sullivan departed, was replaced by Declan Kidney and, in 2009, O'Driscoll finally lifted the Six Nations trophy as a Grand Slam skipper.

NOVEMBER 7

Rugby is the ultimate team game but some individuals appear more equal than others through sheer force of talent – the indispensibles. Gareth Edwards, Colin Meads, Philippe Sella, Martin Johnson etc. Until November 7 1996 it appeared that Jeremy Guscott could be included in that bracket but then England coach Jack Rowell, who had been his mentor at Bath, shocked everyone by picking him on the bench against Italy. Guscott's club-mate Phil De Glanville was captain, so it was a straight choice – Guscott or Will Carling. Rowell went for Carling. Guscott returned against Argentina but was on the bench again in the following Five Nations.

Argentina put a disappointing 1987 World Cup behind them later that year to clinch their first ever series win over a major nation when they saw off Australia 27-19 in Buenos Aires, having drawn the first Test. It was the greatest moment in the career of Cristan Mendy, a replacement wing who scored the match-clinching try. He had feasted against the poor opposition put up by other South American countries, but this series was Mendy's first in the big time. Four tries against Brazil cannot compare to one against the Wallabies...

NOVEMBER 8

The old military-based clichés – "It was a war out there", "they came out all guns blazing", "the little general marshalled his troops" – all seem a little trite when you hear about the real thing. In 1941, New Zealand and South Africa troops based in the Libyan Desert during World War II took a break from witnessing the ravages of conflict to play a game of the sport they all loved – rugby. According to the archives, the men revelled in the match as they stood on the brink of the ultimate sacrifice. Rugby – a uniting force, even in the direst of circumstances.

In 2008, England played a full Test match against a 22nd different international team when the Pacific Islanders descended on Twickenham. Bringing the varied talents of Fiji, Samoa and Tonga together is probably even more difficult than the British and Irish countries unifying as the Lions and England, who had been severely tested by both Samoa and Tonga a year earlier, found the going easier in Martin Johnson's first match as coach, winning 39-13.

NOVEMBER 9

Clashes between the hemispheres have generally gone one way in rugby. Five World Cups to one is the tip of an immense iceberg of achievement by the South over the North, which has been exemplified by the increased regularity of matches in the professional era. November 9 2002 stands as an exception, though. Ireland beat Australia, Wales thrashed Fiji, England recorded 31 points (their biggest score against New Zealand) and France humbled South Africa 30-10. They were four of 10 European triumphs over the South that month.

England v Wales is always special, but a World Cup quarter-final...In 2003, the old rivals clashed in far away Brisbane – as they did in the 1987 last-eight. The Welsh, buoyed by a fantastic performance against New Zealand in their final pool game, set off like men possessed, storming into a 10-3 half-time lead. England's World Cup hopes were on a knife-edge...Enter Jason Robinson's dazzling feet to set up a try for Will Greenwood and 20 points from Jonny Wilkinson. An unconvincing 28-17 victory, but a win's a win...

NOVEMBER 10

A shock win over England was the only highlight of a depressing 1993 for Wales. Three defeats in the Five Nations, pyrrhic victories over Zimbabwe, Namibia and Japan raised little more than a bit of tension but most soul-destroying of all was losing 24-26 to Canada in Cardiff. In over 50 years of rugby, the Canucks had never beaten one of the leading nations in a full Test match but two tries and calm goal-kicking from Gareth Rees beat a Welsh side who had Neil Jenkins' boot and little else. Try-less, and clueless, on the day.

A grim tale about a former France captain...Marc Cecillion appeared in 46 Tests between 1988 and 1995, including two World Cups, and led France to victory over South Africa at Parc des Princes in the last of his five matches as skipper. From hero to absolute zero...In August 2004, Cecillon was arrested after shooting his wife at a "party" and on this day in 2006 was convicted of murder. He is due to serve 20 years in jail.

NOVEMBER 11

They still talk about it in Wales, more than 30 years on...The day the Dragons were "robbed" of victory over the All Blacks. It was 1978, Graham Mourie's tourists had already beaten Ireland in Dublin but were 10-12 down in the dying minutes in Cardiff. At a line-out near the Wales 22, Geoff Wheel was adjudged to have leaned on opposition lock Frank Oliver and referee Roger Quittenton awarded a penalty to the All Blacks. Brian McKechnie slotted the three-pointer, New Zealand sneaked a victory and Wales insisted that Oliver didn't attempt to jump and Wheel couldn't avoid making contact.

In 2000, after 94 years and 34 matches of battling, France and New Zealand competed for a glittering prize – the Dave Gallaher Trophy. The cup commemorates the great All Black skipper killed at Ypres in World War I. Andrew Mehrtens added s special tinge to the inaugural match, equalling his own world record with nine penalties in a 39-26 victory.

NOVEMBER 12

For those with long memories, one of the great sporting images was the great explosions of ticker tape welcoming the Argentina football team in Buenos Aires during the 1978 FIFA World Cup. While the fervour wasn't quite at that level, a gathering of 60,000 saw South Africa play the Pumas in the first-ever rugby international at the River Plate Stadium in 2000. A terrific match, full of enterprising attacking, spawned eight tries and 70 points. It led to New Zealand and Australia visiting the great arena in the succeeding years. Argentina lost each match, but all by narrow margins, and surprisingly have not returned since.

Irishman Shane Geoghegan was never going to reach the heights of playing in top internationals at grounds like the River Plate, but his name resonated round the world of rugby in 2008 for a tragic reason. An estimated 2,000 people attended the funeral of the 28-year-old Garryowen player, who was brutally shot dead in an apparent act of mistaken identity in Limerick, a small city scarred by running battles between rival gangs.

NOVEMBER 13

Some events seem relatively minor but are actually as significant as they come. Take Jason Robinson leading England against Canada in 2004. An experienced international picked to captain his country in an important, but certainly not earth-shattering, match. Jason Robinson... not your archetypal white-skinned, former public/private schoolboy, Oxbridge southerner who seemed to get the role in the dark ages, and he was also playing rugby league four years before. "Billy Whizz" became the first former leaguer to get the plum job in English rugby union.

Robinson was not the only man who had history to contend with in 2004. The Italian rugby team had some vicious numbers from the past to battle against when they lined up against New Zealand in Rome. The seven previous meetings between these nations had been, shall we say, difficult for the Azzurri. Phrased as an aggregate, the score would read 72-462. It was more of the same... The All Blacks were not spooked by a first outing at Stadio Flaminio and ran up 59 points to 10. That's at least 50 hit in seven of the eight matches – Mamma Mia!!

NOVEMBER 14

The 1931/32 South African team was a formidable outfit that completed a Grand Slam tour of Britain and Ireland. Their overall record was played 26, won 23, drew 2, lost 1. That solitary defeat occurred against George Beamish and his stout-hearted Leicestershire and East Midlands (31-20) on this day in 1931. It was a bad day for the Springboks but a personal disaster for their wing Jock van Niekerk. On the long sea journey to the UK, van Niekerk injured his knee attempting to prevent a rugby ball from ending up overboard. He further damaged the knee in the match, was carried off and never played again.

The 1992 Springboks didn't have to contend with unruly seas, but were nowhere near as effective as their forebears. A mitigating circumstance was rustiness from a lengthy period of international isolation but the famed South African "edge" was missing. On a gloomy November day, the dark green shirts appeared in a Twickenham international for the first time in 23 years and were taught a lesson by England, 33-16. It was a sad goodbye to Test rugby for both Naas Botha and Danie Gerber, two 34-year-old legends way past their best.

NOVEMBER 15

This was the day in 1997 when the long march to the summit of world rugby began for Clive Woodward. A weakened England had been soundly beaten in consecutive Tests by Argentina and Australia, today's opponents, the previous summer. Woodward had limited coaching experience but his view was that a fresh approach was required. He selected five new caps – Matt Perry, David Rees, Will Greenwood, Will Green and Andy Long – and a new captain in Lawrence Dallaglio. Woodward's men couldn't breach the Aussie defence, but Mike Catt's five penalties salvaged a 15-15 draw.

Quadrennial events...The Olympics, the US Presidential election, the All Blacks choking in the Rugby World Cup...How the Kiwis must despair – in between World Cups they are generally perceived as either the best or the second best team on the planet, yet have only reached the World Cup final twice in six attempts. In 2003 they faced Australia in Sydney in the semi-finals, having looked like a million dollars in the lead-up. New Zealand made a series of errors, which could only be from the tension of the occasion, and signed off 22-10.

NOVEMBER 16

For decades, rugby union battled against allegations of people being paid to play the game, with suspicion being raised particularly about goings-on in France. Chris Laidlaw, born on this day in 1943, one of New Zealand's great scrum-halves, spent a brief spell with Lyons in the late 1960s. He claimed in a television interview that he had been offered "an apartment and a car", plus "all the food and wine you could need." When asked if there was anything else he required, Laidlaw admitted, ruefully: "I should have said: 'Yes' and given a figure for Francs, but I didn't and played for free."

Scotland have traditionally been tough to beat at Murrayfield, but all too frequently have lacked the killer instinct against the global powerhouses of the game. Since 1981, only once in 23 matches has the Thistle got the better of the Silver Fern, Wallaby or Springbok on home soil when, in 2002, South Africa were humbled 21-6. It was Scotland's first win over the Boks for 33 years and their biggest win against any of the Southern Hemisphere giants.

NOVEMBER 17

Achieving a national record is always something to be proud of, but England's 134-0, 20-try blitzing of Romania in 2001 left a sour taste in the mouth. An England team smarting from missing out on the Grand Slam took out their frustration on totally over-matched opponents to notch their biggest win and score. This was not a match thrown up by the quirks of a tournament draw, Romania were invited to play at Twickenham. Plainly, the fixture should never have happened. Charlie Hodgson will always remember the day, though. He scored an English record 44 points in a Test match.

Team-building exercises have become a feature of modern sporting and business life. Day trips to unusual locations and physical activities are supposed to make people gel. Today, in 2003, the most infamous of the lot was revealed when pictures of South Africa's World Cup squad stripped naked crawling across gravel and standing in a freezing cold lake were released. The footage was leaked by the team's video analyst, Dale McDermott. Coach Rudi Straeuli would soon lose his job but McDermott paid a higher price. Having slipped into depression, he committed suicide in January 2005.

NOVEMBER 18

Inverleith in Edinburgh staged New Zealand's first official Test match in the Northern Hemisphere in 1905. Those "Originals" left their mark on the Scots, winning 12-7, and were the first of many visiting Kiwi teams to enjoy their time in the "Athens of the North". They played a brand of rugby not seen before in Europe – fast, tactical and technical. Skipper Dave Gallaher used the phrase "planned deception" and four tries to one show that the Scots had no answer.

Australians were crying foul (whingeing if you prefer) about some "deception" allegedly thrown at them when Dan Luger's late foray into the Wallaby dead ball area in 2000 won a controversial Test at Twickenham. The score was 19-15 to the visitors deep into injury time when Iain Balshaw lofted a hopeful kick towards the Wallaby right-hand corner. A wicked bounce stunned the defence and Luger was there to touch down. Australia claimed footage offered to the video ref was inconclusive, but the try was awarded and England claimed the Cook Cup for the first time.

NOVEMBER 19

International rugby was, for over a century, slow to look out to the wider world beyond its establishment. The likes of Argentina and Japan were given almost grudging acceptance but viewed as second-class citizens, while little thought at all was put to how the sport could grow elsewhere. How refreshing, in 2005, to see Portugal host Fiji in Lisbon in a full international. Which other sport could bring those countries 11,000 miles apart together? The Portuguese gave the Fijians a game, too, losing by the surprisingly slender margin of 26-17.

Funny how the hard men of rugby can become so attached to a spring-heeled antelope. It was reported on this day in 2008 that the Springbok was to be replaced as the South African rugby team's emblem by the Protea – the country's national flower. A compromise was offered that the Bok could still be used on the shirt, as long as it was not bigger than the Protea – a symbol used by other SA sports teams, including their cricketers. The Bok is a holy grail to some white South Africans, while some blacks see it as a symbol of apartheid.

NOVEMBER 20

The rivalry between England and Wales at rugby has been going on for a very long time. White met Red for the first time in 1881 but, two years before that, Blackheath and Newport crossed swords in the first Anglo-Welsh club fixture between the sides recognised as the unofficial champions of their nations. A bumper crowd of 5,000 was counted and saw Blackheath outclass their opponents by four tries and eight goals to nil. A tradition had started which would be revived by the Heineken and European Challenge Cups well over a century later.

They say that Stade Velodrome in Marseille is one of the most difficult venues to win at for a visiting team. Its high, banked sides and vociferous supporters add up to "nowhere to hide" territory. Argentina walked on to the pitch in 2004. Two tries and a 14-point haul from Felipe Contepomi later and a proud French undefeated record at the ground had gone. A fourth straight win over Les Bleus meant Contepomi and his pals were becoming a bogey team for France. The 2007 World Cup would prove the point.

NOVEMBER 21

Cardiff pulled off one of the greatest victories in their proud history in 1953, when a gripping clash with the All Blacks ended 8-3 to the Blues. The key moment was a sumptuous move instigated by fly-half Cliff Morgan's chip and chase, which culminated with flanker Sid Judd winning a race to the ball to score the only try of the match. The surviving players hold a simultaneous anniversary dinner/breakfast on the Friday before November 21 each year.

From amateur values to professional politics...In 2000, England's preparations to face Argentina were disrupted by the players going on strike in a row with the RFU over pay. Clive Woodward sided with the bosses, while Martin Johnson (who eight years later would become an establishment figure as England coach) branded the RFU "old-fashioned, patronising and arrogant". Woodward gave the players 24 hours to sort it out or face being dropped en masse. The issue was settled the next day. Both sides claimed victory – wasn't it ever thus in industrial disputes?

NOVEMBER 22

The most glorious day in the history of English rugby. On a rainy night in Sydney, England and Australia slugged it out in the 2003 World Cup final. Lote Tuqiri's try was cancelled out by Jason Robinson's, Elton Flatley's goal-kicking matched Jonny Wilkinson's and, at the end of the 80 minutes, the sides were locked at 14-all. Extra time...another penalty each made it 17-17. There were 10 minutes left when England worked the ball into the Aussie 22, this was the moment...Matt Dawson threw the oval to Jonny Wilkinson, the right leg swung, the drop goal was made, England held on and were crowned world champions.

Many believe New Zealand gain a psychological advantage by performing the Haka, others insist it has no impact at all. Richard Cockerill and Ryan Jones are in the former camp. Exactly 11 years after Cockerill eyeballed the All Blacks at Old Trafford, Jones insisted that Wales stood firm at the end of the pre-match ritual in 2008. The All Blacks also refused to budge and referee Jonathan Kaplan tried vainly to get the match started for well over a minute until the visitors finally retreated. Superb...advantage Wales, but New Zealand still won 29-6 on their way to the Grand Slam.

NOVEMBER 23

The commercial boys and girls don't generally waste time in pursuit of money. However, it took England a year after the game went professional to strike a deal with a shirt sponsor. On this day in 1996, Phil de Glanville's side became the first in the 125-year history of the England rugby union team to go into battle with a company name on the lilywhite jersey – BT Cellnet. Thankfully for sports fans, most teams cling on to their evocative names while firms tinker with their identities on a regular basis. BT Cellnet is no more.

"Rugby is a game for hooligans played by gentlemen…" Hmm, there wasn't much evidence of that when South Africa visited Twickenham in 2002. Lock Jannes Lubuschagne's inglorious 11-cap career ended 23 minutes into the match when his vicious assault on Jonny Wilkinson resulted in a red card. Corne Kige's bedraggled Springboks would have lost anyway but what followed was a clinical dissection amid a total loss of discipline, and the skipper was one of the worst offenders as attempted physical intimidation turned into outright thuggery. At least the scoreboard heaped punishment on the Boks…53-3 was their record defeat.

NOVEMBER 24

We have seen conclusive victories in recent years. Mismatched or weakened teams, combined with five points for a try, can lead to big scores. In 1951, a try was worth just three, so it took an exceptional team to rack up 40-plus. The Springboks pummelled Scotland to a then-world record 44-0 defeat at Murrayfield in the first Test of their Grand Slam tour. Scots admitted they were "lucky to get nothing" after a nine-try mauling.

The award of 2008 International Rugby Board Player of the Year was a great end to a fabulous year for Shane Williams. The will o' the wisp received the accolade after his Welsh record-equalling six tries inspired the Dragons to the Grand Slam and three more in five Tests against the Southern Hemisphere heavyweights, including an individual effort of the highest class against the Springboks. Playing in an era with the likes of Bryan Habana, Joe Rokocoko and Sitiveni Sivivatu it would hard enough to be rated the number one wing in the world, for Williams to beat all-comers was really something to blow the chest out about.

NOVEMBER 25

Frustrated fans know how difficult it is to get a ticket for a major international. Twickenham could be sold out several times over for a Six Nations match and it has generally become harder and harder as all-seater grounds have become the norm, but the first all-ticket match was actually one of the ancients. In 1905, Lansdowne Road was designated a full house ahead of match day as news of the adventurous "Originals" spread around the British Isles. Ireland lost that first All Black Test 15-0 and, 104 years later, they still await a first victory over the New Zealanders.

While the Unions coin it in, elsewhere in the rugby world money, or the lack of it, is a very serious issue. In 2008, Newcastle Falcons, the pacesetters when rugby went pro, got themselves into a pickle when a mixture of the economic downturn, some inflated salaries, small crowds and a lack of success on the field combined to leave them with a severe financial black hole. Owner David Thompson scratched around for any takers, found no-one suitable and eventually called a halt, electing to soldier on shoring up the North East club.

NOVEMBER 26

It takes a special talent to make a packed stadium on the other side of the world stand as one to acclaim you, particularly if you are an Australian in Britain. Perhaps Bradman, but alongside "the Don" stands David Campese. Having wowed Murrayfield the week before with two tries, Campo made Cardiff breathless in 1988 with an exhilarating display for the Wallabies against the Barbarians. His try near the end of a 40-22 victory, with mesmeric running and ball-handling, brought a simultaneous gasp from the massed crowd. On just his second tour of the UK, the great Wallaby had been accorded the ultimate compliment.

Campese had long gone from Test rugby when Wales celebrated their first victory over Australia for 18 years in 2005, and their first in Cardiff for 24. Mat Rogers' missed conversion of a Chris Latham try proved crucial at the end of a pulsating encounter, as Wales fell over the line as 24-22 winners. It was a rare terrible time for the Wallabies, who had climbed from the doldrums to enjoy sustained success for two decades. The defeat in the National Stadium was their eighth setback in nine Tests.

NOVEMBER 27

Rugby was in mourning in 1947 when one of its great innovators passed away – Adrian Stoop. The creator of half-back play had served English rugby in many guises – player, captain, selector and president of the RFU. He only played 15 Tests in the early days of the 20th century, but had set a benchmark for how the game should be played. Together with Wavell Wakefield, he became a bulwark of the establishment at Twickenham as rugby grew into a major sport and his name lingers on at his beloved Harlequins' home ground.

Stoop would have recognised that victories over the All Blacks should be treasured. He never played against them, but observed two conclusive defeats...It was to get worse as time progressed. When Sean Fitzpatrick led his side out at Twickenham in 1993 to break Gareth Edwards' world record for consecutive Test match appearances (54), England had enjoyed just three wins in 88 years of matches against the Silver Fern. An English-dominated Lions side had shown the way in Wellington five months before, and the Red Rose followed. The commitment was unrelenting and rarely has the final whistle of a try-less match been greeted with such acclamation...15-9 to England.

NOVEMBER 28

With international teams playing so regularly these days, if you hit a spell of form a mighty number of victories can be built up in a short time. By contrast, in the 1960s it took New Zealand five years to accumulate a world record tally of 17 straight Test victories. Nick Mallett's South Africa finished 2007 with an unbeaten European tour, three early season Tests in 2008 were followed by a Tri-Nations Grand Slam and, in just over a year, the Springboks had won 14 in a row. Victory in Dublin equalled the mark set by Colin Meads et al. However, England denied them sole ownership of the record a week later.

No need for joint ownership of the 2005 International Rugby Board Player of the Year crown. Dan Carter was a runaway winner after majestic displays against the Lions and throughout the Tri-Nations. The concept of awarding a single, subjective prize to a player in a team sport like rugby can be a vexed issue. How do you compare a full-back with a prop, or a scrum-half with a lock? Often it appears that the forwards get the raw end of the deal in a close vote. Few would argue, though, on this occasion.

NOVEMBER 29

William Henry "Dusty" Hare, born on this day in 1952, was a rugby phenomenon. A noted cricketer, his points-scoring feats stand comparison with Jack Hobbs' knack of scoring centuries. Surely no-one will ever get close to Hare's tally of 7,337 points or Hobbs' 199 first-class hundreds. Both sports have changed so radically, with careers being shorter and defences tighter in rugby. Despite his ludicrously consistent performances, Hare was only deemed worthy of 25 England caps spread over 10 years.

A week may be a long time in politics, but three years is a lifetime in rugby. Andy Robinson, Clive Woodward's right-hand man during the 2003 World Cup triumph, was sacked as England coach in 2006. It wasn't a shock, after a disastrous 25 months in charge, but few would have bet that another three years on he would be fulfilling the same role for Scotland...Such is the mercenary world of rugby, where a Kiwi coaches Wales, another New Zealander guides the Wallabies and a South African tries to improve Italy.

NOVEMBER 30

The England rugby union team was a bastion of the white middle and upper class for over a century. A comprehensive school educated player was almost as rare as a black man wearing the Red Rose. Happily, the team is now more representative and one of the standard bearers of inclusivity was popular Bath wing Adedayo Adebayo, born on this day in 1970, who was joined by club-mates Victor Ubogu and Steve Ojomoh as Nigeria-born England internationals in the mid-1990s. The likes of Delon Armitage and Paul Sackey in the current crop continue to break down stereotypes.

Welford Road in Leicester has always been an intimidating place for opponents, but in the dying embers of the 20th century and the dawn of the 21st it was an unbreachable fortress. For almost five years from December 30 1997 the Tigers played 57 games at home, won 52, drew five and lost none. The team that broke the spell was Northampton Saints, the Tigers' bitter East Midlands rivals, who won a Premiership clash 25-12 on November 30 2002. Four Premierships and two Heineken Cups were won by the Tigers during the mighty run.

RUGBY
On This Day

DECEMBER

DECEMBER 1

In 1863, the various rugby governing bodies had yet to form, and the future rugby fraternity were part of the Football Association. Clear differences in interpretation were evident as those early administrators tried to draw up clear rules, but some of the views expressed were extreme by today's standards. At an FA meeting, Blackheath representative FW Campbell railed against a motion to abolish "hacking" proclaiming, in jingoistic terms, that to eliminate the practice would "do away with all the courage and pluck from the game, and I will be bound over to bring over a lot of Frenchmen who would beat you with a week's practice".

Mr Campbell would have no doubt blustered about a huge rugby ball being set up on the Thames embankment where, in 2008, the draw for the 2011 Rugby World Cup was held. Champions South Africa, hosts New Zealand, Australia and Argentina were the top seeds, England, winners in 2003 and runners-up in 2007, avoided the Southern Hemisphere "big three".. Wales were not so fortunate – South Africa, Fiji and Samoa all bring back bad memories for the Dragons.

DECEMBER 2

When Crystal Palace is mentioned most people probably think about a mediocre football team or the premier British athletics track. Football historians will point to FA Cup finals being played at the South London venue, but it was also a location for an historic match for the England rugby team. In 1905, with Twickenham yet to be built, the Palace was selected as the place where England would play the All Blacks for the first time. It didn't go well, the "Originals" won 15-0, but England achieved a 3-3 draw against the Springboks a year later before the Palace was consigned to history as a Test match venue.

Now, you decide...Was rugby a much cleaner game years ago (unlikely), did referees fail to spot suspicious activity or did they simply let lots of things go? In 96 years of Test match rugby only one man was sent off until, in 1967, the great Colin Meads was pointed to the dressing rooms by Irish official Kevin Kelleher for "dangerous play". Had Meads suddenly brought this unnecessary edge to his game? The *Daily Telegraph* wryly observed: 'This was rather like sending a burglar to prison for a parking offence.'

DECEMBER 3

The Barbarians created the concept of throwing together a scratch team to take on an international side, and the famous black and white hooped jersey is the only vehicle through which the idea really works. Various invitation sides have rarely delivered. Take the "World XV" that took on the Springboks in 2006...Very few of Lawrence Dallaglio's side would have qualified on a strict selection of the best players outside South Africa at the time. A motley collection of a few current Test stars, legends past their best, has-beens and never-will-bes were put to the sword 32-7, and it should have been worse.

The 2008 Barbarians against Australia match had a far more meaningful feel about it, and the added lustre of being the first rugby union match played at the new Wembley. Arranged to celebrate the centenary of the 1908 Olympic rugby final, when the Wallabies beat Cornwall (representing Great Britain), the Baa-baas side was strong – Habana, du Preez, McCaw, Burger and Smit to name a few. However, a young Australian side played with utter commitment and triumphed 18-11 in front of almost 44,000. There was criticism of the pitch, after serious injuries for props Matt Dunning and Sekope Kepu from losing their footing at scrums. Great stadium, but Twickenham it isn't.

DECEMBER 4

The Heineken Cup – surely the pinnacle of ambition for all European clubs. Not to everyone. Bourgoin held a different view in 2004, preferring to concentrate their resources on the French Championship. Having lost their opener at Bath, the French club decided to rest their first-choice players and ran up some embarrassing results that could have skewed the qualification process. They lost 34-0 at home to perennial Italian makeweights Treviso and then, on December 4 2004, they were humiliated 92-17 by Leinster in Dublin.

A Frenchman who always gives his best is Philippe Saint-Andre. He won 69 caps, captained his country, enjoyed success as a coach at Gloucester and then guided Sale to the Premiership title in 2006 but, on this day in 2008, Saint-Andre decided that the end of the season would be time to leave Stockport for a return ticket to France and "different challenges". This would turn out to be a highly rewarded post on the Cote d'Azur as sporting director at Toulon, where Jonny Wilkinson and other luminaries would come under his wing. Nice work if you can get it – Bon Chance, Philippe!

DECEMBER 5

The hullaballoo and razzmatazz surrounding international rugby at the highest level...So how did it all start? Well, from a humble hand-written letter...In 1870, four Scottish Clubs (Edinburgh Academicals, West of Scotland, Glasgow Academicals and University of St Andrews) decided to write to Blackheath as representatives of "the whole footballing interest of Scotland" to lay down a challenge to "any team selected from the whole of England." The gauntlet was picked up and in March 1871 it all began, the Scottish side winning by a goal and a try to a try. The letter had promised the Sassenachs a "hearty welcome". Yeah, right...

A promising player from Port Elizabeth pitched up at Bath in 1992 who would have an amazing career in English rugby. Mike Catt was accepted into the close-knit family at The Rec and made his club debut on December 5 1992. His English parentage soon brought him to the attention of the selectors and he won his first England cap in 1994 as a replacement against Wales. He would go on to seal the 2003 World Cup triumph when he kicked the ball off the park to condemn Australia to defeat and in 2009 he played, at the age of 37, for London Irish in the Premiership final.

DECEMBER 6

In December 1994, we were still eight months away from the official declaration that people could be paid to perform in rugby union, and thus the rehabilitation into the fold of former players who had fled to rugby league. Until then, the 13-a-side code was held at arm's length, like a nasty smell under the nose of the union administrators. Enter Adrian Spencer, who produced an anomaly as the first former leaguer allowed to appear at Twickenham. Spencer had played in the RL Varsity Match for Cambridge (unpaid) and now came on as a replacement for the light blues in the union version.

Whatever your background, Twickenham was the place to be on this day in 1997 as England and the All Blacks played out an epic Test match. It was the second of two internationals between the two sides and, having won easily at Old Trafford, New Zealand were overwhelming favourites to seal a 2-0 series. What followed were the first signs of something stirring for England under Clive Woodward, as his side took the game to the feared ABs and secured a thrilling 26-all draw.

DECEMBER 7

When a meeting of the Rugby Football Union's "Club England Committee" is given more coverage than most matches you know that rugby has arrived as a media sport. The hounds of truth were on the case in 2006 as Rob Andrew presented a report to the body on England's autumn internationals and subsequent sacking of Andy Robinson. Would Brian Ashton be recommended for the top job? We didn't find out immediately (that's not the RFU way), but the answer was "yes". The cycle was repeated when Ashton was sacrificed in the summer of 2008 to make way for Martin Johnson. Rugby – the new football, with added committees.

The ivory tower at Twickenham is a far cry from the sequins and glitter of ballroom dancing – although some might say there's as much nifty footwork around certain issues at the former as in the latter. Austin Healey was prancing with the best of them in the 2008 *Strictly Come Dancing* series until the former Blundellsands scrum-half met his own personal Waterloo when he lost a "dance-off" to TV presenter Lisa Snowdon. The 51-times capped England international thanked the programme for allowing him to "be in something so amazing".

DECEMBER 8

This was the day in 1984 when Australia arrived as a world rugby union force. England, Ireland and Wales had been vanquished, only Scotland stood between Andrew Slack's men and history as the first Australians to complete a Grand Slam tour. But this was, in theory, the hardest of the four – the Five Nations Grand Slam champions at Murrayfield, where the Wallabies had only won once before, in 1947. But now they had Mark Ella and David Campese...Campese scored twice and Ella's try completed a full personal set against each of the Grand Slam opponents as Australia won 37-12. What a way to end his Test career, at the age of just 25.

Want to know how sport has changed in 20 years? In 1987, six months after raising the World Cup as New Zealand captain, David Kirk played in the Varsity Match for Oxford. It would be impossible to imagine the last three world champion skippers – John Smit, Martin Johnson and John Eales – sacrificing years of professional rugby for student life, but that's how things were in the amateur era.

DECEMBER 9

There is more than one way to nail a Grand Slam tour. Do it with a swagger (1984 Wallabies), by physical intimidation (1960/61 Springboks) or by clinical dissection (1978 All Blacks). The latter case was, remarkably, the first-ever clean sweep of the British Isles by New Zealand, at the sixth attempt. The man responsible for uniting some powerful personalities into a cohesive force was skipper Graham Mourie. The Taranaki man led by example in the denouement, a hard-fought 18-9 victory over Scotland. Although Welshmen still claim the All Blacks got lucky at Cardiff with a disputed late penalty.

It's a long way from Samoa to Gloucester and to the 1995 tourists from the South Pacific it must have seemed like a different planet when they lined up to face the South West at Kingsholm. The temperature on the pitch surface during the match was a staggering -12°C! It was a bit nippy, alright. Skipper Pat Lam would soon become more accustomed to the occasional harshness of the British winter through accepting a contract with Northampton.

DECEMBER 10

Drug scandals rear their ugly head all too often in sports such as athletics and cycling, where a string of high profile performers have been caught cheating. However, UK Sport figures from 2003 to 2008 suggested rugby union has the highest volume of offences – perhaps mitigated by the number of players tested, but no less worrying. Lessons have yet to be learned as, eight months after the damning stats of 62 positive tests came out, Manchester prop Marshall Gadd was suspended for two years after testing positive for stanozolol.

While Gadd suffered his fate, one of England's loyal servants left Test rugby on his own terms...Josh Lewsey, 2003 World Cup winner, had been left out of England's pre-Six Nations squad and felt the writing was on the wall for his international career. He opted to call it a day after 10 years, 58 caps (including three for the Lions) and 22 tries. Four months later he decided that season 2008/09 would be the full stop to his club career for Wasps. The Sandhurst graduate left the rugby scene with more medals than an army general.

DECEMBER 11

Raeburn Place in Edinburgh was the venue for the first international game in 1871, but 13 years previously, on this day, it was the scene of a schools match that would become rugby's longest running annual fixture. Edinburgh Academy hosted Merchiston Castle, playing the match under 20-per-side Rugby School rules. Merchiston had only just taken up the new game and apparently "did not fully understand all its rather complex rules." The Academy claimed a win, but the result was disputed. However, Merchiston has had much the better of the 230-odd matches since, with twice as many victories.

Whatever happens to another student player, Chris Catling, he has achieved a feat that will go down in the annals of the game. In 2008, the Oxford University wing scored the first hat-trick of tries in a Varsity match for 88 years, as the dark blues saw off those of a lighter hue from Cambridge 33-29 in a thrilling spectacle at Twickenham. For many involved the annual shindig will be the highlight of their rugby lives. Catling, though, aspires to turn pro and he might have a future judged on his startling acceleration and footwork. Watch this space...

DECEMBER 12

Ned Barry, who died aged 88 on this day in 1993, played only one Test for New Zealand but the flanker was the pioneer of a rich rugby legacy. His son, Kevin, also played for the All Blacks (in non-Test action) and Ned's grandson, Liam, packed down alongside Michael Jones and Zinzan Brooke against France to earn a full cap. The Barrys are the only family to provide three generations of All Blacks, but sadly Ned passed away two years before Liam matched his achievement.

With all manner of people to pay these days – players, coaches, physios, masseurs, you name it – balancing the books is almost as important as winning matches. As such, a long-term broadcasting deal is vital for all concerned. In 2008, with the financial world on its knees, Heineken Cup organisers pulled off a coup by agreeing an extended, four-year deal with Sky Sports. The competition has grown exponentially over the years, but TV coverage has seen the mightiest shift. From just the semis and the final in season one, eight matches from every Pool weekend, plus all the knockout fixtures are now shown live across the world.

DECEMBER 13

Where would sport be without the occasional character who stands out from the crowd? Rugby has had its fair share, with World War I veteran Stan Harris, born on this day in 1894, a particularly ubiquitous chap. Harris was picked for the Lions tour of South Africa in 1924, which was handy as he was playing for the Pirates club in Johannesburg at the time. He would later settle in the Republic and become its amateur light-heavyweight boxing champion, represented South Africa in Davis Cup tennis and water polo and be acclaimed as a ballroom dancing champion.

JPR Williams was also never one to shirk a challenge but, in 1978, even the great full-back was powerless as he became victim to a piece of thuggery. Playing for Bridgend against the All Blacks, Williams became stuck at the bottom of a ruck. New Zealand prop John Ashworth proceeded to stamp twice on the face of the stricken JPR. The sickening incident led to 30 stitches in his cheek but, typical of the man, he came back on the pitch to finish the game. JPR said there was no apology from Ashworth, only a bottle of wine sent 30 years later...Cheers, a year for every stitch...

DECEMBER 14

Some are born to thrill with their skill, others find fame as a coach, while others make their name sitting behind a desk...Today, in 1991, Bernard Lapasset, at the age of 44, became the youngest president of the French Rugby Federation. He progressed to the biggest job in his profession when named the International Rugby Board chairman in 1995, taking on the role again in 2008 having overseen the successful 2007 World Cup. From triumph to disaster...he courted controversy through the Experimental Law Variations, most of which failed to achieve their aim of making it into the law book and threatened to split the rugby world.

One of the most eagerly awaited debuts in rugby history occurred in December 2008 when Dan Carter made his debut for Perpignan in a Heineken Cup match against Leicester. Carter had been lured to the South of France for a lucrative six-month sojourn. Day one went well, Perpignan triumphed 26-20 with 16 points for Carter, but disaster struck seven weeks later when the fly-half suffered a ruptured Achilles tendon that abruptly ended his spell in Europe.

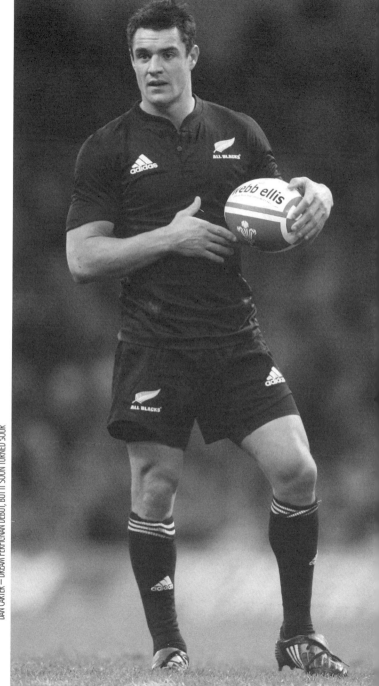

DECEMBER 15

Parents of rugby players know all about ferrying your nearest and dearest to rain-soaked fields, standing on windswept touchlines, the endless washing of kit and cleaning of boots...So it must be double the trouble if you have twins. The only doppelgangers to play together for the All Blacks, Alan and Gary Whetton, came into the world in Auckland on December 15 1959. Gary made the first impression at international level in 1981 while slower learner Alan came into the fold in 1984. They would both play every match during the 1987 World Cup, where they earned winners' medals at their home ground – Eden Park.

If sheer weight of numbers has anything to do with it then rugby had better be prepared if China ever gets its act together. The sport is growing in the world's most populous country – where there are over 300 people for every one New Zealander – despite only being 20 years old. It was December 15 1990 when the first rugby club was formed at the China Agricultural University and progress has been such that China has moved into the top 50 in the world rankings.

DECEMBER 16

The most famous try-that-never-was happened in 1905 when New Zealand were denied a potential Grand Slam-winning score against Wales in Cardiff by referee John Dallas. The Scot ruled that Bob Deans had not reached the line, despite most observers concluding that it was an obvious try. Dallas was wearing regular shoes rather than boots, so couldn't keep up with the play. The All Blacks lost 3-0, it was the only match they failed to win on a 32-match tour during which they scored almost 1,000 points – phenomenal at any time but truly extraordinary in the early 20th century.

They left it late, but at Twickenham in 1967 there was no doubt about an All Blacks victory over a Barbarians side that included a trio of future legends making their way in the game – Gareth Edwards, Barry John and Gerald Davies. It was 6-6 in injury time when Baa-baas full-back Stuart Wilson missed touch. Brian Lochore drove his team upfield and from the ensuing ruck a training ground move created the overlap for wing Tony Steel to score – practice made perfect.

DECEMBER 17

Overall, the use of technology to help judge borderline decisions has been of huge benefit. The "Television Match Official" has prevented miscarriages of justice occurring, but the system is not foolproof – human error will still creep in. The "video ref" can only adjudicate on whether a try has been scored. He can't advise on any incident leading up to the vital moment. Thus, when Ulsterman Andrew Trimble's foot-in-touch was missed by the touch judge, as he completed a try scoring pass to Kevin Maggs against Saracens in 2005, the TMO should have kept quiet or been overruled by the main official. Neither happened, the try was disallowed and Sarries won 18-10.

Imagine Ewan McGregor leaving a film set to appear for Scotland at Murrayfield or Mel Gibson trotting out in a Wallaby shirt after finishing off a movie...Rahul Bose is a famous Bollywood actor who used to also play for the India rugby team. In 2005, he finished shooting *Daastan* and then took time out to coach some Kashmiri youngsters. Despite Bose and its prominent place in rugby history through the Calcutta Cup, the sport has yet to catch on in India.

DECEMBER 18

We often hear commentators describe heroic defensive play on the rugby field with the vivid description: "He put his body on the line." For today's professionals it's their job, for the likes of Irishman Tommy Crean in the late 19th century it was a pastime – something to be enjoyed before taking on far more important (and dangerous) events. Crean toured South Africa with the Lions in 1896 and stayed on to see service in the second Boer War. On December 18 1901, Crean earned the Victoria Cross at the Battle of Tygerkloof for tending to wounded comrades directly in the line of fire incurring severe, but thankfully not fatal, blows himself.

To more prosaic issues...The Aussies have always envied the South Africa and New Zealand competitive structure below international level. Until Super rugby appeared, there were just two teams in Australia of any quality below Test level – New South Wales and Queensland. They have been joined by the Brumbies and Force, but where is the Aussie Currie Cup or NPC? A bold plan was hatched for an Australian Rugby Championship where all below Wallaby level could compete and raise standards. It folded on this day in 2007 after the first and only season incurred a crippling $4.7m loss

DECEMBER 19

Those of pensionable age are the only ones who can recollect seeing Wales beat the All Blacks. Way back in 1953 the Principality saw its side's third and last defeat of New Zealand, inspired by the mesmeric Cliff Morgan and his centre sidekick Bleddyn Williams. The duo had already been involved in a momentous victory for Cardiff over the tourists and now it was time for the All Blacks to take their medicine once again. Ken Jones and Sid Judd (who had also scored for Cardiff) were the try scorers.

Scottish victories against Australia have been almost as rare as Welsh ones against New Zealand. The last tartan success inflicted on the Aussies at Murrayfield came on a wintry December afternoon in 1981. Home advantage was everything on that day with the Wallabies unable to conquer both spirited hosts and their discipline in the biting cold. Australia scored three tries to one but still lost 24-15. Andy Irvine played a captain's hand with five penalties to see his side home.

DECEMBER 20

The 1969 South Africa tour of Britain simply should never have happened. The full horrors of apartheid were being unleashed and the world at large was questioning why such encouragement should be given to a racist regime. It was the day of the Test against England and the Springboks were filing on to their coach; a protester leapt into the driver's seat and proceeded to pull away. Players jostled the hijacker and the bus crashed into half a dozen cars. Eventually the tourists arrived at Twickenham, amid a torrent of abuse, and would lose 11-8. The match was secondary, South Africa would not return for 23 years.

In 2006, England were still world champions but in name only. Eight out of 11 Tests that year were lost, and coach Andy Robinson had been sacked. So where would the cavalry come from? As with the three previous England bosses, the new man would have Bath connections – Brian Ashton. Ashton was recognised as the most innovative backs coach in England and his team began to play more expansively, hit the buffers against South Africa on tour and again in the World Cup but bounced back to make the final. Suspicions that Ashton was keeping the seat warm were correct as he was dismissed just 18 months after being appointed.

DECEMBER 21

Murrayfield is used to poor weather – it's in Scotland after all – and is prepared for the worst. A typical December day dawned in Edinburgh in 1994 as Scottish Exiles and North & Midlands prepared for an Inter-District match. They turned up at HQ only to find a frozen pitch – how could this be? Seemingly, the great and the good had forgotten to turn on the under soil heating...Er, when would you be thinking of using it if not when the temperature is below freezing? All was not lost, by a strange quirk the practice ground was frost-free. So, an important domestic fixture was played on a park pitch outside a multi-million pound arena.

Rugby players and weddings...There have been a few examples of oval ball stars getting into alleged strife at nuptials. On this day in 2008, All Black flanker Adam Thomson attended a wedding in New Zealand and was charged with assault by the woman he accompanied, children's TV presenter Joanna Margaret Holley. The case was thrown out when Holley admitted it was a "misunderstanding". The year before, England's Olly Barkley was claimed to have brawled at Matt Perry's big day. The case was also dismissed.

DECEMBER 22

In 1951, South Africa took on Wales in Cardiff, bringing with them an awesome reputation from a 44-0 obliteration of Scotland and 17-5 dissection of Ireland. They were steaming towards a Grand Slam. A then-record crowd of 53,000 saw the Springboks notch the only score of the first half through a try by wing Chum Ochse. South Africa added a penalty and eventually Wales ditched their obsession with kicking and ran with the ball, leading to Bleddyn Williams dotting down near the posts. All too late, resolute Bok defence kept them out for a 6-3 win. Wales won their own Grand Slam the following spring.

There's no escape for today's stars...In 2008, the Rugby Football Union stepped up its fight against drug-taking by accepting the World Anti-Doping Agency's "Athlete Whereabouts Requirements". This effectively means that England players must let the authorities know where they are in advance so, if selected, they can comply with out of competition drug testing. For those familiar with advertising in the 1970s, it's the Martini syndrome – "Any time, any place, anywhere".

DECEMBER 23

An early Christmas present for Madame and Monsieur Gachassin during the dark days of World War II in 1941, their son Jean was to become a French rugby hero. The diminutive maestro from the foothills of the Pyrenees claimed fame by appearing for France in every back-line position, except scrum-half, during his 32-cap career. Remarkably, in 1967 Gachassin was selected in consecutive Tests at centre, full-back, wing and fly-half. Gachassin was elected president of the French Tennis Federation in February 2009.

Gachassin was proof that small can be effective, but I'm not sure that equates to Premiership grounds. Rotherham clambered into the top flight in 2000 via a tortuous play-off process and December 23 of that year saw the kind of fixture they worked so hard for – Leicester at home. A 4,000 crowd crammed into Clifton Lane to see Martin Johnson, Austin Healey, Martin Corry et al claim a 27-9 victory on their way to the successful defence of their title. Such a spectacle can no longer happen, as Premiership capacities must be well over 4K and the legendary double-decker bus press box would be deemed not good enough.

DECEMBER 24

Christmas Eve...A chance to prepare for the big day, or even put your feet up if you've got a match on Boxing Day. Competitive sport on December 24 is now little seen...Not so in 1888 when the first Kiwi team to tour the UK, the New Zealand Natives, were sent to play Swansea. They won 5-0 and had little time to recover before taking on Newport on Boxing Day, then Cardiff three days later and Bradford on New Year's Day. So it continued...a match every two or three days for a manic 74 games in 176 days around Britain.

Pragmatism before pride – you don't often get those characteristics in that order. On Christmas Eve 2008 plans were revealed in the media to revamp the European Challenge Cup (aka rugby's Europa League) and one of the bigger advocates was a man representing those clubs most likely to lose out. The second tier competition had begun to be dominated by English sides so three teams eliminated from the Heineken Cup would now play in the quarter-finals. "English dominance of the Challenge Cup was becoming bad for the competition," Premier Rugby chief executive Mark McCaffery nobly declared.

DECEMBER 25

Christmas Day 1872 in Calcutta, a group of ex-pats fancy a spot of fun in the sun to work off the excesses. What better than a game of "rugger"! So, 20 players representing England and 20 from Scotland, Ireland and Wales battled in Bengal. This apparently "social" game led to the creation of rugby's first international trophy and, 125 years later, was contested by professionals. The Calcutta Football Club was formed in 1873 but the climate soon put paid to rugby in the sub-continent. However, the Calcutta Cup, created with the melted down club funds, lives on.

Parents can be so embarrassing...On Christmas Day 1916 a baby boy was born in Llanelli. The people charged with giving him a first name to be proud of, perhaps overcome with emotion, plumped for "Christmas". Christmas Davies soon figured that life would be somewhat easier if he used his middle name – Howard (which must be the only instance of Howard being preferable to anything). Davies went on to play six times for Wales at full-back either side of World War II. He was no turkey, but hardly a cracker...

DECEMBER 26

Those Victorian sporting pioneers had their own idiosyncratic ways. Boxing Day 1857 in Edinburgh and the new Academicals club play their first match at a venue which would host the historic first international 14 years later – Raeburn Place. The opposition is Edinburgh University, it's 25-a-side and would last FOUR weekends. Well, why not, there was nothing much on the telly.

The 1912/13 South African tourists beat Scotland, Ireland, Wales and England, conceding just three points across the four Tests. However, they had a far from unblemished record. Newport, London and Swansea, on Boxing Day, lowered the Springbok colours. The latter were the only one of 27 opponents to prevent the Boks from scoring, with DJ Thomas' try dividing the teams. Torrential rain caused makeshift drains to be cut across the pitch. St Helens was hardly a bowling green but good enough for the All Whites, who had also defeated the 1908 Wallabies.

DECEMBER 27

Friary Field, Hartlepool may appear to be a nondescript location but it was there that rugby's most famous touring club played its first match, on this day in 1890 – the Barbarians. A cherished dream of William Carpmael came to life when a team drawn together by the love of the game ran out in the now famous black and white shirts, dark shorts, and each wearing the socks of their various clubs, to play Hartlepool Rovers. The kit sums up the club, a set of individuals attempting to play as a team.

The Premiership's progression continued in 2008 when a record 50,000 crowd saw Harlequins play Leicester at Twickenham. It wasn't that long ago that only a few committee men would regularly watch Quins. Now, though, they took a punt on The Stoop being too small, this was an opportunity to go across to the big place on the other side of the A316 and make pots of money for Cancer Research wearing a one-off pink and white kit. Even the match went (almost) to plan – a late Ugo Monye try and Nick Evans conversion produced a 26-all draw.

DECEMBER 28

This was when it really started to go horribly wrong for Jonny Wilkinson. Just five weeks after his drop goal sealed the World Cup, the fly-half suffered the first in a gruesome list of injuries. While playing for Newcastle against Northampton in 2003, Wilkinson went in for a tackle on Bruce Reihana and finished in agony on the turf. "Soft tissue damage" to his right shoulder was the verdict and there were no alarm bells ringing for a while. The weeks ticked by and in February he was operated on, ruling him out of the Six Nations. It's been calamity after calamity ever since.

It may well come, but Wilkinson has so far managed to avoid injury from a head-butt. Something similar was an unusual form of Christmas greeting favoured by Sale flanker Luke Abraham to Bath centre Alex Crockett in 2008. The all-pervading eye of the citing commissioner cottoned on to it and Abraham was told to attend a disciplinary hearing charged with "striking". It's such a flimsy term for a needless, aggressive act. A few weeks later Abraham was banned for eight weeks.

DECEMBER 29

Traditions are fantastic to maintain, but some can't survive the march of progress. In 1909, Leicester played the Barbarians for the first time, as part of the Baa-baas' Christmas tour. The match took the place of the regular match with Scottish team Fettes-Lorettonians in the Tigers' schedule and ended in a 9-all draw. It became entrenched in the calendar for almost a century. However, the professional era first shifted the match to spring and now it has disappeared as an annual event. Only 8,000 took up what was once the hottest ticket of the season in March 2006, leaving Welford Road half-full.

Saracens are pinning their hopes on a veteran of the Premiership scene – Brendan Venter, born on this day in 1969. The former Springbok centre is a fierce competitor who transformed London Irish from also-rans into cup winners during his time as player/coach. His appointment at Sarries brought rumours linking half the South Africa squad with Watford, although Venter insisted that he wasn't intent on pillaging the Boks to curry favour with London-based South Africans – a key market for him and the club owners.

DECEMBER 30

The New Year honours list is traditionally transmitted to the media on December 30 and published or broadcast the next day. In 2003, the sporting alumni were headed by England's World Cup winners. The concept is a puzzling issue for many people, with its hierarchical structure. All members of the squad were made MBEs apart from skipper Martin Johnson (CBE), Jonny Wilkinson and Jason Leonard (both OBE). Wilkinson had only been granted MBE status 12 months before, an upgrade in just a year – he must have done something a bit special.

Wilkinson's medal in the 2002 list at the age of just 23 made him usurp Gareth Edwards as the youngest rugby player to be honoured by the Queen. Edwards was named an MBE in 1974 and, in 2006, was lifted up the ladder to become CBE. Quite why it took the powers-that-be so long to do this, nearly 30 years after the great man retired, is beyond reason. Still, the humble Welshman said all the right things: "I couldn't believe it. I read the letter about three or four times. I thought they'd sent it to the wrong person."

DECEMBER 31

The last day of the year was the first of their lives for two of the all-time great open-side flankers. Jean Pierre Rives was born in the rugby hot-bed of Toulouse in 1952 and quickly established that, despite his relatively diminutive stature, he was more than a match for any of the grizzled forwards in French club rugby. His trademark blonde hair swaying in the breeze was a familiar sight during the late 1970s and early 1980s, as he exhibited courage and determination by the bucket-load in a monumental 59-cap career.

Less of a showman, but no less feared than Rives, has been All Black skipper Richie McCaw, who was born in North Otago at the height of the Frenchman's powers in 1980. Some have claimed that McCaw gets away with daylight (or floodlit) robbery on a rugby pitch, but no-one can deny that the teak-tough South Islander is as fine a reader of the game as there is in the modern era. Not the quickest on his feet, his sharpness of brain makes him arrive at the breakdown in the first tranche more often than not. He manages to spirit the ball back for the All Blacks so regularly that it makes some wonder if he stays within the laws.